creating chefs

creating chefs

a journey through culinary school *with recipes and lessons*

by carol w. maybach

with glenn humphrey

::

illustrations by erik tieze

THE LYONS PRESS :: Guilford, Connecticut
An imprint of The Globe Pequot Press

The Lyons Press is an imprint of The Globe Pequot Press.
10 9 8 7 6 5 4 3 2 1
Printed in China
Designed by LeAnna Weller Smith
ISBN 1-59228-183-4

Library of Congress Cataloging-in-Publication data is available on file.

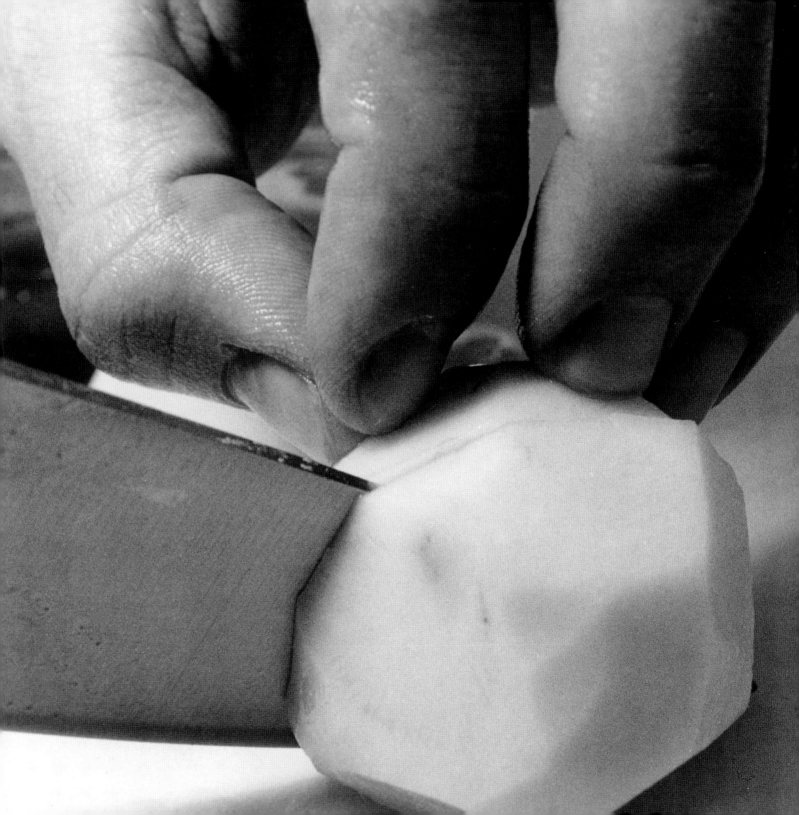

FOR ANNA AND ERIN, SO THAT YOU WILL GROW UP TO DISCOVER ALL THE BEAUTIES AND POSSIBILITIES OF WOMANHOOD.

DEDICATED TO PHYLLIS WIECHMAN, WHO WAS THE GREATEST TEACHER OF ALL.

CONTENTS

INTRODUCTION

" Always have enough time in your life to do something that makes you happy, satisfied, even joyous. That has more effect on economic well-being than any other single factor. "

—Paul Hawken

For those who know food, cooking is not a job, it's a love affair. It's not the prestige that brings them to the kitchen, it's not the corner office, it's definitely not the paycheck. But in the hearts and minds of chefs they do have it all. What more is there than to come to your work every day in awe of the creations that come from your hands: to watch magic happen in front of your eyes, to feel nectars flow through your fingertips, to allow yourself to be seduced by every smell that leaves the pan and competes for your attention, to abandon your senses to the absolute beauty that lies before you in the form of food waiting to be transformed?

To cook well does not exclusively depend on your ability to be moved by food. What does it take, then, to turn someone's all-consuming passion into a skill for life; to turn interest into an art form? To mold the hearts, minds, and movements of a young cook into a promising chef, ready to take on the world of food?

By devoting themselves to the education of our young cooks, the chefs in this book are changing food in America. They are the educators behind the next great chefs. It is through their tutelage that people begin their journeys to travel the world and impact cuisine with their inspirations. It is here that people begin their dreams to become the next Julia Child, Thomas Keller, or Alice Waters.

Although I had more modest aspirations than to achieve the status of The Great Ones in the kitchen, I came to culinary school with no less of an enchantment with cuisine. After years of immersion in teaching and academia, it suddenly dawned on me that I should eventually be teaching what I adore, and I am hypnotized by the beauty of food. Food depends on life, sustains and takes life, enhances, documents, influences, and affirms life. But the most fascinating aspect of food is its connection to all aspects of living.

For example, during travels domestically and throughout the world, I have found that food acts as a cultural ambassador of sorts, connecting us to the land, the seasons, the traditions, the livelihoods, the lifestyles, the art and history of the people. When food customs or recipes are shared, minds and hearts meet simultaneously. The mutual understanding is like owning a golden key to the lives of new people: It opens the door to their greatest devotions; it allows us an intimate peek into coveted family secrets. Finding opportunities to cook in new places, seeking out food artisans who preserve the heirloom methods of making products, visiting organic farmers' markets, eating family-style or at least lingering over dinners that last for hours in homes or restaurants with local people–all these experiences afford us not only great pleasure, but also the opportunity to embrace diversity.

There is something magical about knowing on which wildflowers the bees are feasting, or when certain fruits or truffles are in season. Identifying the good or bad years of a particular vintage connects us to the human spirit as we feel elation and the sorrow ebb and flow in response to local weather patterns. During years of bad crops, we are connected to farmers and vintners as their best-laid plans are overwhelmed by the power of nature. Celebrating good years of food and wine brings forth new images of great art and music from the region that resonate in our bodies as we savor every delicate nuance. Breaking bread together has its own way of bringing the world's people together on a one-on-one basis, with its own beautiful, real, and natural diplomacy.

I found a similar communion in culinary school. When the simple four-letter word *food* was uttered, people came together with equal levels of enthusiasm. But their sources of inspiration all stemmed from their own unique experiences. Some brought to the table their love of science, others their fascination of history or philosophy, or nutrition, or art, or even spirituality, but all were linked together by that simple notion of food and their deeply seeded desire to create. Despite our own diversity, we were united behind the stove by our devotion to our "great thing," the beauty of food, and our desire to bring it to its most graceful form. It was and is truly a quest for the grace of great things.

I came to school to learn how to better express myself through my food. Completely parallel to my reasons for photographing people and food, my drive to cook is an attempt to bring out the most beautiful, fascinating, and complex facets of the subjects at hand. The best artists in any medium are those who can simultaneously bring out the depth and mystery of a subject without losing its simplicity. I wanted to do that in my cooking, but first I needed to learn the fundamentals of technique that would allow me to express myself in the kitchen with clarity and finesse. Learning to cook food perfectly, applying the proper technique to the food in hand, is the way to revere its simplicity. Its depth and complexity come from learning to taste

in isolation, and then to layer flavors to add interest and meaning to the dish. The secrets I wanted to uncover were how to combine flavors in ways that made sense. I own a boatload of cookbooks that teach me what to cook; I wanted to know how to cook with inspiration, flavor, meaning, and depth.

This book was created in response to that desire. By examining the inspirations and life lessons offered by each chef, I learned to draw upon my own instincts, experiences, and motivations to bring out the best in my cooking. By looking at cooking almost as if it were a sort of culinary hermeneutic circle, I began to understand each chef's cooking by referencing his or her own worldviews. I also found the reverse to be true: Chefs' worldviews can be constructed, in part, by looking at their cooking. The result was a revealing education that illustrated Anthelme Brillat-Savarin's concept and took it one step farther: We are what we eat, and we cook who we are. Like a talented linguist who can pinpoint geographic markers in a speaker's sentence, good cooks can pinpoint regional influences on people's lives when their recipes are deconstructed. As these chefs share their recipes, specifically designed to give even the most technically challenged individual a feeling of success, they allow a glimpse into the parts of the world that have helped to influence their cooking. Perhaps it is a heavy dose of French tradition, or maybe the influence of the American Southwest, or perhaps it is a memory elicited from the food that brings back childhood in a mouthful.

The key to a great culinary education is to let the inspiration drive you to learn outside the classroom. I would run home every day, not just to read the required material, but also to pore over answers to my questions by referring to great culinary, literary, artistic, and philosophic minds from my library shelves. As a result, I had not only the chefs from this book answering my questions, but also many other great teachers: Harold McGee addressed my scientific queries on how food reacts on the stove; M. F. K. Fisher inspired me through her beautiful prose; Bo Friberg taught me how to bake; Brillat-Savarin helped me envision the goddesses of the gastronomic world; Georges-Auguste Escoffier walked me through the kitchens of tradition; Maguelonne Touissant-Samat taught me the history of food; Edward Weston inspired me to reconsider the peppers behind my camera lens; Vivaldi prompted me to listen yet again to his masterpieces that perfectly capture the natural world. Philosophers Thoreau and Emerson, poet Rainer Maria Rilke, and educators Robert Grudin, John Dewey, Paulo Friere, and Maxine Greene rounded out the Chautauqua that happened every evening in my living room, with "guest lectures" from a host of other chefs, writers, and artists who were occasionally invited to share in the dialogue. There is always more to learn: That is why the world is heavenly, why cooking is divine.

The joys of reaching deeply in culinary school can be truly symbiotic if you find a teacher who completely understands your passion. With one aching to learn and one yearning to teach, it's hard to imagine a more satisfying relationship. Robert Grudin wrote in his beautiful book on creativity and innovation, "We cannot understand beauty without participating in it. . . . The insight gained from our efforts or those combined with someone else's teaching . . . fills us with unspeakable delight and seems to renew the world."

This book is an ode to great educators and great chefs. It is also an opportunity for us all to deepen our insights: to understand the people behind our food, to examine the inspirations behind our cooking, to learn that food is born out of the lives of those who create it for us, with all of their wisdom, experience, and heart. It could also serve as your inspiration to examine your own life, to bring together your own experiences, and to do what you love to do: to live, to cook, to love, to eat.

:: **CWM**

ADVICE FROM A STUDENT

- **Genuflect to freshness.** Start with fresh, local, seasonal, and preferably organic ingredients that are harvested at their peak of ripeness. Use them as soon as possible to capture their greatest flavor and nutrition.

- **Never have a dull knife.** Razor-sharp knives increase efficiency and decrease injuries.

- **Use a kitchen scale to measure dry ingredients.** The only way to guarantee accuracy during baking is to ensure that you are using the exact amount every time. Measuring by weight and not by volume is the way to get professional results.

- **Invest in great knives and pans.** Put your money into the best basics you can afford. Instead of buying gadgets, learn to use your basic tools well.

- **Preheat your pans on the stove before adding fat.** The combination of a hot pan and hot fat is the way to ensure that your food is cooked properly when it first enters the pan.

- **Use clarified butter when the recipe demands it**. Clarifying butter is simply a process of melting it on low heat and skimming off the milk fats as they rise to the surface. The elimination of these fats allows the butter to be heated to a higher temperature without burning–affording the benefits of oil, but with the flavor of butter.

- **Learn the traditional ingredients** that characterize culinary customs at home and in different regions around the world. Cooking within these flavor profiles allows you to understand world cuisine as well as fuse across cultural lines with intelligence.

- **Turn your kitchen into a flavor laboratory.** Try all different flavors in isolation, then combine them in as many ways as you can to inspire your next creation.

- **Begin with the best stock you can make.** The boost in flavor is worth the time it takes to make it correctly. If it's worth doing, it's worth doing well.

- **Make a commitment to the product and yourself that you will bring out the food's greatest assets.** Dedication to natural flavor keeps you focused on the best that food has to offer, and marries you to the practice of cooking it perfectly every time.

- **The plate is truly your palette:** color, texture, flavor, balance, contrast, context, pattern, form, light, shape, space, perspective, design, rhythm, point, and line all help you develop your art, define your style, and speak with food as your medium.

- **Learn the science behind the cooking** so that you know why things in the kitchen are behaving as they do.

- **Keep your food safe.** Wash your hands, sanitize your workstation, avoid cross-contamination, and keep food below 40°F or above 140° so that it is out of the danger zone for food-borne illnesses.

- **Learn to maximize all products:** Use trimmings to boost flavor elsewhere, for instance, or to make creative garnishes.

- **Strain your sauces.** Luxurious texture brings sensuality to your food.

- **Taste, taste, taste.** Taste throughout the process of cooking so that you are in control of your product.

- **Mise-en-place is the secret to happiness.** Read and reread the recipe, gather everything you need in advance, arrange your food and tools in a way that makes sense. Being organized keeps you centered and is the only way to ensure that things are timed perfectly.

- **Create dining experiences** that encourage people to slow down and savor your food as well as the company that surrounds them.

- **Stay connected to your senses** as well as your instincts so that you are always cooking from the heart.

:: **C W M**

culinary basics I

INSTRUCTOR: CHEF GLENN HUMPHREY

I WAS COMPLETELY IMMERSED IN A WORLD OF ACADEMIA WHEN I WOKE UP TO THE REALIZATION THAT I HAD TO COOK.

My passion for cuisine was too strong: I couldn't just teach education anymore, I had to teach what I adored. But to teach about cuisine or how to cook well, you need to abandon all pretenses and start at the beginning, to hone your basic skills in the kitchen. Culinary school was the place to begin, and Chef Humphrey's class was the perfect starting point. With absolute charisma, he whisked up our culinary dreams, embraced them, and showed us how to turn our aspirations into real skills in the kitchen. His phenomenal depth as a chef allowed him to deconstruct our cooking until the emphasis was where it should be: on mastering the basics. We learned to sauté, braise, roast, broil, poach, fry, grill, and steam to perfection. The rigorous course included every-

thing from palate development to the proper selection, storage, fabrication, and cookery of every type of food, and our instructor's enthusiasm left us begging for more. Chef Humphrey attributes his abilities in the kitchen to the inspiration he gains from riding his Harley. On his bike, all of his senses become heightened: "I bring these feelings to the kitchen and elicit that same sense of freedom to find my sense of smell, flavor, and texture fully alive." His strength taught me to rely on my senses, to listen to my food. His grace taught me the beauty of organized movement born of careful mise-en-place (preparation for cooking). His commitment to each and every student solidified my conviction to teach. :: **CWM**

REFLECTIONS OF A CHEF

THE INFLUENCE OF CHILDHOOD ON COOKING

The journey of becoming a chef takes a lifetime. Along the way you build memories of flavors and flavor combinations; then you learn to draw upon all your experiences to create your own signature for each plate.

My most vivid memories of food go back to when I was between 4 and 14 years old, growing up where my dad worked, on the Johnnycake Charolais Ranch in Connecticut. The owner of the ranch would throw extravagant parties in huge tents with chandeliers and elegant people, with row after row of incredible cars lining up to drop off the guests. It was very F. Scott Fitzgerald-ish. But what was most striking about those times are my memories of the food. By that age I had watched Julia Child on TV, but the food at those parties was almost larger than life. They would make a huge New England-style clambake in an enormous pit oven. Once they got the fire going, I watched how they loaded the massive pit with all this incredible food, then covered it up to cook for the whole day. Even though it was done in a barn environment, boy, the smells coming out of that pit, I just kind of hung out there most of the day. When it was finally ready, they'd pick up shiny new shovels and dig down through all the clams, and the steamers, and down through the corn, the potatoes, the lobster, and the chicken. It's probably the first time I was mesmerized by cooking. Now I can't cook lobster without thinking about those days. I usually try to do a lobster feast at least once a year, and now there are piles of kids watching me as we load in the lobsters.

MEMORIES FROM CULINARY SCHOOL

Culinary school became an obvious choice for me to pursue my ambitions. One of my favorite memories from my years at the Culinary Institute of America, CIA, was bringing a group of classmates to the ranch to see what fresh food was all about. It was there they first cooked eggs that were still steaming from the warmth of the chicken. We'd

studied meat fabrication at CIA, so we went out to watch the cattle. I grabbed a marker,
ran to a cow, and said, "Watch this!" I drew all the primal cuts of beef right on its body.
I felt between the ribs to see if I could find the space between the fifth and sixth ribs of
the chuck, the neck, the rib section, there was this little flap for the flank steak, until
the whole cow was drawn. Then we just sat and watched how it moved, every muscle.
I wanted to teach them what I learned on the ranch: why some cuts of meat are tough
and others tender.

LESSONS FROM THE FIELD

You don't have all the answers when you leave culinary school. You will continue to be
tested and pushed to bring out your best work in the jobs you have after graduation.
It's only when you master the food and the responsibility that you move from being a
cook to becoming a chef.

I was fortunate enough to work for a chef early in my career who forced me to
accept responsibility for the entire restaurant. Front of the house, back of the house, all
of the managerial aspects of the restaurant: It's all crucial to the success of the business. It's not all about The Food.

THE INFLUENCE OF OTHER CHEFS

The chefs I refer to for inspiration in cooking are those who emphasize mastering the
basics. Fernand Point emphasized perfecting a skill by trying it out 25, 30, 40 different
times. Thomas Keller, Jean-Louis Palladin, Jean-Georges Vongrichten, they all understand the very essence of food. The idea is to simplify cooking instead of making it
more dramatic—just get down to the core of what's important. Bring out the best qualities of the food itself. Period. A dish may only need three or four things to bring out its
potential.

GLENN HUMPHREY

COOKING SECRETS

Salt is a powerful tool in the kitchen. It brings out flavors that need to be emphasized. It knocks back flavors that got a little carried away. You just have to know which type of salt to use and when to use it. Only use enough to create what I call the "succulence of the food": When you feel that kind of watering in your mouth, that's it, you've hit it right on.

THE ROLE OF THE ARTS

A good meal is like a symphony. You start out with that overture and Boom! You're off and running. It calms down a bit as you have your salad; then you start building again as you go through the entrée. In this course all the other components start playing, the high notes here, the low notes there, and Bam! The dessert. The Grand Finale.

Visual art comes into play in my vegetable carving. Whether I'm carving daikons into a staircase based on Escher's drawings, or apples into birds, or turnips into the most delicate of calla lilies, I appreciate the beauty of each one I make.

Literature has always been a part of my cooking and my teaching. What I read gets tied into a package so when I come to class, I can put myself into a frame of mind of Mexico or Germany when I'm cooking foods from those countries. You have to put your whole self into your cooking, and that means bringing everything you've ever done into the kitchen.

THE CHEF'S LESSON

ROULADE OF PORK TENDERLOIN WITH ASPARAGUS AND MUSHROOMS IN FRAGRANT ROSEMARY CREAM SAUCE

(SERVES FOUR)

Chef Humphrey's pork tenderloin recipe is a good lesson in the effects of brining on meat. I tried this recipe both ways: Without brining, the meat was delicious, but with brining the entree was sublime. The brining process is very simple, and worth the extra step. :: **CWM**

PORK INGREDIENTS

2 to 2½ pounds Pork Tenderloin
2 quarts Water
½ cup + 2 tablespoons Salt
¼ cup + 2 tablespoons Sugar
2 tablespoons Butter, unsalted
8 ounces Mushrooms, finely chopped
4 Shallots, minced
14 Asparagus Spears, trimmed,
    blanched, shocked
1½ cups (8 ounces) Manchego
    Cheese, shredded or grated

SAUCE INGREDIENTS

1 cup Madeira Wine
2 tablespoons Shallots, minced
2 teaspoons Rosemary, minced
2 cups Heavy Cream
Kosher Salt and White Pepper

ACCOMPANIMENTS

Jasmine Pear Pilaf (recipe follows)
4 Button Mushrooms, sautéed

PROCEDURE

1. Trim all fat, sinew, and membrane from the meat. Slice lengthwise along the side of the tenderloin, but do not cut all the way through, to butterfly the meat and create a thinner, wider surface. Place between sheets of plastic wrap and carefully pound out to ³⁄₈ inch.

2. Combine the water, salt, and sugar to create a brine. Place the meat in the brine for at least an hour, not to exceed 3 hours. The brining allows the protein structures to become swollen and softer, resulting in a more juicy and tender piece of meat.

3. Meanwhile, heat a sauté pan and add the butter to melt. Over low heat, add the chopped mushrooms and shallots to the pan and cook slowly, stirring constantly, until the mushrooms have a soft, even consistency.

4. Remove the meat from the brine and spread the mushroom mixture across the top.

5. Place the asparagus on top, spacing evenly between each spear. Leave 1 inch of space at both ends of the meat. Press grated cheese into the spaces between the spears.

6. Carefully roll the end of the meat closest to you over the first asparagus spear. Continue to roll the meat into a tight cylinder shape. Thread a skewer along the exposed end of the meat to make a seam and keep the shape intact.

7. Refrigerate for 15 minutes to firm, and preheat the oven to 350°F.

8. Sear the meat in a hot sauté pan with about ¼ inch of hot oil until it is evenly browned. Transfer the meat to an ovenproof dish or half-sheet pan.

9. Bake for approximately 30 minutes, until internal temperature is 145°F. This allows for 5-10 degrees of carry-over cooking. Let the meat rest for 10 minutes in a warm place.

10. Meanwhile, pour the oil out of the sauté pan and deglaze with the Madeira.

(continued)

(Roulade of Pork Tenderloin
continued from page 6)

:: Chef's Note

In order to achieve a velvety smooth texture in the rosemary sauce, be sure to strain it through a chinois or a fine strainer lined with cheesecloth.

11. Add the shallots and rosemary and allow the wine to reduce by half.

12. Add the heavy cream, stir lightly, and reduce the sauce to nappe—just thick enough to coat the back of a spoon. Strain, and season to taste with salt and pepper.

13. Slice the meat in medallions. For each serving, arrange the medallions around a portion of the Jasmine Pear Pilaf. Drizzle the sauce in front and garnish the dish with a mushroom.

JASMINE PEAR PILAF

(SERVES FOUR)

In Culinary Basics, each aspect of a meal is covered in class from start to finish. For example, with the Jasmine Pear Pilaf, we discussed the types of rice, the choices of pear, the importance of using unsalted butter, the basics of a good chicken stock, the advantages of kosher salt, and the meaning of the "pilaf" method of cooking rice. :: **CWM**

INGREDIENTS

1 Bosc or Comice Pear
2 tablespoons Butter, unsalted
1/4 cup Shallots, chopped
2 cups Jasmine Rice
4 cups Chicken Stock or Broth, heated
Kosher Salt and Pepper

:: Chef's Note

The "pilaf" method of cooking rice involves briefly sautéeing the rice in hot fat before cooking it in hot water or stock.

PROCEDURE

1. Preheat the oven to 350°F. Peel and dice the pear into 1/4" x 1/4" cubes. Set them aside in a cool-water bath.

2. Heat an ovenproof pan on top of the stove over low heat. Add the butter and allow it to melt. Add the shallots, cover, and allow them to sweat for approximately 1 minute. Do not allow the shallots to brown.

3. Add the rice and stir to coat the kernels with fat.

4. Add the hot stock, cover the pan again tightly, and place it in the oven for 10 minutes.

5. Drain the cubed pear. Remove the pilaf from the oven, add the drained pear, cover, and place back in the oven for 10 more minutes.

6. Remove the pilaf from the oven and let it stand for 5 minutes. Uncover the pot and season with salt and pepper to taste.

BLANCHING/SHOCKING ASPARAGUS:

- Bring a large pot of salted water to a boil. (Use enough salt to make the water taste like the sea.)
- When the water's at a full boil, drop in the asparagus. (Don't cover or it will increase the acidity and make the asparagus turn drab.)
- After a few seconds, when it becomes vibrant green, take out asparagus with tongs and plunge it into ice water in order to set the color.

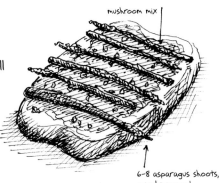

mushroom mix

6-8 asparagus shoots, evenly spaced

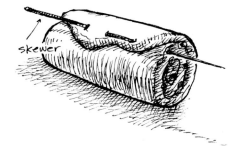

skewer

SEARING PRINCIPLE:

- The searing process quickly raises the surface temperature of the meat to approximately 300-400°F. At this temperature, the color and flavor of the meat intensifies. However, searing does not "seal the pores" of the meat, as is commonly but incorrectly described in many "Kitchen Wisdoms." Therefore, searing does not affect the loss of natural juices during cooking, but it does improve the color and flavor of the meat.

CARRY-OVER COOKING:

- Since the outside of the meat is hotter than the inside as it cooks, the process of conduction continues even after the meat is taken out of the oven. This results in the continued cooking of the meat caused by the heat retention in the tenderloin. Allow 5-10 degrees for carry-over cooking.

PLATING PRINCIPLES:

- Lean medallions against pilaf to increase height and interest.
- Garnish with an edible, cooked product that is included as an ingredient in the recipe. In this case, use a sautéed mushroom on top of the pilaf.
- Only drizzle on enough sauce to complement the meat; don't overdo it.

Keep sauce off edge of plate

THE CHEF AS TEACHER

THE REWARDS OF TEACHING

Teaching is all about passion. It's my goal to make people want to get up in the morning to see what more they can learn that day. I love to see people lean forward in their chairs, actively involved in my lectures in Culinary Basics. I can see the excitement in their faces, I watch their expressions. It's all a part of being a teacher.

The culinary educators I know have worked in restaurants all their adult lives and then moved into education for a life change. Suddenly they are saddled with the awesome responsibility of shaping people's lives, not just teaching them how to cook. Some are better at it than others. To me, it's an opportunity to pass on a legacy of experience and knowledge that I've come to know: lessons about life, about food, about classical techniques, about cooking from a base of knowledge that Escoffier brought to the table. You can't learn all of that just being out in the field. You have to study the techniques in order to operate from them.

I teach people to love and respect food, taste everything at all stages of cooking, pay attention, and do their best to understand the food they are cooking.

PALATE DEVELOPMENT

My biggest teaching secret is opening up my students' minds to how food should taste, teaching them how the chemical reactions of taste work. I help them understand the essential elements of flavor and how those elements can be combined to create different effects on the food. Once people understand this, they can build everything else.

The point of palate development is to learn how to balance flavors so that your food ends up with the level of depth and complexity that you intend. We start with a sampling of pure flavors that help students learn where the sensations of taste take place: sweet on the front of the tongue, salty then sour on the sides of the tongue, bitter and hot in the back. We taste from the front to the back of the tongue, but we flavor from the back to the front. It's crucial to know how to counter flavors. For example, if something is too sweet, you add tartness; if it is too salty, you dilute it or counter with sweet and sour flavors; if it's too sour, add

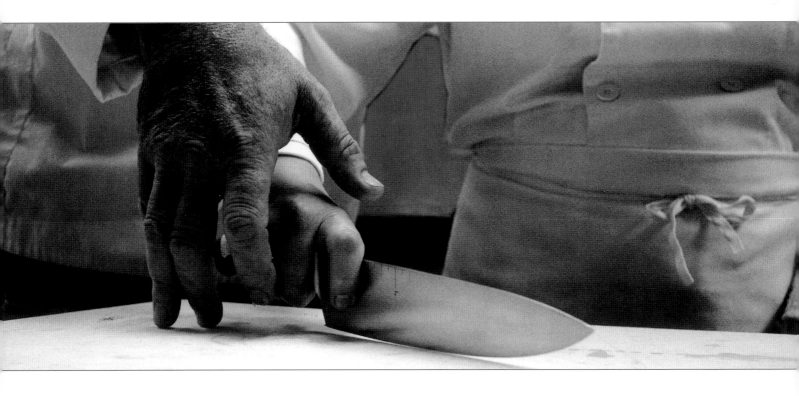

salty and sweet ingredients; if it's too bitter, add acidity; if your food is too hot, add bitter or base to negate the acid. The idea is to bring together a flavor profile that is individually balanced in the dish and collectively balanced throughout the course of a meal.

TEACHING A PHILOSOPHY OF FOOD

The true essence of a dish is not born out of a recipe. It comes from the inspirations and thoughtful techniques used every time a cook holds on to a beautiful piece of food. Students learn that the art begins when that food is treated with respect, and lovingly brought to its new form. Something out there died for us to eat it: Our reverence is its 21-gun salute, its requiem. Each moment in the kitchen gives a new opportunity for inspiration that is brought to that individual dish. When I'm cooking at home, I don't take shortcuts because I can't; I know deep down inside what I want it to be. I just give it the honor it deserves.

A DAY IN THE CLASSROOM

Humor plays a very important role in my class. If I can get people laughing, then they are relaxed and able to accept new ideas. I'll always poke fun at myself, too, simply because I'm not perfect and I want people to understand that. I look at the people around me and try to draw them in by enjoying the subject myself. I put quotes on my board every morning to set the tone for the day, to underscore a discussion or a particular technique. I have been collecting quotes for years, from Teddy Roosevelt to Tom Waits. I use them every day to deepen the learning and help people learn about life. I like to use the quote from Bryan Miller, "The qualities of an exceptional cook are akin to those of a successful tightrope walker: an abiding passion for the task, courage to go out on a limb, and an impeccable sense of balance."

The things I choose to teach are based on the value of the lesson, the importance of the techniques, the significance of the styles, and the impacts of the variations possible. One demonstration that takes people out of their mind-set is introducing them to a classic wine, shallot, chipotle cream sauce that goes as well on filet mignon as it does on vanilla ice cream.

SEEING THE POTENTIAL IN YOUNG CHEFS

Potential in the kitchen takes many forms. For those who are naturals, it's all about how they move in the kitchen; it's a fluidity that sets them apart. They may not do well on tests but they make something once or twice and then they've got the procedure down pat. Some people are better at tests, some have professional experience, others just have an intuition for it. Some students will show their potential just by talking about it; I can see their desire and see that they really know what it takes. Our job is to nurture them all.

We don't graduate chefs, we graduate culinarians, who then may become chefs.

ADDITIONAL RECIPES

TENDERLOIN MEDALLIONS ROBED IN A CITRUS CHIPOTLE SAUCE

From Chef Robert McCullough

(SERVES EIGHT)

In addition to Chef Humphrey's roulade, here is another wonderful way to prepare tenderloin. This recipe gives the pork a tangy southwestern spice. For a milder sauce, remove the seeds from the chipotles; for a spicier sauce, leave them in. Just remember never to wash a chipotle, or you will lose much of its beautiful flavor. :: **CWM**

PORK INGREDIENTS

2, 2¼-pound Pork Tenderloins, fat and
   silverskin removed
Salt and Pepper, to taste
Vegetable Oil for searing

SAUCE INGREDIENTS

6 Chipotle Chiles, canned, stemmed, drained
5 cloves Garlic, fresh, peeled
4 Shallots, peeled
½ cup Cilantro, fresh, leaves only,
   loosely packed
2 tablespoons Thyme, fresh, leaves only
¼ cup Orange Juice, freshly squeezed
2 tablespoons Lemon Juice, freshly squeezed
2 tablespoons Lime Juice, freshly squeezed
2 teaspoons Cumin, ground
1 teaspoon Ginger, ground
1 teaspoon Cinnamon, ground
¾ cup Vegetable Oil
Kosher Salt and Pepper

PROCEDURE

1. Preheat the oven to 325°F. Season all sides of the pork with salt and pepper.

2. Heat a large sauté pan and add just enough oil to coat. Allow the oil to get very hot. Sear all sides of the tenderloins until the surface of the meat is completely golden brown. Remove the pork from the sauté pan and set aside.

3. Put all the sauce ingredients except the oil, salt, and pepper into a food processor. Puree until smooth.

4. While the processor is still turning and the lid is still on, slowly pour the oil down the funnel. It should be poured in a stream as thin as a pencil lead in order to achieve a thick emulsion. Season to taste with salt and pepper.

5. Smooth the chipotle mixture on to all sides of the pork. Put the pork on a rack in a roasting pan, uncovered, and roast until it reaches an internal temperature of 145°. This allows the meat to rise an additional 5-10° during carry-over cooking.

6. Transfer the pork to a plate on the counter and allow it to rest for 5-10 minutes in order for the juices to settle into the meat. Slice and serve as medallions fanned on the plate.

:: Chef's Note

Roasting is a dry-heat method of cooking: A cover is not placed on the roasting pan or moisture will become trapped, resulting in a steaming process. Meat should be basted only with fat, not liquids or broth; otherwise moisture will leach out of it. Basting with fat actually increases the juiciness of a piece of meat.

YUKON GOLD-ENCRUSTED SEA BASS WITH ALBA WHITE TRUFFLES, MAYTAG BLUE CHEESE, AND CITRUS VINAIGRETTE

From Chef John Deflieze

(SERVES FOUR)

In this recipe a refreshing citrus vinaigrette dresses a potato-wrapped sea bass to result in an entrée fit for a special occasion. If white truffles are out of season, white truffle paste is a perfectly acceptable replacement. :: **CWM**

PROCEDURE

1. Using a mandoline slicer, slice the Yukon Gold potatoes paper-thin lengthwise. Be certain the slices can completely surround the width of each piece of sea bass. Place the slices in a bowl of melted clarified butter.

2. Wash the sea bass portions and pat dry with a paper towel. Season both sides with salt and pepper.

3. Heat a sauté pan and add clarified butter to cover the bottom of the pan.

4. Remove the slices of potato from the butter. Add them to the pan in a single layer to warm over low heat for approximately 15 seconds, until the potatoes just begin to wilt. Do not allow them to brown. Remove the potatoes from the pan to cool slightly. Turn off the heat under the pan.

5. Completely wrap each portion of fish with one layer of potato slices, overlapping them slightly to ensure that the fish is entirely encased. Tuck the ends of the potato beneath each sea bass portion.

6. Preheat the oven to 350°F.

7. Reheat the sauté pan. When the butter is hot, put the fish portions in the pan, with the potato ends still tucked beneath. Cook over medium-high heat without moving the pan until the potatoes are golden brown on one side. Carefully turn the fish to the other side. When the second side is light brown, transfer the fish portions to the oven to finish cooking.

8. Meanwhile, whisk together the lemon, lime, and orange juice. Slowly incorporate the oil by pouring it in a stream as thin as a pencil lead, whisking constantly. Season to taste with sugar and salt.

9. When the sea bass has reached an internal temperature of 120°, remove it from the oven. Place each portion atop a bed of greens on a warm plate, sprinkling with the vinaigrette. Crumble ½ ounce cheese around the base of the fish as well as a few red peppers. Finish the dish with 3 white truffle slices on each portion.

SEA BASS INGREDIENTS

2 large Yukon Gold Potatoes, peeled
Clarified Butter
4, 6-ounce portions Chilean Sea Bass, cut in 2"-wide strips
Salt and White Pepper, to taste

CITRUS VINAIGRETTE INGREDIENTS

1 Lemon, freshly squeezed
1 Lime, freshly squeezed
1 Orange, freshly squeezed
½ cup Extra-Virgin Olive Oil
Superfine Sugar
Salt

ACCOMPANIMENTS

Tatsoi Greens, Micro Greens, or Baby Arugula
2 ounces Maytag Blue Cheese, crumbled
2 tablespoons Red Bell Pepper, brunoise or finely diced, and lightly sautéed
12 White Truffle Slices

:: Chef's Note

The texture, flavor, and creamy soft yellow interior of Yukon Gold potatoes make them work well for many cooking purposes. In this case, their ability to keep their shape during the cooking process, even when they are thinly sliced, makes them an excellent choice.

To ensure that the potatoes encase the fish in this dish, be certain to slice them as thinly as possible; soak them in clarified butter; overlap them as you wrap the fish; sauté the fish with the edges of the potato tucked underneath; and allow the potatoes to brown undisturbed before carefully turning them once.

culinary basics II

INSTRUCTOR: CHEF JANETTE SINCLAIR

BY THE TIME I REACHED CULINARY BASICS II,
I ALREADY FELT A CHANGE IN MY THINKING AND COOKING.

Returning to the basics of cooking made me think anew about the basis of my food philosophies. I wanted to understand flavor from an historical perspective, one that started with the early beginnings and evolved to a contemporary view. In Culinary Basics II, we continued to learn about basic cooking methods and studied food from the beginnings of mankind through Careme and Escoffier's influences on modern fare. Although an historical examination of race, class, and gender is beyond the realm of culinary school, I found that conversations with Chef Sinclair helped to shape my own perspectives on authenticity. I discovered that we both enjoyed seeking out the world's freshest flavors and tasting them in the milieu in which they were born. Like an artist with a palette of basic colors, a cook with genuine gastronomic experience obtains a spectrum of primary flavors that can be mixed and matched with wisdom to create entirely new hues. As we explored the fundamentals of French cooking, we saw how its principles could be applied to all of the world's great cuisines. By understanding how to stay true to each culture's unique flavor combinations, we could add the French methodology as a variation, rather than as a form of culinary colonialism dominating a culture's flavor profile. It became clear to me where regional, historical, and geographical traditions stopped and my own personal inspirations and input began. :: **CWM**

REFLECTIONS OF A CHEF

THE WORLD TRULY IS MY OYSTER

I am a nomad at heart. It is my life passion to search the world for the freshest, most amazing ingredients and to learn authentic recipes from real people.

When I was 20 years old I moved to Taiwan to teach English and to learn about Chinese cooking. I chose to live in an older neighborhood of Taipei because it allowed me to become completely immersed in the culture. I steered clear of the Americanized grocery stores. I lived with a family that had originally lived on the mainland of China but had moved to Taiwan during the Cultural Revolution. The mother had passed on all her cooking knowledge over the years to her daughters. So when I cooked with my family, I learned about generations of tradition from the mainland to Taiwan.

My kitchen consisted of a stove with one flat burner for heating liquids and one curved burner designed to hold a wok. That was it. There were no ovens, as traditionally those are reserved for professional bakers. I went out and purchased a tiny refrigerator. Despite its miniature size, it still cost about $600. Refrigerators are very hard to come by in Taiwan because everything you cook is fresh, so there is no need for refrigeration. When I would go to the markets with my Asian family, I would choose a live chicken and the vendor would kill it on the spot. The vegetables that were displayed in the market at 6 A.M. had been picked at 4 that same morning. The food was unbelievably fresh.

I got turned on to a wonderful collection of cookbooks titled *Fu Pei Mei*. The beauty of that collection was that they were written in Chinese and English, which allowed me to read them myself as well as take one to the market, point to ingredients in the recipe, and say, "I want this." That way I could find everything I needed on my own.

Gathering all of those ingredients at the market was the first step in a very long process of preparation for each dish. Chinese cooking forces you to perfect your mise-en-place. There is no other way to begin a recipe unless everything is completely prepared in advance. You have to be meticulously organized because Chinese cooking is done very quickly once the heat actually hits the pan. To me, one of the greatest secrets to Chinese cooking is using oyster sauce and plenty of garlic. The garlic is minced very finely and mashed into a paste. Combining those two ingredients is the key to creating great garlic sauce. Nyo Row Mien—beef and noodle soup made with miso, lots of cilantro, and a deep, rich beef broth—is one of my favorite Chinese dishes from that time in my life. They had little food vendors on nearly every corner in my neighborhood selling that soup, and to this day I crave that aroma and comforting taste. Squids-on-a-stick were another favorite of mine that I used to pick up outside of the National Palace—and I still dream about the bento boxes I used to order on the train as I would go to teach my English classes. They were filled with pickled vegetables, rice, a barbecued, braised pork chop, and the most amazing black tea eggs made with five-spice seasoning. I was a kid in a candy store there because every dish became my new favorite meal.

I moved to Mexico for the same purpose: to absorb the nuances of traditional cooking from real families. By living in one location, I learned how to create dishes with a more thorough understanding of the heirloom recipes, ingredients, and techniques used in that particular region. It was a very intimate perspective. Consequently, Rick Bayless's and Diana Kennedy's documentations of Mexican cooking have been very inspirational to me, since their lifework focuses on similar visions.

When I was living there, I would walk down the beach with my daughter, who was very young at the time. We would stop to talk with fishermen to find out the best location for the freshest seafood. When I found a great tip on lobsters, I went right to the source and convinced one fisherman to deliver his freshest lobsters to me twice a week. He would bring them straight to my door as soon as the boats came in. So for well over a year, my daughter and I ate lobster twice a week. Her passion for seafood became evident when we would go into restaurants in the area after a full summer of that beautiful shellfish. The waiter would look at her and ask if she'd like to see a kid's menu and she, at five years old, would respond, "No. But I will have six oysters on the half shell and the fried calamari."

COOKING SECRETS

Perhaps I got my wanderlust from my father. He goes to Alaska on yearly fishing trips and brings home fresh salmon. Even though I'm not a big salmon fan, I found a wonderful combination that brings together complementary flavors. The idea is to combine strong flavors with a fish that has strong flavors of its own, in a way that doesn't make the fish or the seasonings stand out as overwhelming.

First I brine the salmon with salt and maple syrup and let it cure in the refrigerator

JANETTE SINCLAIR

for 10 hours. Then I cold-smoke it with alder wood. The chips are available in shops that specialize in barbecue. It's a wonderful way to tie the rich, complex flavors together. After I cure it in the refrigerator, I put it in to cold-smoke. If you don't own a smoker you can heat the wood chips put them in the bottom of a hotel pan, place a rack over the top of the coals, and place ice wrapped in aluminum foil on top of the smoking wood. Next, place a second rack on top of the ice pack and the fish on top of the rack. Cover the entire pan with aluminum foil. The pan is put over heat that will allow it to remain at a consistent temperature of 70-85°F. Let it sit to absorb the smoke for about 10-15 minutes. When it is ready, the wonderful flavors will be absorbed, and it will be ready for the cooking process of your choice.

THE TAO OF FOOD

I see food and life through the lens of my Buddhist philosophy. To me, it's not a religion; instead it's a way of being. Whether I am traveling or at home in my kitchen, I draw upon those philosophies to inform my experience. It's what allows me to look at every opportunity to get the very most out of every lesson I possibly can. It also provides a framework for me to see the world. I see food as an extension of the Earth with one of its roles being the provision of sustenance for us. We, too, have a role to help the food sustain its own life; our lives are interconnected. I appreciate the opportunity to take food at its most perfect state and work to accentuate its own glories by applying just the right techniques. Simple is not easy. To make simple, perfect food is very, very difficult.

THE UNIVERSAL HIGH

The people who cooked with me on the line understood the euphoria that cooking brings to my soul. Although I love being a chef educator now, I definitely left a part of my heart on the line. Maybe I'll always be a line cook at heart. There was one team in particular that I worked with that will remain my favorite group of cooks. As a five-person team we would put out 200 to 250 covers a night. We were so tightly choreographed that the entire evening, every night, was just a flow of movement. As we would walk out the door after work we would be so pumped—it was a great natural high. It's an emotion that is really only understood by other chefs. We were so connected that we still keep in touch with each other.

A FAMILY OF CHEFS

We are very much a profession that looks out after our own. Despite the overwhelming number of chefs out there in the world, for some reason chefs feel a respect and a kinship toward one another that connects us all. That unspoken regard makes our industry feel like a small, tight community. We all learn from each other, we revere each other's work, we care about each other's livelihoods. Even chefs who scream at their cooks, care desperately for the people who work for them.

THE CHEF'S LESSON

FRESH MARYLAND CRAB CAKES

(SERVES SIX)

Chef Sinclair's lesson is one of balance. The freshest of ingredients are always preferred, but items such as live Maryland blue crab are not always available. This recipe balances the ideal with suggestions for real alternatives that still result in a wonderful crab cake. Balance also comes into play when adjusting the texture of the cakes. To hold their shape, the cakes need to be bound with bread crumbs and egg in a way that keeps them together without becoming too soggy. For extra flavor, try adding lemon zest and cayenne pepper to this recipe. :: **CWM**

INGREDIENTS

8 cups Lump Crabmeat, preferably from
    freshly boiled Maryland Blue Crab
1/4 cup Butter, unsalted
1/4 cup Yellow Onions, small diced
1/4 cup Celery, small diced
1/4 cup Green Peppers, small diced
Kosher Salt
1/2 teaspoon White Pepper
1 1/2 tablespoons Prepared Mustard
1 teaspoon Worcestershire Sauce
1/2 cup Mayonnaise
2 cups Fresh White Bread Crumbs
2 whole Eggs, beaten
1 tablespoon canned Pimiento, drained,
    small diced.

PROCEDURE

1. For fresh crabs: Maryland blue crabs are purchased live. They are plunged live, all at once, into a pot of boiling water seasoned with 1/4 cup Old Bay Seasoning and 2 tablespoons salt per gallon of water. Then they are covered and cooked for 10–12 minutes, or until the shells turn bright red. Remove and cool. Open the shells and pick out the crabmeat. Try to keep the crabmeat in lumps as large as possible. Include the mustard-colored tomalley (liver), that is tucked into the recesses of the shell and the meat, to intensify the flavor of the crab.

2. For precooked crabs: King crab legs, Dungeness, and snow crabs are more widely available. The meat from these crabs may also be used for making crab cakes, although there will be some difference in texture and flavor.

3. For canned crabs: Choose the best grade available, preferably the type of canned lump crabmeat that comes refrigerated.

4. Regardless of the form of crabmeat you are using, place the crabmeat in a colander, drain it well, then transfer it to a large mixing bowl. Discard the liquid. Be sure to search carefully through the crabmeat to remove any remaining shell particles.

5. Heat a sauté pan, then add the butter and allow it to melt. Add the onions, celery, and peppers and sauté until they are al dente. Do not allow them to brown. Remove the vegetables from the heat and allow them to cool slightly.

6. Salt the crabmeat to taste, then add the cooled, sautéed vegetables into the bowl with the crabmeat.

7. In a separate bowl, combine the white pepper, mustard, Worcestershire, and mayonnaise. Mix until well blended. Add to the crabmeat mixture and stir gently.

(continued)

(Fresh Maryland Crabcakes
continued from page 24)

:: Chef's Note

A live crab weighing 1 pound will provide, on average, 1 cup of meat. Be sure all the crabs are alive at the time of purchase as well as at the time of preparation. Cook live crabs the same day you purchase them. If you buy king crab, 1 pound of crab legs is approximately 1½ cups; for canned crab, one 7½-ounce can of crab is equal to 1 cup of crabmeat. Crab cakes should taste as though they came straight from the sea, so choose the best crab you can find for this dish.

8. Add the bread crumbs and mix gently. Then stir in the eggs a little at a time, until the crab cake mixture is bound but not too wet. Stir in the pimiento.

9. Using a medium-sized ice cream scoop, portion the crab cakes into equally sized balls. Flatten the cakes until they are shaped into patties 3" in diameter; place on a sheet pan lined with parchment paper. Refrigerate for at least 4 hours but not more than 24 hours. When the cakes feel firm, they are ready for grilling.

10. Just before serving, coat a preheated grill with vegetable spray. Place the cakes on the grill and cook for 4-5 minutes per side, or until lightly browned. The cakes are completely cooked when the internal temperature reaches 165°F.

11. If you prefer to cook the crab cakes slightly ahead of your serving time, keep them on a prepared sheet pan in a 165° oven for 20 minutes or less.

TOSTADAS DE MAIZ AZUL CON CEVICHE (CEVICHE ON BLUE CORN TOSTADAS)

(SERVES SIX)

In this lesson we learn that the proteins of seafood are denatured when they are marinated in citric acid. This denaturing process is the also the primary scientific effect that takes place when heat is applied to food. In Culinary Basics the fundamental knife cuts are also taught, and precision is expected throughout the course of the culinary school program. Uniform cuts ensure even cooking. In a dish such as ceviche that is not cooked, knife cuts are important because the uniformity greatly enhances the presentation. :: CWM

PROCEDURE

1. Using 2 plastic or stainless-steel bowls, place the shrimp in one of the bowls and the whitefish in the other. In a third small bowl, dissolve the salt in the lime juice. Pour half the juice over the shrimp and the other half over the whitefish.

2. Allow the fish and shrimp to marinate until they have a "cooked" opaque appearance, 45-60 minutes. Drain well and discard the liquid.

3. Combine all the ceviche flavoring ingredients in a large mixing bowl. Stir to mix well.

4. Add the drained fish and shrimp to the ceviche mixture. Gently mix the ingredients without crushing the whitefish.

5. Crisp the tortillas in oil just before serving. To do this, heat a heavy skillet and add 2 tablespoons vegetable oil. When the oil is hot, fry each tortilla on both sides for just a few seconds. Repeat this process until all of the tortillas are crisped.

6. To serve, lift the ceviche out of the bowl with a slotted spoon to eliminate any extra liquid. Fill each tortilla with a generous scoop of ceviche. Garnish with slices of avocado and whole cilantro leaves.

FISH MARINADE INGREDIENTS

1/2 pound Shrimp, peeled, deveined, small diced
1/2 pound Whitefish, small diced
1 tablespoon Kosher Salt
1 1/2 cups Colima, or Key Lime Juice, freshly squeezed

CEVICHE FLAVORING INGREDIENTS

4 Roma Tomatoes, small diced
1 small White Onion, small diced
1 Serrano Chile, minced
2 tablespoons Cilantro, fresh, chopped
1 tablespoon Mexican Oregano, minced
1 tablespoon Tomato-Based Salsa
1 tablespoon Sugar
3 tablespoons Colima, or Key Lime Juice, freshly squeezed
2 tablespoons Kosher Salt

ACCOMPANIMENTS

6 Blue Corn Tortillas, crisped in hot oil
Avocado Slices, dipped in lime juice to maintain their color
Cilantro Leaves, whole, for garnish

:: Chef's Notes

Colima limes are the genetic fathers of the key lime. They come from the coast of Mexico near Jalisco, the home of tequila. Colimas are very flavorful and aromatic with a large amount of highly acidic juice. They can be kept fresh for 2-3 weeks if stored in a jar of water in the refrigerator.

Use very fresh fish for this recipe. If whitefish are unavailable, use pompano, red snapper, or sole. If you do not have a juicer, you can increase the amount of juice squeezed from each lime by rolling the fruit back and forth between your palms, then piercing the limes with a fork and placing them in the microwave on medium for 10-20 seconds.

- Simmer crabs for about fifteen minutes in water and crab boil.

- When crabs are red, remove and chill.

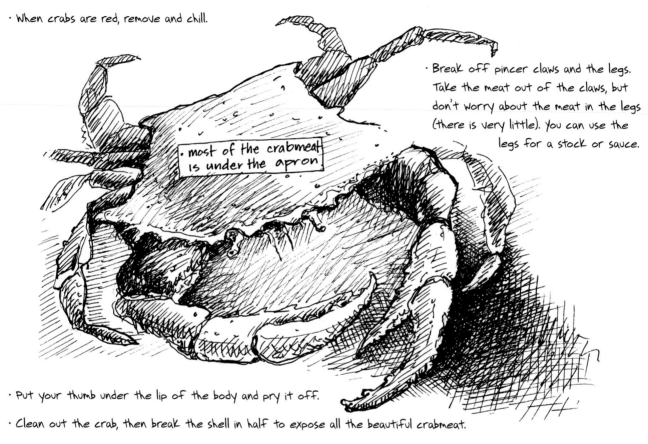

- Break off pincer claws and the legs. Take the meat out of the claws, but don't worry about the meat in the legs (there is very little). You can use the legs for a stock or sauce.

· most of the crabmeat is under the apron

- Put your thumb under the lip of the body and pry it off.

- Clean out the crab, then break the shell in half to expose all the beautiful crabmeat.

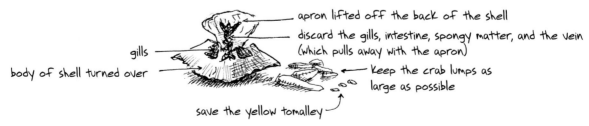

apron lifted off the back of the shell

discard the gills, intestine, spongy matter, and the vein (which pulls away with the apron)

gills

body of shell turned over

Keep the crab lumps as large as possible

save the yellow tomalley

FOR THE CEVICHE:

· Since "ceviche" comes from a verb meaning "to saturate," this dish uses a saturation method of "cooking." The acid in the limes actually denatures this fish and gives it an opaque appearance.

BLUE CORN TOSTADAS:

· The tortillas used to construct these tostadas are made from a blue corn that has a rich, nutty flavor. The sun- or fire-dried corn is treated with wood ash, which brings out its blue color.

· Yellow corn tortillas can be used as a substitute in this recipe, but this will change both the texture and the visual appeal of this dish.

· If you make the tortillas yourself, the blue cornmeal is available in specialty markets or the gourmet section of some grocery stores.

CHOICE OF UTENSILS:

· Be sure to marinate the ceviche in a plastic or stainless steel container, otherwise the acids in the lime will react with the metal. With aluminum bowls, the acids can actually start to dissolve the metal.

THE CHEF AS TEACHER

THE GIVE AND TAKE OF TEACHING

Teaching is an art that I was absolutely meant to do. I don't know how many people can say they are doing what they were meant to do. Teaching means sharing a part of myself. Every six weeks when I get a new class, I give away a piece of who I am to 40 different people, and every six weeks I get that back tenfold. But to me, that's what it's all about.

THE SOCRATIC METHOD

My father taught me that good teaching is not about stating great things, it's a matter of posing great questions. His lessons will always be with me.

When I was 17 my dad bought me the shell of a Pinto station wagon. Not the whole car, just the shell. His words to me were, "You'll need to find an engine for it, but you can use my machine shop to put it in. Happy birthday." He knew the gift would push me to grow and force me to ask the right questions until I surpassed even my own expectations. Life is not about being given all the answers. It's about being secure enough to say, "I don't know it all, but I trust myself and the world around me to go looking for the answers I need."

THE SURPRISE OF A CULINARY EDUCATION

People, especially younger students, think they are coming just to learn the information and techniques outlined in the curriculum. They do learn that, but they usually end up learning more about themselves as people; it's inevitable because so much growth is possible in a culinary curriculum. If you are motivated and learn the lessons deeply, you are challenged on every level: physically, intellectually, and creatively.

MY CUP IS FULL

The students I find most challenging to teach are the ones who come to school after a great deal of experience in the field and bring with them an attitude that there's not much more to learn. At those times I find it helpful to refer to a little

story from a book called *Zen and the Art of Martial Arts*. Here Bruce Lee, the martial-arts icon, recounts the story of a professor who goes to visit a Japanese Zen master in the martial arts. But shortly after the master starts to teach, he stops the lesson and takes the professor inside for a cup of tea. The master begins to pour the tea into the professor's cup and continues to pour long after the cup is full, and tea begins running out all over the table onto the floor. Finally, after moments of hesitation, the professor becomes quite perplexed and asks for the master to stop, pointing out that his cup is full. The master responds that it is for this very reason that he could not teach this professor about the intricacies of the martial arts. His cup was full. You cannot be open to new lessons if you feel you know it all already.

THE BEAUTY OF UNIQUE THOUGHT

I want to learn from my students as much as I want to teach them what I know. Creativity comes from unique thought. How can you ignore the fact that every student brings in his or her own unique perspective on cooking? You can't possibly have all the same thoughts, so there are always new ways of combining flavors and applying techniques. There's always more to learn from each other.

ANALOGIES FOR COOKING

I find artistic analogies to be helpful when I teach, not just because they have perfect parallels, but also because they reach out to all kinds of students with all different frames of reference. People listen when you speak their language. If students have a theatrical bent, I use that theme as I teach palate development. I help them see food a little differently when they place some ingredients in a starring role in the performance and other food or flavors in supporting roles.

It works just as beautifully to use musical analogies to teach about cooking within regional themes. For example, I may start with a lesson focusing on a morel mushroom. If I look at that mushroom as a solo, it is beautiful on its own. I can take a little oil and roast it to get a bit of complexity in that flavor, but it would primarily emphasize one particular type of taste in your mouth. Then I think what flavors would harmonize with that mushroom, such as butter or duck fat. If I were cooking within the regional theme of the Périgord area of France, I would choose duck fat for the dish. The regional theme is the recurring pattern that I would refer to in order to add other harmonizing flavors, since I can look to that region to see what other ingredients are traditionally used. The harmonizing chords that you add to the dish bring complexity whether you choose dissonant or consonant flavors to characterize the dish. Once you know your ingredients and the ways they can combine together, it's like the work of an accomplished musician who knows where the notes are on the keyboard, and no longer needs to read the music.

Finally, you can draw upon literary analogies to understand how to make a statement with your food. If you imagine your dish as a story line, you can decide what the moral of the story would be after your creation. Let's take that same morel mushroom as the lead character. Perhaps you want to bring out the earthy, more rustic qualities of the mushroom. Your story line would speak of life in the countryside, or the raw beauty on a farm. Or perhaps you want to emphasize a more formal side of the same mushroom and tell the tale, "These morels are haute cuisine and they only belong on the plate with foie gras and puff pastry." You are the author: The message is up to you.

Even lessons on restaurant ownership are perfectly suited for artistic analogies. Without a doubt, the restaurant owner is an entertainer. Regardless of how a workday has played out, The Show Must Go On. When the doors open on time to a hungry audience, they don't care if your dishwasher got drunk and didn't come in, or if your line cook is awaiting bail, or if your featured item didn't come in at the airport. They are ready to be entertained, no matter what. As a line cook, you are a performer in that grand production and you have to learn how to stay in character for the entire length of the performance. You have to be professional, because your emotions come out through your food. You have to keep it together and come into the performance with your mental mise-en-place primed. You have to be ready every night to give a performance that deserves a standing ovation.

ADDITIONAL RECIPES

GARLIC SALMON HACHÉ

From Chef Joel Brookstein

(SERVES FOUR)

The distinct flavor profile of these salmon patties offers an alternative to traditional crab cakes. Garlic is a good choice to combine with salmon since its pungency holds up to the strong salmon flavor. :: **CWM**

INGREDIENTS

1 pound Salmon, boneless, finely minced
2 Eggs, beaten
1 Shallot, minced
1 teaspoon Garlic, minced
1 teaspoon Italian Parsley, chopped
1/2 teaspoon Kosher Salt
1/4 teaspoon Black Pepper, freshly ground
3/4 cup Fresh Bread Crumbs, or as needed
1/4 cup Milk, or as needed
3 tablespoons Vegetable Oil for sautéing

:: Chef's Notes

If you prefer a strong salmon flavor, choose fresh, wild salmon for this dish. For more subtle flavoring, use farmed salmon–which, although it tends to be more fatty, has a less pungent flavor. To remove the bones, drape the salmon across the back of a mixing bowl, run your hand along the surface to find the bones, and use tweezers or a strawberry huller to pull them out. Then use a very sharp French knife to cut the salmon into a fine mince to result in a patty with a delicate texture.

A whole shallot is the whole globe, not just a clove from inside.

PROCEDURE

1. After checking the salmon for any remaining bones, combine it with the eggs, shallot, garlic, parsley, salt, and pepper in a large mixing bowl.

2. Add the bread crumbs and milk alternately, a little at a time, in order to adjust the consistency of the mixture. It needs to be just wet enough to hold together when squeezed into a patty. If the patties are too wet, the shape will deteriorate when they are fried.

3. Use an ice cream scoop to divide the mixture into even portions. Shape each portion into a patty that is 3" in diameter and 1/2" thick.

4. Preheat the oven to 150°F.

5. Heat a nonstick sauté pan over a medium-high flame. Pour in the oil and allow it to heat.

6. Fry the patties until they are golden brown on each side, approximately 3-4 minutes per side.

7. Transfer the patties to the oven to hold for a maximum of 20 minutes before serving.

SPICY FRUIT SALSA IN A SOUTHWESTERN MARINADE

From Chef Kevin Flynn

(SERVES SIX)

A variety of entrées from the Southwest are enhanced with this fruity salsa that delicately combines savory, sweet, sour, hot, and salty components. :: **CWM**

PROCEDURE

1. Combine the fruit, tomatoes, onions, jalapeño, cilantro, lime juice, and lemon juice. Mix well, then season with salt and pepper to taste.

2. Cover and put in the refrigerator for at least 3 hours to allow the flavors to combine. Serve cold with your favorite meat, poultry, or fish.

INGREDIENTS

½ cup Dried Fruit, small diced (dried raspberries or blueberries work nicely)

4 ripe Italian Plum Tomatoes, peeled, seeded, small diced

½ cup Red Onions, small diced

1 teaspoon Jalapeño Pepper, minced

2 tablespoons Cilantro, fresh, leaves only, chopped

1 tablespoon Lime Juice, freshly squeezed

1 teaspoon Lemon Juice, freshly squeezed

Kosher Salt and freshly ground Black Pepper

:: Chef's Note

The word *salsa*, "sauce" in Spanish, has evolved to mean an accompaniment made with a range of flavors from tomatoes to fruit. Since this salsa is fresh, it should be kept in the refrigerator, wrapped tightly, for no longer than 5 days.

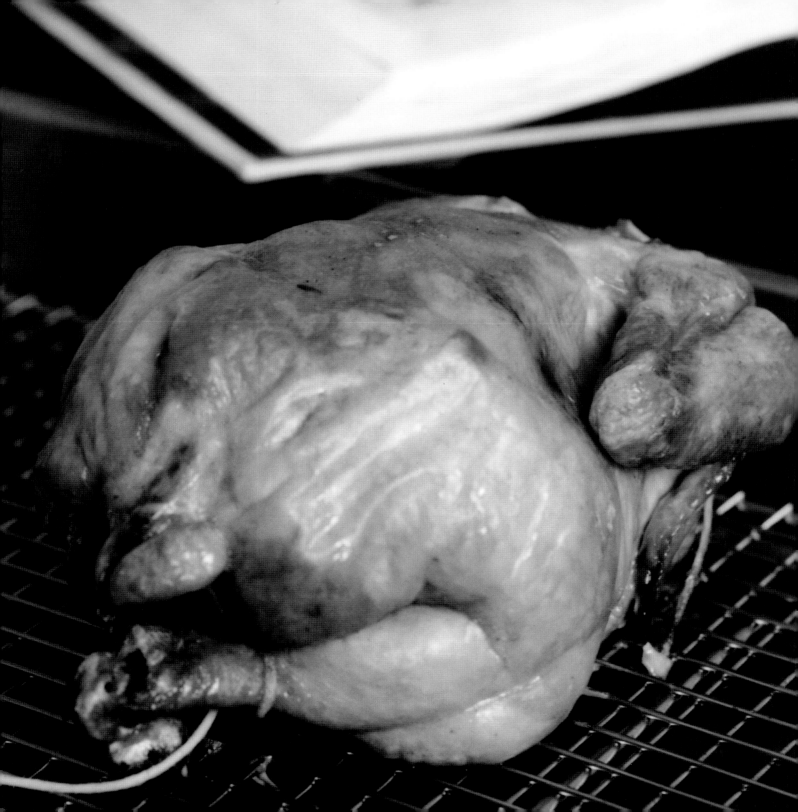

meat fabrication

INSTRUCTOR: CHEF JEAN-MARIE RIGOLLET

I MUST ADMIT THAT BEFORE I BEGAN A COURSE IN MEAT FABRICATION, I DIDN'T FEEL A NATURAL AFFINITY TOWARD BUTCHERY.

The carving of meat seemed gruesome and macabre. But with the depth and joie de vivre that Chef Rigollet brought into the classroom, I soon learned to relax and respect the importance of the class. I realized that it was virtually impossible to cook from a position of wisdom without knowing an animal's muscular and skeletal structure. To know an animal's movements allowed me to understand the texture contained in the cuts of its meat, which in turn taught me to determine which time, temperature, and technique would bring out its finest features. In class, we also learned the processes of brining, curing, smoking, and aging, which added further options to the chef's palette. In addition to teaching the basics of how to purchase and process beef, pork, fish, and poultry, the class also focused on charcuterie—sausages, forcemeats, pâtés, and terrines that utilize nearly every part of the animal. The ways of the West inspired Chef Rigollet to move to America. His deep appreciation for the land, the food, and the native people was evident in all he did. The gifts he brought to his students included lessons on carefully fabricating all forms of meat with the least amount of waste; the joy to appreciate every aspect of cooking; and the finesse to make every movement in the kitchen purposeful and precise. :: **CWM**

REFLECTIONS OF A CHEF

COMING TO AMERICA

When I first arrived in this country, at 25 years old, my attitude was, "I am a French man. Oo-la-la, listen to me, I am from France. Let me show you how things are done in the kitchen." I had to mellow significantly. I was cocky, aggressive, and condescending. It was wrong that I was being so stupidly French when I came to America. There are many different ways to be French.

I began in this country as a chef at the Arizona Biltmore Hotel and later started my own restaurant. We had amazing clientele, including Stevie Nicks, Megadeth, Don Ameche, the prince of Greece. I cooked for Sting's wedding. Other regular guests included members of the Boiche family, who were dear friends of Nancy Reagan. When President Reagan was in office, I eventually cooked for him, too. It was an evening complete with the FBI, sniffing dogs, and an army of taste testers.

My restaurant was very successful, but I knew when the time came to sell the business. I needed a change for my own well-being; it was taking too much out of me. It was clear the time had come to follow the dream that originally brought me to America: to go out in the desert and immerse myself in Western Life. So one day I gave my wife power of attorney, sold my restaurant, hooked up my horse trailer, and started The Lost Frenchman Outfitter, a culinary adventure business taking people on horseback to the desert: camping, riding, and cooking on the open range.

On horseback I could experience the ancient roots of food and civilization. After a long rain I would go out for morning rides in the desert to discover evidence of the Ancestral Puebloans who lived in those parts 800 to 900 years ago. I could find holes in the rocks where they ground their corn, fire pits where they burned corn for their ceremonies, and peach pits buried in the sand that fell from ancient orchards. A fossilized egg once rolled down from the top of a mesa. The treasures of the past seemed to be making themselves known to the passions of my present life. It fulfilled the cowboy part of my soul.

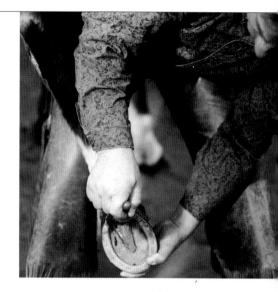

FOOD ALFRESCO

Food becomes a totally new experience if you take your meal outside. The roast lamb you made for lunch is blah when eaten inside, but take that same plate into the air of the countryside or garden and the difference is astonishing. It takes on a new beauty because that is where you are meant to live. Food should be experienced in the midst of the terroir: the dirt, the air, the fragrance of nearby blossoms.

THE PLEASURES OF SLOW FOOD

In order to fully appreciate food, you have to slow down, savor every nuance, every morsel, every aspect of the food itself. Let your passion be unleashed on your tongue.

You also have to seek out the sources for your food to be certain the plants and animals were allowed to live as full of a life as possible. Quality of life does not happen in enormous feedlots involved in the mass production of meats. Something is definitely lost there. When chickens and dairy cows are constantly pushed to produce more and more, the animals, the land, and the quality of the food all suffer. We need to support the small farmers who nurture the plants and animals we adore.

The closer you are to the food, the more you appreciate it. You can honor food if you get up at 5 A.M. with your flashlight to find the chickens still asleep in the hay. Then you go outside before the sun comes up and apologize to the chicken before you take its life and put it in boiling water, pluck it, clean it, and burn your hands in the process. That's chicken with integrity instead of just getting in a case of chickens on ice. It's up to us as chefs to see food as a beautiful part of life.

ON GRATITUDE

Being a responsible chef all has to do with gratitude. You should learn gratitude in this business. There are places where people don't have the abundance that we do, who live life on the other end of the extreme, who die from their need for food. When I throw something in the garbage that still has some use, I apologize quietly for those who didn't get to eat that day. That someone could die of starvation while we have such a bounty is to me completely unjust. I cannot stand to watch people waste.

If we can be selective of only what we truly need, only then can we live life at the right pace and in the right measures. The same is true for food, sex and love, or whatever else: Live life to the fullest but don't overdo.

COOKING SECRETS

One of the most important cooking secrets is how to cook with less waste and more flavor. A valuable lesson is using a remouillage to maximize the flavor and usage of expensive items. A remouillage is a "rewetting" of the stock ingredients. When you make lobster stock, for example, in a remouillage, you would strain the ingredients from the stock instead of throwing them away immediately. Strain out the lobster shells using a big spider strainer and put them in a large colander set over a second rondeaux pan. Then, using a china cap strainer, strain the stock itself into another pot. The sediment that is left in the china cap is then put back with the shells. Allow the shells and sediment to drip from the colander into the rondeaux for 3-5 minutes, until the last drop lands in your rondeaux instead of in the garbage. Then you wash the shells with some of the reserved

stock and draw out a weaker stock, which you later combine with the richer version. After all your stock is recovered, combined, and reduced, you've increased your production of lobster bisque by 20-30 percent.

MEMORY AND CONTEXT

Good cooking brings back memories of something lost, something from the past. On a rainy day, a boring afternoon, you think of your mother and the French toast that she made for you as a child. You make it right at that moment and she's there with you again.

Olive oil, shaved garlic, chopped tomatoes, cracked black pepper, aromatic herbs, freshly made pasta: It's the simple flavors that take me back to my life in France. There everyone was always dreaming about what we would eat next. My friends and I would look at each other and say, "We need this dish," and we'd know exactly where to go get it. We'd walk down to George's restaurant for his special dish or wherever we needed to go to satisfy those desires.

THE BLENDING OF ARTISTIC INSPIRATIONS

Food has a way of intertwining with the arts in a way that enhances both the flavor and the art experience. When I dance and it's elegant, it's all about champagne, caviar, hors d'oeuvres, and foie gras. But if it's a good salsa beat it's about chimi-churi salsa, jerk pork, and lovely spicy-smelling ladies.

JEAN-MARIE RIGOLLET

With architecture, I am attracted to buildings of ancient times. When I visited the old temples in the Greek islands, I once licked the corner of an outside wall to taste the salt from the sea that surrounds them. I love to ingest life. The older I get, the more I am in a hurry to sample it all over again. The beauty of old, wonderful buildings reminds me of how many lives have walked on this earth, how many celebrations have taken place in their halls, how the traditions of food and life continue through the ages.

THE CONNECTION OF LITERATURE

Literature connects you in a way that balances you as a person and a chef. In order to be happy, you have to have your head connected to the ground. Literature grounds you in that way by bridging your experiences to those of the rest of humanity and the natural world. When I read Alfonse Daudet's *Letters from My Windmill*, I hear the shrill call of locusts in the trees, I smell the salt as it seasons the air, I feel the warmth of the sun on the leaves dancing in the vineyard, I absorb the graceful motions of the fig and olive trees as they sway in the afternoon breeze. It creates an appreciation for the world.

SOUL FOOD

Music is food for the soul. It captures the biggest moments in time, the big battles and historical events. Music works to get all the senses tuned in and connected at the same time. I love cooking to baroque music. I can see everything those composers wrote, I can see it. The big castles, the lord of the land, I see the feasts, the hunt, the killing, I see huge kitchens with 200 people cooking with simple instruments. No hygiene and dogs everywhere, but that was life. Music makes my cooking come alive.

COOKING AS LOVE AND ART

Cooking is an artful expression of love. Through our creations, people's eyes light up. It's definitely a form of art for us to express ourselves that way, a very brief form of art. The writer has her books, the painter has his paintings, but the chef has only the memory of the creation and the smile of the guest. Our art results in an intimate expression of feelings and nourishment. It's a rush when you combine all the right elements. It's important to use the best ingredients you can find. Use beautiful wine. Don't drink cheap. Don't cook cheap. When you use all your senses in your art—your touch, your sight, your smell, your taste, your hearing—it evolves into something emotional. Why not? You feed your soul and body in a way that elicits desire, passion. That is art. That is love.

THE CHEF'S LESSON

FAISAN AUX CAPRES (PHEASANT IN LEMON-CAPER SAUCE)

(SERVES FOUR)

In Meat Fabrication class all types of meat, fish, and poultry are fabricated into specific, manageable cuts. The muscle groups are examined to distinguish the characteristics that affect the culinary preparation. For example, the pheasant breasts in this lesson are from a less exercised portion of the bird, so they will stay tender in this quick method of preparation. They do not need the prolonged moist method of cooking required for tougher cuts. For extra juiciness, you can insert a teaspoon of duck fat or a piece of unsmoked bacon under the skin of each breast. :: **CWM**

INGREDIENTS

3/4 cup Butter, clarified
4 Pheasant Breasts
Kosher Salt and freshly ground Black Pepper
1/2 cup All-Purpose Flour
1 cup Dry White Wine
1/2 cup Capers, drained
1 Lemon, freshly squeezed
4 Anchovy Fillets, rinsed, pureed
2 tablespoons Butter

:: Chef's Note

This recipe elicits memories of great hunts that took place on my aunt's private woods in France. She has her own flock of birds for hunting, and the pheasants are particularly wonderful. This simple preparation enhances the tender pheasant with a classic French sauce that brings moisture and flavor to the dish. Roasted potatoes would go nicely with this entrée.

PROCEDURE

1. Preheat the oven to 375°F.

2. Heat an ovenproof skillet on the stove. Add the clarified butter and allow it to get hot.

3. Quickly season the pheasant breasts with salt and pepper and dredge them in a pan of flour to coat all surfaces. Gently shake off any excess flour.

4. Immediately add the pheasant to the pan, skin-side down, and allow the pieces to brown nicely without disturbing.

5. When the meat is golden brown on all sides, add the wine, capers, lemon juice, and anchovies to the pan. Turn the pheasant to coat well.

6. Cover and place the pan in the oven for approximately 20 minutes, or until the juices from the pheasant run slightly pink. The internal temperature should reach 150°. Do not overcook or the pheasant will become dry.

7. Remove the meat from the pan and set aside on a warm serving plate to rest. Whisk the butter into the pan juices to enrich and slightly thicken them. Adjust the seasoning. Serve with the warm pan juices drizzled over the top of each serving of pheasant.

COQUILLES SAINT-JACQUES AUX RAISINS ET AUX NOIX (SEA SCALLOPS WITH SCOTCH-SOAKED RAISIN WALNUT SAUCE)

(SERVES FOUR)

This is an excellent lesson in creating flavor while maintaining the texture of the main ingredient. The preparation allows the flavors to marry in the creamy sauce without making the scallops rubbery. If you are lucky enough to find farm-raised sea scallops in the shell, keep the roe for flavor and the shells for presentation. The shells can be washed and stored for use when only shucked scallops are available. The name Coquilles Saint-Jacques comes from early times when St. Jacques wore a scallop shell as his personal emblem. :: **CWM**

INGREDIENTS

18 Walnut Halves
1 cup Raisins
1 cup Scotch, your preferred brand
¼ cup Butter, unsalted
24 large Sea Scallops, washed, patted dry
¼ cup Crème Fraîche (see note)
Sea Salt and White Pepper

ACCOMPANIMENTS

4 cups cooked Basmati and Wild Rice, mixed
    after cooking
Reserved Sea Scallop Shells, optional, for
    garnish
Red, Black, or Champagne Grapes for garnish

:: Chef's Note

Crème fraîche can be found at specialty food stores, but you can also make your own. Heat 2 cups heavy cream to 100°F and stir in ¼ cup buttermilk. Pour the mixture into a plastic container, cover, and let it sit in a warm location for 24 hours. Transfer the crème fraîche to the refrigerator for a few hours to allow it to thicken. It can be kept covered and refrigerated for up to 2 weeks.

PROCEDURE

1. Toast the walnuts in a hot, dry skillet. Remove them from the heat when they just begin to turn dark brown. Put the walnuts between 2 pieces of paper towel and roll them back and forth to remove the skins. Reserve the nutmeats and discard the skins.

2. Soak the raisins in the Scotch for 1 hour. Strain, reserving the Scotch and raisins in separate containers.

3. In a large saucepan, melt the butter and add the scallops. Sear the scallops briefly on each side, then remove the pan from the stove. Add the reserved Scotch to the pan and return it to the heat. Tip the pan carefully and ignite the Scotch. Allow the liquor to flambé the scallops. If the flame does not die down after about 20 seconds, put a lid on top of the pan for 1-2 seconds to smother it. At this point, remove the scallops from the pan and set them aside.

4. Add the walnuts, raisins, and crème fraîche to the pan containing the Scotch. Whisk together over low heat and reduce until the sauce is nappe.

5. Return the scallops to the sauce just before serving to quickly reheat. Do not leave the scallops in the sauce too long or they will become rubbery. Add salt and pepper to taste.

6. Serve over a bed of basmati and wild rice, with each rice cooked separately, then mixed together and seasoned just before serving. To plate up the dish, put a scoop of the combined rice in the center of the plate, arrange the shells around the base of the rice, if desired, and spoon the scallops with the sauce on top of the shells. Drizzle extra sauce on top of the rice. Garnish with a small cluster of fresh grapes on the side.

COOKING WITH PHEASANT:

· Pheasants are actually the most widely-consumed feathered game in the world.

· Recipes for pheasant date back as early as the 14th century.

· Hunting for pheasant is obviously the way to ensure a fresh bird with robust flavor. The next best option is to choose a free-range pheasant from a reputable butcher specializing in game meats. The free-range pheasants eat varied diets that result in a very flavorful meat, particularly in comparison to the flavor of caged birds.

· Hanging birds for an average of three days before roasting has long been a controversy. This is only done when a bird is still in plumage and is not yet eviscerated. This practice is losing favor in European as well as American kitchens due to a preference for less gamey tasting meats.

· Although hens are smaller than cocks, they are a better choice for roasting because they have more meat on their carcasses and the meat tends to be more tender.

· The breast of the pheasant is always the most tender. Pheasants use their legs extensively, which results in tougher leg meat. To deal with this difference in tenderness, the legs can be detached and cooked separately using a longer, slower cooking method. They may also be reserved for use in stocks, soups, and sauces.

- Pheasants are very lean and tend to be dry if cooked without additional fat. To increase the juiciness of the meat, you can lard the bird with bacon or insert duck fat underneath the skin before it is placed in the oven.

- When cooking pheasant, it's better to undercook rather than overcook. Look for the juices to run pink when pricked in the thigh.

ABOUT SCALLOPS:

- The reason scallops have such a firm texture is because they move and travel underwater significantly more than their other mollusk friends. This results in a much stronger muscle.

- The Coquille Saint-Jacques is considered a "great scallop" and is much larger in diameter than queen, Iceland, or bay scallops.

- Bay scallops are very sweet with a delicate flavor, and are in season from October until March.

- Calico scallops are easily turned from tender to rubbery since they generally arrive at the fishmonger partially cooked.

- Sea scallops are the type most commonly found in markets and have a rich sweet flavor. Look for scallops that are labeled "unsoaked," as these will have more of their own natural flavor. Always be sure to smell them unwrapped to ensure that they still have a fresh, not fishy aroma. Their color should be slightly pink or a milky white shade.

- If you buy scallops with the shell on and observe a little coral-colored sac, leave this attached as it contains the roe and will bring added flavor to the dish.

THE CHEF AS TEACHER

TEACHING AS RECONNECTION

Teaching is an incredible immersion. It's like opening a box filled with family pictures. I get a chance as a teacher to peek into that box and see parts of people's lives, to experience new perspectives. It puts me back in touch with parts of myself that I didn't even realize I'd forgotten. It's almost like a trip to the past 40 years of my life, just being involved with my students. It's completely fulfilling.

THE FREEDOM TO CREATE

In order for my students to truly create, I have to step back as an educator to some extent to allow them room to experiment. Freedom begets creativity. I may not agree with what comes out of their efforts, but they need that feeling of carte blanche in order to produce something new. Less is more when it comes to the direction of a creative process.

EXERCISES IN FLEXIBILITY

I build opportunities into the day that force people to deal with change. Constant change is a part of life in and outside of the kitchen. I add demonstrations to watch in the middle of production time so that people have to completely switch gears, leave their stations, and come to watch what I am producing. It forces people to deal with many priorities at once.

It's also important to help people learn how to deal with pressure: It's a tremendous force in the kitchen that creates many opportunities for humility. A humbling experience is always a good lesson. Humility is like a good friend that reminds you of the tremendous work that you have in front of you, a reminder of the consequences you face as a result of your life choices. Pressure is a good thing, too. It wakes you up from your own laziness, your denial, or fears; it stirs the pot; it forces you out of your comfort zone. When pressure is present, you can choose to fight it, trust it, or enjoy it. The key is to learn how to use its edge to improve your efficiency.

THE STRENGTH OF IDEALS

It's imperative to offer lessons in accountability. Being a chef puts you at the helm of responsibility in directing people's lives as well as controlling the flow of resources in and out of a kitchen. You are faced with constant challenges and temptations to take the easy way out. You have to be very strong in order to truly live by your ideals.

BEAUTY TO AN INSTRUCTOR

I'm the kind of instructor that looks at the people almost more than the food. Beauty to me is all in the intention of the cook. I look at who made a plate of food. How hard did they work on it? Did they make it out of necessity or did it come from the heart? Did they have a glow on their faces as they cooked it because they enjoyed where they were and what they were doing? What was their emotional state when they cooked it? If it's presented with eye contact and a beautiful smile, you can see the pride and sincerity. If they enjoy bringing it to you, that food is already beautiful.

ADDITIONAL RECIPES

RHUBARB-GLAZED DUCK BREAST WITH JALAPEÑO AND PINE NUT STUFFING

From Chef Chris Francis

(SERVES FOUR)

I found this preparation of game to be remarkable. The sweet, shiny rhubarb glaze on the duck is contrasted with the roughly textured stuffing. The combination of savory, spicy, and tart flavors is bridged together by the rum-butter richness. This is also lovely served with Jasmine Pear Pilaf (see page 8). :: **CWM**

STUFFING INGREDIENTS

3½ tablespoons Butter, clarified
¼ cup Red Onions, minced
1 Jalapeño Pepper, seeded, minced
2½ cups Granny Smith Apples, peeled,
    cored, small diced
¼ cup Dark Rum
1½ cups Pine Nuts

DUCK INGREDIENTS

4 Duck Breasts, trimmed (preferably Magrets)
Kosher Salt
1 tablespoon Vegetable Oil

RHUBARB GLAZE INGREDIENTS

3 tablespoons Rhubarb Jam
¼ cup + 3 tablespoons Pineapple Vinegar
    (see note)
¼ cup Balsamic Vinegar
3 tablespoons Sugar

PROCEDURE

1. Trim the duck breasts of any extra fat. Lightly score the top of the remaining fat with a chef's knife to create a diamond pattern in the skin.

2. Make a small cut on the side of each duck breast. Insert your finger into the hole to stretch the duck breast slightly and create a small pocket. Be careful to stretch gently so that the breast will not rip. Place the breasts in a small bowl, cover with plastic wrap, and put it back into the refrigerator until needed.

3. Sanitize your hands, knife, cutting board, and countertop.

4. To prepare the pine nuts, heat a dry sauté pan, add the nuts, and allow them to toast. Stir constantly until the pine nuts begin to turn light brown. Remove them from the stove and pour them onto a plate so the hot pan does not continue cooking them.

5. After the nuts have cooled slightly, place them in a plastic bag and crush with a rolling pin. Set aside.

6. In a large, hot sauté pan, add the clarified butter and minced onions. Stir constantly until the onions are slightly softened.

7. Add the minced jalapeño. After a few seconds, add the diced apple. Sauté for approximately 1 minute.

8. Take the pan off the heat and pour in the rum. Return the pan to the stove and allow the rum to cook off. When the rum is reduced to au sec (almost dry), set the pan off to the side to cool.

9. Combine the pine nuts and apple mixture when both are cooled.

10. Retrieve the duck and salt the surface of the meat and inside the pocket. Insert the apple/nut mixture into the pocket of the duck, but do not stuff it too full. Close the open end by weaving a wooden skewer or toothpick through the duck flesh.

11. Preheat the oven to 350°F.

12. Heat an ovenproof sauté pan on the stove over medium heat, add the oil, and allow it to get hot. Place the duck in the pan, skin-side down, and sauté the breasts until the skin is crisp. Pour off the excess fat in the pan. Turn once and place the pan in the oven.

13. While the duck is cooking, quickly combine the glaze ingredients and pour the mixture into a separate, prewarmed sauté pan.

14. Stir constantly over medium heat until the glaze has a syruplike consistency. Remove from the heat and pour about $1/4$ cup of the glaze into a separate small dish. Reserve the rest of the glaze in the pan, off the heat.

15. Approximately 3-4 minutes before the duck is done, or when the internal temperature reaches 139°, evenly brush the tops of the duck with the $1/4$ cup of glaze. Continue cooking the duck until the breasts are rare to medium rare, a total of approximately 10 minutes in the oven. The internal thermometer should read 140-145° when the duck is removed from the oven. Remove the duck from the pan and place it on warm serving plates.

16. Gently reheat the reserved glaze. Drizzle glaze on the front of the plate and serve immediately.

:: Chef's Notes

Magrets are the breasts from Moulard ducks. They are preferred for this recipe because the breasts are bigger, which makes them easier to stuff. If you can't get those, you can substitute Muscovy or Pekin duck.

Pineapple vinegar is available in specialty food stores, but it tastes fresher if you make your own. To do this, combine equal parts white or cider vinegar with fresh pineapple puree and heat the mixture to the boiling point. Cover and refrigerate for up to 36 hours, then strain off the flavored vinegar.

GRILLED VENISON WITH BOURBON CREAM SAUCE

From Chef Chris Francis

(SERVES FOUR)

Venison is also a very lean game meat. The quick method of preparation used in this recipe is suitable for steaks because they are a tender cut of meat. This rich bourbon sauce brings moisture as well as full-bodied flavor to a hearty entrée. :: **CWM**

VENISON INGREDIENTS

4, 5-ounce Venison Steaks

MARINADE INGREDIENTS

2½ cups Teriyaki Sauce, low sodium
1 cup Worcestershire Sauce
½ cup Bourbon, of choice
½ cup Brown Sugar
1 tablespoon Garlic, minced
1 teaspoon Tarragon, fresh, minced
1 teaspoon Basil, fresh, minced
1 teaspoon Cayenne Pepper
½ teaspoon Onion Powder
½ teaspoon Oregano, fresh, minced
Black Pepper, freshly ground

SAUCE INGREDIENTS

Marinating Liquid, above
1 pint Heavy Cream
2 tablespoons Butter, unsalted
Salt and Pepper

:: Chef's Note

Be careful not to cook venison past the point of medium rare or it will become tough and dry. When choosing the meat, consider New Zealand farm-raised venison, which has a notably milder taste.

PROCEDURE

1. Combine all the marinade ingredients in a small saucepot. Cook over medium heat, stirring constantly, until the sugar is dissolved. Remove the pot from the heat and allow the marinade to cool.

2. Submerge the venison steaks in the cooled marinade and refrigerate for at least 2 hours, turning every hour.

3. Just before cooking, preheat the grill and coat the grates with nonstick spray. Remove the steaks from the marinade, blot dry, and place directly on the hot grill. Turn the steaks over only once during the grilling process. Cook over high heat until medium rare, approximately 2–2½ minutes per side for a 1¼" steak. The internal temperature should read 125–130°F. Remove the steaks from the heat and allow them to rest for a few minutes in a warm location in order for the juices to be absorbed.

4. While the steaks are on the grill, strain the marinade into a saucepan. Over high heat, reduce the sauce by two-thirds, until it is nappe. Stir occasionally. Set aside in a warm location.

5. In a small saucepan over medium-low heat, reduce the cream by half, stirring constantly. Just before serving, whisk the warm cream into the reduced marinade. Finish by whisking in the butter. Season to taste with salt and pepper. Serve the sauce drizzled in front of the venison steaks on the plate.

saucier

INSTRUCTOR: CHEF WILLIS GETCHELL

SAUCES ARE ROMANTIC TO ME.

Nothing is more luxurious than liquids allowed to deepen in flavor, to shine with pearl-like translucence, to thicken so that the sauce will cling to the entrée with a soft robe of moisture and richness. Even the name, *Saucier*, rolls off your tongue. I couldn't wait to cook in Chef Getchell's kitchen, where we would learn the secrets of great sauces, soups, and stocks coupled with the beauties of a perfectly sautéed dish. In class, it soon became evident that his devotion to the most beautiful foundations in life—great food, art, literature, music, and above all, family—was a perfect metaphor for the lessons he taught in Saucier. He taught us the secret to great French cooking: The foundation of great cuisine is wonderful, deeply flavorful stock; it is the key to all other richness in the savory side of the kitchen. From that building block, we learned to create outstanding soups with layers of vibrant flavor, as well as velvety sauces that teased, complemented, contrasted, or married the other flavors on our plates. He demonstrated that the integrity involved in cooking requires a devotion to the best principles from start to finish. That dedication to a core of flavor has stunning results. Chef Getchell, a former talent scout for a record company, likened the sensation of presenting a great meal to the applause a band receives when it appears on stage: "When you put a dish in front of your guests, suddenly there's a hush from the crowd. Your emotions are poised to explode with delight as they shower you with adoration. I marvel at that split second of silence." :: **CWM**

REFLECTIONS OF A CHEF

LIFE IN THE RECORD BUSINESS

Working with a record company in the 1970s meant being swept up in the British musical invasion. The punk-rock frenzy was the embodiment of wretched excess. Life on the road was fast and destructive; it was too good a time. I left the recording business to begin as a cook, the only other skill I knew at the time. On the one hand, it gave me a whole new lifestyle in which to live out my ambitions. On the other, it reminded me enough of the recording industry to keep me engaged. Cooking represented immediate gratification and the chance to entertain a crowd.

The best chefs remind me of the best musicians from that era. Elvis Costello is one of my favorite singer-songwriters. Like a great chef, he does what he wants. He doesn't sit down to write hits. He writes what inspires him, not just what sells. He's not afraid to try new things. He's done things with tenors, quartets, even with a three-piece power trio doing hard punk rock. For musicians and great cooks, you have to be willing to risk, to mix things up in order to turn out something truly unique.

INTRODUCTIONS THROUGH THE WRITTEN WORD

I began my career as a cook working at a little French bistro. The chef threw me a copy of Julia Child's two-volume set *Mastering the Art of French Cooking* whenever he wanted me to try something new. I devoured those books; they gave me great confidence. For example, after reading a seven-and-a-half-page description of lobster bisque, I was certain I could attempt that luxurious soup on my own. It began my addiction to great culinary literature.

Much later in my career, I did an apprenticeship with a chef in Philadelphia who owned a 10,000-volume private collection of obscure cookbooks. He even had an original cookbook from Thomas Jefferson's collection. Chefs from all over the Delaware Valley used to come to research culinary questions in his library. Whenever I would walk the crooked stairway up to the library, past the old dog and cat that guarded the chef's residence over the restaurant kitchen, I would be filled with new questions that I couldn't wait to have answered in the volumes of culinary literature before me. Because Fritz, the library owner and chef, knew that I eventually wanted to be a culinary educator, he would "require" me to return to the kitchen after my research in his library to teach the rest of the kitchen staff what I had learned. Those moments with great literature fueled my imagination and began a lifelong love affair with books and cuisine.

ANALYSIS AND THE LAYERING OF FLAVORS

One of the biggest "ahas" for me in the process of learning was understanding how to be analytical. When Fritz would come up to me and say, "Research six or seven different duck preparations for next week," I would head up to the massive library. Meanwhile, he would order in the duck and together we would compare the best recipes. He would begin by leaving the creations up to me, and then he would pop in and out of the

kitchen saying "try this" or "try that." Then he would join me side by side and we would taste all the different nuances, one right after the other. Finally he would have me try the same flavors in different combinations. It was then, at last, that I completely understood the layering of flavors that can happen on a plate. I also learned to analyze foods that I don't enjoy to truly understand what it is that I don't enjoy about it.

By being so precise it is possible to isolate the specific reactions that are repulsive— which is much more helpful than generalizing the dislike from the entire food itself. I share an aversion to cucumbers with Alexandre Dumas, who wrote *The Three Musketeers* and *The Count of Monte Cristo*. He said the best thing you can do with a cucumber is to peel it, scoop the seeds out, slice it really, really thinly, add a little sugar, a little salt, a little vinegar, and then dump it in the trash.

PRACTICE MAKES PERFECT

In the early days of my career I built my confidence by practicing my techniques at home so that I could be solid when I came to work. I'd practice flipping food in a sauté pan with a slice of bread. Then I'd practice with dried beans to get used to moving small pieces as one mass. I would practice while my roommates from those days watched television in the same room, and they'd complain, "Aw man, he's doing the thing with the beans again." But it worked, and I mastered the technique of veggie tossing, despite the lack of support. I would go out and buy a flat of eggs and practice flipping them until, again, my roommates would say in disgust, "Throw those away, we're not eating eggs again tonight. Beer and eggs don't work." Despite the less-than-enthusiastic response, I mastered the egg thing, too. At work, I'd volunteer to take on extra work, I was so eager to learn. I made hollandaise with 30 eggs so often, I could do it with my eyes closed. It's the mastering of the basic techniques that builds the foundation of a great chef.

EXPERIENCE AT ALL LEVELS

Working at a major casino is a perfect training ground. There are so many venues; if you are motivated, the plethora of choices allows you to work in every position imaginable.

I got my first position at a casino when I took a job at Caesar's in Atlantic City. I moved through the casino, seizing every opportunity to learn. I milked everything there was to know from sauciers to line cooks, managers to sous-chefs, pastry chefs to chefs de cuisine. I learned until I had an opportunity to work in those positions myself. From the butcher shop to bakery to banquets, I cooked in every position. My days were filled with work. I'd cook 11 P.M.-7 A.M. at the hotel. Then at 8, I would head to the little French bistro where I first began cooking to help with their lunch shift until 1 P.M. Then I'd crash on the beach for a few hours before I'd go back and do it all over again.

SUCCESS AND THE ULTIMATE MENTOR

My persistence paid off when, after years of cooking and managing at every venue in the hotel, I was offered a position in fine dining at the gourmet seafood restaurant of the Trump Castle as their chef de cuisine. This was during the heydays of the casinos; 90 percent of my business was made up of high rollers who were comped at the restaurant. As a result, I was able to do unbelievable things and charge ridiculous amounts of money for the things we created. The beauty of the position, however, was not in the money itself, but in the creativity that budget afforded us.

We could create whatever we dreamed. We would get 5-pound lobsters and stuff them with half a pound of crab imperial and charge $125 for them. We couldn't get enough of them in to fill the demand. It was a time of unsurpassed creativity and opulence.

But more importantly, it was in that position that I found one of my greatest mentors, Katsuo Seguira. Seeing him use his knife was like watching Stevie Ray Vaughan play a guitar solo. On the line he would come behind you and show you how to do a technique, then he would watch you do it. He would say, "In my country you learn things three times: when you see it, when you do it, and when you teach someone else."

THE FINAL HORIZONS

I also worked as the sous-chef at the Sands Hotel. The Sands had the exclusive contract with Frank Sinatra and featured many other big stars as well, including Cher, Liza Minnelli, Whitney Houston, Bill Cosby, Willie Nelson, Johnny Cash, Waylon Jennings, and Kris Kristofferson. My job was not only to be responsible for the room service for all the other guests, but to direct the food and service for all the butlers and VIPs as well.

We would get pages of notes for requests for Mr. Sinatra's dressing room and suites. He would always order all different flavors of Lifesavers candy as well as bowls and bowls of candy to have out for people who came to visit him. His standing order was bottles of Gentleman Jack, which was an upscale version of Jack Daniels, that he would always drink with one ice cube.

WILLIS GETCHELL

But Mr. Sinatra wasn't difficult to cook for if you knew exactly what he wanted. I seemed to be the only cook who could make his food the way he liked it. He loved silver-dollar pancakes, burned bacon, and well-done steaks.

Willie, Waylon, Johnny, and Kris all wanted home cooking: pot roast, chicken potpie, fried chicken, and other food that was easy to make so that it tasted like home. Cher ate very healthy foods, and she traveled with her own personal chef who showed me a few pointers. Whitney Houston was a very kind guest to have at the hotel. She stayed at the oceanside property down the beach from the hotel. I would bring her Chinese cooking and she would stay to chat as I sautéed the soft-shell crabs for her dinner. It was amazing to look back at that point in my life and realize how far I'd come from the kid "doing the thing with the beans again."

COOKING SECRETS

Cher's chef gave me great tips on maximizing flavor without fat. Cher was very health-conscious but she did like bacon. So he would blanch her bacon first in hot water for about a minute to get most of the fat out of it and then cook it. Then he would save the blanching water, put it in the refrigerator, take the fat off it, and use the liquid to make soup for her. It was a fabulous way to incorporate an enormous amount of flavor without all the guilt.

THE CHEF'S LESSON

CREAMY BRIE SOUP WITH TOASTED BUTTERY CROUTONS

(SERVES SIX)

In Saucier we learn that the secret to superb soups and sauces begins with a commitment to high-quality ingredients, particularly when it comes to stock. Since stock is time-consuming to make, I have a ritual of "simmering on Sundays," and freezing the stock in zipper-lock bags to use throughout the week. If you need an alternative, use the Kitchen Basics brand of stock and "refresh it" by simmering it with fresh mirepoix, a bouquet garni, and some browned bones, just long enough for it to reduce slightly and deepen the flavor. :: CWM

SOUP INGREDIENTS

1 head Garlic, unpeeled
¼ cup Butter, unsalted
½ cup All-Purpose Flour
6 cups Chicken Stock (see page 78)
1 tablespoon Butter
¼ cup Carrots, peeled, julienned
¼ cup Celery, small diced
6 ounces Brie, rind removed
¼ cup + 2 tablespoons White Wine
¼ cup Heavy Cream
¼ cup Mushrooms, sliced
Salt and Pepper

ACCOMPANIMENTS

3 tablespoons Chives or Scallions,
   freshly chopped
Toasted Buttery Croutons (see note)

:: Chef's Note

Freshly-made croutons are wonderful. Preheat the oven to 400°F, cut off the crusts of an unsliced loaf of bread, and cut the bread into ½" cubes. Heat a large sauté pan, add 3 tablespoons clarified butter, and add the bread cubes. Toss to distribute the butter and pour onto a sheet pan in a single layer. Bake until crunchy and golden brown, tossing occasionally.

PROCEDURE

1. Roast the garlic: Cut off the top one-fourth of head to expose the cloves. Drizzle with olive oil and roast at 350°F for 30-45 minutes, or until cloves are soft and the juices run brown. Squeeze to release the garlic from its paper skins. Reserve and mash 6 of the garlic cloves. Wrap and store the remainder.

2. In a large stockpot, melt the butter and incorporate the flour gradually, whisking constantly. Be certain the whisk and pot are not made of aluminum, or the mixture will become discolored. Stir this mixture, which is known as a roux, until it has the aroma of cookies baking.

3. Slowly whisk in the chicken stock. Bring the soup just to a boil, then immediately turn the heat down for the soup to simmer. Reduce the soup by a third or until its consistency is nappe, skimming off any foam or impurities.

4. During the reduction, heat a sauté pan on low heat and add 1 tablespoon butter. Add the carrots and celery, cover, and allow them to sweat for 2 minutes. Remove the pan from the heat. Set the carrots and celery aside on a separate plate.

5. After the soup is done reducing, strain it through a chinois, or fine strainer. Return the soup to the stove on low heat and add the Brie. Using a heat-resistant spoon, stir constantly to avoid scorching.

6. When the cheese has melted, slowly whisk in the wine and add the carrots and celery. Simmer and stir until the vegetables are almost al dente, 3-4 minutes.

7. Meanwhile, warm the heavy cream in a separate saucepan. Add the mashed, roasted garlic and the sliced mushrooms to the soup, stir, and simmer 1 more minute.

8. Stir the warm cream into the soup and adjust the seasonings with salt and pepper.

9. Serve garnished with freshly chopped chives or scallions and crisp, buttery croutons.

SEARED FOIE GRAS WITH GINGER-INFUSED RASPBERRY RHUBARB COULIS, BALSAMIC REDUCTION, AND SAVORY CORN MADELEINES

(SERVES SIX)

All it took was one heavenly bite to know that foie gras was a splurge I would indulge in whenever I could afford it. I melt like a pool of duck fat every time my mouth gets an opportunity to embrace this amazing product. :: **CWM**

BALSAMIC REDUCTION INGREDIENTS

1 cup Fig Balsamic Vinegar
1 tablespoon Superfine Sugar
Kosher Salt and freshly ground Black Pepper

COULIS INGREDIENTS

2 tablespoons Butter, unsalted
1, 1" piece Ginger, fresh, peeled
3½ cups Rhubarb, fresh, medium diced
1 cup Red Raspberries, fresh
½ cup Superfine Sugar
¾ cup Chicken Stock (see page 78)
¼ cup Apple Juice
1 teaspoon Lemon Juice, freshly squeezed
Superfine Sugar
Kosher Salt and freshly ground Black Pepper

FOIE GRAS INGREDIENTS

1 pound Grade A Duck Foie Gras, fresh
Sea Salt and freshly ground Black Pepper

ACCOMPANIMENTS

3 cups Mâche or Baby Greens, washed
1 cup Red Raspberries, fresh
Savory Corn Madeleines (recipe follows)
1 tablespoon Crystallized Ginger, brunoise

PROCEDURE

1. Place the foie gras in a bowl of ice water for 10–15 minutes to firm the lobes and draw out the blood.

2. Remove the foie gras from the water and separate the two lobes with your hands. Remove and discard any veins, fat, or sinew. If the foie gras consists of a single lobe, make one cut through its center with a sharp, thin knife that has been heated in hot water, then dried. Then remove any visible veins, fat, and sinew.

3. When the foie gras is clean, cut the lobe(s) into ½" slices. Wash and dry the knife as needed.

4. Wrap the foie gras tightly in plastic wrap and place it in the refrigerator.

5. Begin the balsamic reduction by reducing 1 cup of fig balsamic vinegar over medium-low heat until it has a light syrupy consistency.

6. Turn off the heat and immediately stir in 1 tablespoon superfine sugar. Season to taste with salt and pepper. Pour the reduction into a squirt bottle and set aside in a warm-water bath.

7. Meanwhile, take the foie gras back out of the refrigerator and set aside on the counter to come to room temperature before searing.

8. To make the coulis, heat a sauté pan over medium-low heat. Add the butter and allow it to melt. Add the ginger, rhubarb, raspberries, ½ cup superfine sugar, and chicken stock to the pan. Stir gently, then simmer for approximately 5 minutes until the rhubarb is tender.

9. Remove the pan from the stove. Remove and discard the ginger, add the apple juice and lemon juice, and puree until smooth in a blender.

10. Season to taste with superfine sugar, salt, and pepper. Pour the coulis into a squeeze bottle and set aside in a warm-water bath.

11. Heat a large, nonstick skillet over high heat. Remove the foie gras from its wrapper and season each slice with salt and pepper.

12. Working quickly, place the slices in the pan and cook for about 30 seconds per side to create a lightly crisp exterior and a rare interior.

13. Immediately place the seared foie gras on a bed of mâche or other baby greens. Drizzle the coulis around the front part of the plate, and squirt the balsamic reduction in its own little dots in between the drizzles of coulis. Place 3 fresh red raspberries in the coulis on each plate. Lean one of the madeleines next to the foie gras to give the plate some height and finish with 1/2 teaspoon brunoise crystallized ginger sprinkled on top of the sauces on each plate. Serve immediately.

SAVORY CORN MADELEINES

(SERVES SIX)

Chef Getchell chose to include corn in these madeleines because it is delicious, but also as a "play" on the way geese and ducks are raised for foie gras production. Arguably, it was in ancient Egypt that ducks and geese were first force-fed corn in order to fatten their livers and prepare them for foie gras production. The practice continues today. Moulard ducks, however, whose livers are also used for foie gras production, also fatten themselves naturally when they prepare for their migratory flights. :: **CWM**

PROCEDURE

1. Preheat the oven to 350°F. Generously butter a madeleine baking pan, then chill it in the refrigerator.

2. Combine the dry ingredients and set aside.

3. In a large mixing bowl, combine the beaten egg, melted butter, and buttermilk. Whisk the ingredients together until they are just combined. Do not overmix.

4. Distribute the batter evenly in the prepared madeleine pan.

5. Bake immediately for 15 minutes or until the madeleines are golden brown and shrink away from the sides of the pan.

6. Immediately loosen with the tip of a knife, then transfer to a rack to cool.

INGREDIENTS

5 tablespoons All-Purpose Flour
1/4 cup Cornmeal
3 tablespoons Masa Harina, or Corn Flour
1 tablespoon Sugar
1/4 teaspoon Baking Powder
1 pinch Kosher Salt
1 Egg, beaten
1 1/2 tablespoons Butter, melted
5 tablespoons Buttermilk

:: Chef's Note

Madeleine baking pans are just like muffin tins only with elongated, shell-like patterns imprinted in each mold. The name madeleine supposedly comes from a story in the 18th century when a duke visited a castle in France; he became smitten with a peasant girl named Madeleine and was equally impressed by the little cakes she made.

MY THOUGHTS ON THE FUNDAMENTALS OF FRENCH CUISINE:

- Because stocks play such an important role, the utmost care is given to developing the flavor profile of each of the ingredients used to make them.

- Like nurturing a lasting relationship or raising a child, there is first a thoughtful contemplation of each ingredient's best qualities. Then, a patient process takes place that exemplifies those beautiful aspects as the product simmers and prepares to offer its best self to the world.

- Along the way, as a stock is prepared, a chef's ideology is exposed. Although chefs adhere to certain steadfast principles, their interpretations of those recipes offer insights into their individual food philosophies. Just as a conductor brings emotions to an audience through his or her interpretation of a great classic, the same deeply seeded desire to elicit an emotional response happens in a kitchen as a chef interprets a recipe.

- Whether it is an aria capturing the beauty of the Earth's resources, or a recitative reflecting the resonation of an incredibly deep flavor, the oratorio of a great stock reflects the composer in the kitchen. The art lies in the interpretation. The beauty lies in the passion of one's concern.

- Onion skins are either rescued in or banished from the stock. Bones are either washed of impurities or coveted for their flavor, clarity be damned. Mirepoix and sachets have ingredients that are either embraced or shunned. Why has there never been an opera based on the life and loves of a CHEF? The metaphors in the kitchen are endlessly intoxicating...

THE MOTHER SAUCES:

(now there's a great basis for the female leads in the kitchen opera!)

· From stocks come the next building blocks in French cuisine, the "mother" sauces. These five sauces give birth to an endless array of other smaller sauces, all with the primary function to complement and marry the other players on the plate.

· Fernand Point said, "In the orchestra of cuisine, the Saucier is the soloist."

MOTHER SAUCE:	THICKENER:	LIQUID:
BÉCHAMEL	· WHITE ROUX equal parts by weight of butter and flour, cooked till it smells like cookies baking	MILK
VELOUTÉ	· WHITE or BLOND ROUX blond roux is basically white roux cooked longer, until it is slightly darker and has a nutty aroma	WHITE STOCK (veal, chicken, or fish)
BROWN SAUCE (ESPAGNOLE)	· BROWN ROUX roux cooked even longer until it is light brown and smells like popcorn	BROWN STOCK
TOMATO	· OPTIONAL ROUX tomato puree acts as its own thickener	TOMATO PLUS STOCK
HOLLANDAISE	· EGG YOLKS	BUTTER

THE CHEF AS TEACHER

THE VALUE OF GOOD TEACHING

If I can inspire others the way I was inspired by good teaching mentors, I will be satisfied that I have done my job well. The value of good teaching can go a long way in the food business. Some people are more willing than others to allow themselves to be taught new things. But if you are open, the lessons can greatly improve your technique, deepen your knowledge, and make you an effective businessperson in your career. If you take it one step farther and learn to train people well yourself, you can directly increase the revenues of your establishment by boosting the skills of your own workforce.

I fully recognize how important it is for other mentors to enter the lives of my students. I'm not egotistical enough to think they could learn everything from me. So when it comes time for externships, even though it's not technically my job to help with securing externship sites, I'll do everything in my power to honor any request for help. An awesome placement may mean an opportunity for the student to find his or her own mentor of a lifetime.

COMPARISON AND THE MAGIC OF NAPA

I try to bring the joys of my own learning back into the classroom to share with my students. One of my more recent learning revelations occurred while comparing wines in the vineyards of the Napa Valley. Wine tasting in the middle of the vineyard has no comparison in my experience. To sip the wine, smell the dirt, then sip the wine again to discover the terroir is mind-blowing. The difference in the wine is remarkable after that one simple connection to the earth: You can truly isolate the individual flavors that the terroir brings to the wine. It's important to look for ways to allow comparisons of products even in the classroom. It may not be Napa, but if it teases out new discoveries, that's what education is all about.

PEARLS OF WISDOM

It's wonderful to encourage my students to examine their own culinary history and use it to enhance their cooking. Whether it's memories of wild strawberries

sold from a roadside stand or fresh fish fried on an open fire, understanding the cooking that formed the foundation of their food memories will help them build context into their cooking. They can build on old traditions and find ways to make the flavors in their food bring back memories from long ago.

FREEDOM THROUGH ORGANIZATION

I try to teach my students to start with a plan, think as far in advance as possible, and come to the kitchen mentally ready to rock. Once people are organized they can have the luxury of being spontaneous. It's only then that their spontaneity can bring amazing results.

BRAVERY IN THE KITCHEN

One thing I try to encourage in my own classroom is something has helped me throughout my career as a chef: I learned to screw things up without fear. In fact, I relished opportunities to make mistakes so that I had the chance to discover what exactly went wrong and why. The license to experiment is learning at its best. It gives you a chance to rework something over and over again until you own the new technique. Now I look at the whole world with a kind of "Zen and the Art of Kitchen Maintenance" point of view that puts more emphasis on the wonder of everyday life. I question everything. I encourage my students to do the same.

THE CONFIDENCE IN A FINISHED DISH

Since students have a chance to bring up dishes every day for grading and critique, they also have daily opportunities to grow in their confidence about their own tasting skills. Great chefs should be like great painters or artists. They have to know when to stop drawing one more fluffy cloud. A great chef needs to know when there's enough butter or cream; to have the ability to stand back and say, "Okay, this dish is finished."

IDENTIFYING MY DESIRE TO TEACH

Teaching allows me the opportunity to tie all my experiences together to jump-start the ambitions of other people. I enjoy teaching because when I make hollandaise, I still get a thrill when it comes together in my bowl. I want others to find the same enjoyment. I get some kids who come into school riding a mental skateboard. It's up to me to inspire them enough to jump off that board and find a new wave to ride: one that turns them on to how cool it is to learn things at a deeper level.

LESSONS ON STOCK

Each chef has his or her own view of what constitutes great stock. Although stock appears to be a basic recipe, there are many nuances that can be adjusted to affect the final outcome. Before you begin to experiment with your own stock, it is important to keep in mind a few universal principles:

1. A clear, clean appearance is desired in stock. This is not achieved by straining, it is only achieved through the proper cooking methods described in the stock's recipe that allow the stock to become clarified.

2. Clarification happens when the proteins coagulate and attract other particles suspended in the liquid.

3. A protein complex called *albumin* is a valuable ingredient in stock due to its ability to form a mass of particles when it is exposed to a very slow application of heat. Albumin is found in things such as blood, egg whites, and in some vegetables such as leeks.

4. If you wash bones and meat before they are used in stock, although your stock will be clearer, you will lose a great deal of flavor. Some chefs choose clarity and prefer a milder flavor, others accept a slight amount of cloudiness in order to bring out a deeper flavor profile.

5. Stock will also become cloudy if it is boiled instead of simmered. Boiling also reduces the flavor by destroying the aromatics in the stock. The stock is at the proper simmer at about 185°F, when it forms small bubbles that come up from the bottom of the pan, causing a slight turbulence but breaking just below the surface. Without the slight turbulence particles in the stock will remain at the bottom of the pan and will cause the stock to burn. However, if the heat is turned on too high, boiling will occur which blends the particles in the stock back into the liquid, resulting in cloudiness. In a description of the bubbling process, it is said to let the stock "smile in its simmer, rather than to let it boil or laugh out loud."

6. The particles in the stock are also removed through a skimming process called depouillage. In this process, the stockpot is placed just slightly off-center from the flame on the stove to allow for the circulation of the liquid to force the particles to one side of the pan, where they can be easily skimmed off the top of the surface. These impurities are in the form of fat and scum that should be completely removed and discarded.

7. Use very cold water to make a stock—a 4 to 1 ratio of water to ice. So, if a stock calls for 5 quarts of liquid, use 4 quarts of water and 1 quart of crushed ice.

8. Stock should be cooled in an ice bath so that it reaches a temperature of 40°F in less than 4 hours.

9. There are three basic elements of a stock. They include: the primary flavor base, or nourishing elements (such as bones from meat, poultry, and fish, or from vegetables); the aromatics (such as a bouquet garni or sachet, and the vegetables used in the mirepoix); and the liquid (such as water or a remouil-lage). Occasionally a fourth element, seasoning, is added when salt is used in rare circumstances, but this is the exception rather than the rule.

10. Since sizes differ, be sure to weigh the mirepoix ingredients to be certain you are using the proper proportions.

11. Basically there are three types of stock: neutral stock, white stock, and brown stock. Generally speaking, neutral stock refers to vegetable stock, white stock refers to stock in which the bones are not browned in the oven first, and brown stock refers to stock made with roasted bones.

12. The final reminder is to use great care when creating stocks. Start with high-quality ingredients and follow the directions precisely. Great sauces can only be derived from the highest-quality foundation.

:: CWM

WHITE STOCK (VEAL, BEEF, OR CHICKEN)

(MAKES ONE GALLON)

This stock is good for dishes such as white sauce, fricassees, and poached dishes. :: **CWM**

INGREDIENTS

3-4 stems Parsley
⅛ teaspoon Thyme
4 Peppercorns
1 clove Garlic
1 Bay Leaf
5 pounds of Bones (Chicken, Veal, or Beef),
   cut into 2-3" pieces
4 quarts Cold Water
1 quart Crushed Ice
4 ounces (1 cup) Onion, peeled, quartered
4 ounces (1 cup) Leek, cut into 1" pieces
4 ounces (1 cup) Celery, cut into 1" pieces
4 ounces (1 cup) Carrot, cut into 1" pieces
2 tablespoons Butter, unsalted

PROCEDURE

1. Place the parsley, thyme, peppercorns, garlic, and bay leaf into a piece of cheese-cloth that is large enough to completely surround the ingredients. Tie the top of the bag closed with a piece of string 9" long to form the sachet.

2. Put the bones in a large stockpot and add the cold water and ice.

3. Bring the contents just to the boiling point, then immediately turn the stove down to a simmer at approximately 185°F. Make sure the pot is positioned just slightly off-center from the flame of the stove.

4. Skim the scum off of the top of the stock as it rises to the surface. If your pot is positioned properly, the scum should gather at one side of the pot.

5. Sauté the mirepoix (the onion, leek, carrot, and celery) in the butter until it is golden, then add it to the stock.

6. Add the sachet and tie the end of the string to the side of the pot, making it easy to remove later.

7. Simmer the stock 6 to 8 hours for veal or beef, or 3 to 4 hours for chicken. Skim frequently.

8. Strain the stock by carefully pouring ladles full of stock through a cheesecloth-lined china cap or fine strainer.

9. Cool the stock in an ice bath until it reaches 40°F, about 4 hours or less.

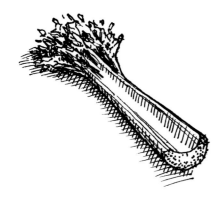

BROWN STOCK (VEAL OR BEEF)

(MAKES ONE GALLON)

A brown stock is used in such dishes as meat glazes and gravies. :: CWM

PROCEDURE

1. Roast the bones in a 350°F oven.

2. Meanwhile, place the parsley, thyme, peppercorns, garlic, and bay leaf into a piece of cheesecloth that is large enough to completely surround the ingredients. Tie the top of the bag closed with a piece of string 9" long to form the sachet.

3. Put the mirepoix (onion, leek, carrot, and celery) into a large bowl and mix in the tomato paste. When the bones are very light brown, add the mirepoix mixture to the roasting pan and continue the roasting process until the bones are golden brown.

4. Meanwhile blacken, or brûlé, the 2 pieces of onion by placing them in a hot sauté pan until the bottom surface begins to turn black. Turn and repeat on the other side. Remove and set aside.

5. Put the browned bones in a large stockpot and add the cold water or remouillage and ice.

6. Deglaze the roasting pan with some of the water from the stock pot or the optional red wine. Scrape all liquid and browned bits into the stockpot.

7. Bring the contents just to the boiling point, then immediately turn the stove down to simmer at approximately 185°F. Make sure the pot is positioned just slightly off-center from the flame of the stove.

8. Add the sachet and tie the end of the string to the side of the pot, making it easy to remove later. Float the onion brûlés in the stock as well.

9. Skim the scum off the top of the stock as it rises to the surface. If your pot is positioned properly, the scum should gather at one side of the pot.

10. Simmer the stock from 6 to 8 hours. Skim frequently.

11. Strain the stock by carefully pouring ladles full of stock through a cheesecloth-lined china cap or fine strainer.

12. Cool the stock in an ice bath until it reaches 40°F, about 4 hours or less.

INGREDIENTS

5 pounds of Bones (Veal or Beef), cut into 2-3" pieces
3-4 stems Parsley
1/8 teaspoon Thyme
4 Peppercorns
1 clove Garlic
1 Bay Leaf
4 ounces (1 cup) Onion, peeled, quartered
4 ounces (1 cup) Leek, cut into 1" pieces
4 ounces (1 cup) Celery, cut into 1" pieces
4 ounces (1 cup) Carrot, cut into 1" pieces
1/2 cup Tomato Paste
4 quarts Cold Water or Remouillage
1 quart Crushed Ice
1 cup Red Wine (optional for deglazing)
1/2 Onion, peeled, cut horizontally in half

ADDITIONAL RECIPES

BLACK-EYED PEA AND WINTER VEGETABLE SAUTÉ

From Chef Leigh Blakemore

(SERVES SIX)

In Saucier it is not only the preparation of stocks, soups, and sauces that is focused on in class. The art of sautéing is also an element of the curriculum. This sauté has an option: If you want a quick side dish to accompany a meal, the recipe can be made with canned black-eyed peas without an enormous loss in quality. However, if you enjoy cooking and eating slowly, as I do, you can always cook these black-eyed peas from scratch. I love to watch and smell the simmering peas and garlic as they slowly cook on the stove. Starting the beans from a dry state takes only a bit more time, your senses become engaged, and the subtle differences in your product are what good cooking is all about. :: **CWM**

INGREDIENTS

2 tablespoons Butter, unsalted
1 cup Black-Eyed Peas, dried
2 cloves Garlic, peeled
1 medium Sweet Potato, peeled, small diced
2½ tablespoons Olive Oil
1 medium Yellow Onion, small diced
4 cloves Garlic, minced
1 Red Bell Pepper, seeded, small diced
1 Jalapeño Pepper, seeded, minced
1 teaspoon Thyme, leaves only, fresh, chopped
Salt and freshly ground Black Pepper

:: Chef's Note

This is a delicious accompaniment to roast chicken or pork. You can add other vegetables to this dish, but match the vegetables to the season in order to maximize freshness, sustain local agriculture, and bring symmetry into your cooking.

PROCEDURE

1. Heat a saucepan over medium-low heat and add the butter. When it has melted, add the black-eyed peas and peeled garlic. Immediately cover the ingredients with water, increase the heat to high, and bring the mixture just to a boil. Turn the heat back down and allow the mixture to simmer until the black-eyed peas are tender, 25–30 minutes. Drain, reserving the peas and discarding the garlic. Set the peas aside in a warm location.

2. Add the diced sweet potato to a pot of boiling salted water. Reduce the heat slightly and cook for 4–5 minutes, until fork-tender.

3. Pour the sweet potato into a colander to drain. Leave to steam-dry until there is no more steam rising from the surface.

4. While the sweet potato is drying, heat a sauté pan and add the olive oil. Allow the oil to heat, add the onion, and sauté over medium heat until translucent.

5. Add the garlic, bell pepper, and jalapeño and sauté for another 2 minutes or until the onion just starts to brown.

6. Gently stir in the drained black-eyed peas, reserved sweet potatoes, and fresh thyme. Heat through, then season with salt and pepper.

SWEET POTATO CROQUETTES

From Chef Randy Foote

(SERVES EIGHT)

This side dish provides a crunchy texture to a meal. These croquettes also add a good source of vitamin A since sweet potatoes are high in beta-carotene. :: **CWM**

PROCEDURE

1. Preheat the oven to 400°F.

2. Put the sweet potatoes on a parchment-lined sheet pan and bake until they are soft and nicely browned.

3. Fill a deep, heavy saucepot with peanut oil until it is 2½" deep. Make certain the pot is deep enough to contain the oil splatters when the batter is added later on. Preheat the oil to 350°.

4. Peel and mash the sweet potatoes. Put them in a mixing bowl and add the garlic, scallions, bell pepper, and shallots. Mix well.

5. Add the bread crumbs and eggs, adjusting the consistency of the mixture so that it is not too wet or dry and easily holds its shape when pressed into a ball.

6. Adjust the seasonings with sugar, salt, and pepper to taste.

7. Using a small ice cream scoop, drop by scoopfuls into the hot fat and deep-fry until the croquettes are golden brown. Test to be certain your frying time allows the center of the croquette to be cooked thoroughly.

8. Drain the croquettes on a rack to make certain the air circulates around them so that they can retain their crunchy texture.

INGREDIENTS

3½ pounds Sweet Potatoes, unpeeled, cut in half
Peanut Oil for frying
2 tablespoons Garlic, minced
¼ cup Scallions, thinly sliced
½ Green Bell Pepper, brunoise or finely diced
2 tablespoons Shallots, minced
3½ cups Bread Crumbs, fresh
3 Eggs, beaten
Sugar
Salt and Pepper

:: Chef's Note

Sweet potatoes are actually not scientifically related to other forms of potatoes. Instead they are related to the morning glory family. They were actually discovered by European diners before regular potatoes. Members of Columbus's crew were introduced to them in Haiti in 1492. It wasn't until about 40 years later that they discovered the glories of the regular potato.

nutrition / management

INSTRUCTOR: CHEF FRITZ PASQUET

WE ALL MISSED OUR CHEF'S KNIVES A GREAT DEAL WHEN WE HAD TO SET THEM ASIDE FOR SIX WEEKS TO STUDY NUTRITION AND MANAGEMENT.

I can vouch for the fact that chefs go slightly nuts when they can't cook in class every day. Moving and creating in the kitchen is a daily requirement. But the lessons Chef Pasquet brought to the classroom every morning helped to make up for our lack of activity over the stove and cutting board. His lectures covered topics such as how to adhere to dietary recommendations and develop healthy yet delicious menus and recipes, and he taught us how to identify the structure and characteristics of vitamins, minerals, carbohydrates, proteins, and fats. His lessons were especially meaningful when he added fascinating stories from his own life experiences as an inspiring

chef, a health-care professional, and an amateur musician. Even Chef Pasquet's deep love of jazz heightened my appreciation for nutrition. Jazz is an art form that requires both range and depth of musical knowledge. A great jazz player combines a thorough understanding of musical form with the confidence to deviate from that form, an ability to improvise and come up with a completely new tune much in the same way an emerging chef crafts a new dish. Chef Pasquet's lessons inspired me to start with a great basis of flavor and build upon it with my own repertoire of healthy variations. The results blew me away. :: **CWM**

REFLECTIONS OF A CHEF

GROWING UP IN THE WHITE HOUSE

Life around me throughout my formative years was filled with incredible events. My father, who'd immigrated from France, was with the Secret Service and also served as an interpreter to Presidents Truman, Eisenhower, Kennedy, Johnson, and Nixon. He retired from his post before Nixon's second administration. I'll never forget watching the whir of motion in the kitchens as the White House staff prepared for major events. Despite my naïveté, it was a spectacular childhood. My most memorable moments came with the Kennedys when they brought in the chefs from France.

My father was a food and wine connoisseur. His closest companions were, when I was growing up, the world-renowned chefs at the helm of the White House kitchens as well as many of the famous chefs in Washington including Jacques Pépin, René Verdon, Ferdinand Lavat, Claude Bouchet, and Jean Frances. As a family, we would frequent the great restaurants of the D.C. area, having lunch at The Guards, the Shoreham Hotel, or the Jockey Club where Bobby Kennedy and all the senators would dine as well as Chet Huntley, David Brinkley, and other members of the news teams. We would also go out with the chefs to other famous old restaurants like the Flagship and Haussner's in Baltimore. My life was constantly surrounded by fabulous cooking.

My father's friends became very close to our family. After school René and Ferdinand would pick us up and take us swimming at the Ambassador Hotel until my dad got off work. One time when my mother had gallbladder surgery, they came to our house to cook the whole time that she was in the hospital. I had no idea how amazing this all was at the time; it was just our life. I remember being completely blown away by René's flourless chocolate cake. I was only 12, but I remember being stunned that there was no flour in those unbelievably wonderful things.

THE PRESIDENTIAL PALATES

One of President Kennedy's favorite dishes was a stuffed chicken breast with cheese and prosciutto like a Cordon Bleu. President Johnson, being from Texas, was big on barbecues. He brought in a big, wonderful African American chef and held western-style barbecues on the White House lawn. The Nixons brought in German chefs with all their wonderful pastries and rich German food. President Nixon couldn't get enough of sourdough dumplings, schnitzel, and knudel. It seems I retained more food knowledge than political strategizing from those wonderful years of my life.

A POSITION WITH CLAUDE BOUCHET

When I was 13 years old my father began to appreciate my like-mindedness when it came to food. He discussed with Claude the possibility of having me apprentice with him in the kitchen at the Shoreham Hotel. He agreed as a favor to my father, and I went to shadow Claude throughout the kitchen. He definitely ran his kitchen in the old style, keeping his cooks in line with an iron fist. He demanded perfection from everyone. But Claude was very gentle with me as a family friend. The entire kitchen staff was extremely helpful because I was a kid and they knew I was under his wing. Since I was required to stay directly behind him at all times, he gave me an official title for my new position. I was to be known as the Secretary of the Posterior, which was particularly funny given that we were right there in the midst of Washington politics. At the time, I didn't pick up on the joke. I was just pleased that I had a big title.

The area I concentrated the most on was the garde manger station. I remember Claude discussing with me the importance of presentation. It was there that I learned the brilliance of adding art to a plate. The transformation of carrots, tomatoes, cucumbers, and zucchini into exotic sculptures allowed me to see food taken to an entirely new dimension. He showed me how to bring color and form to every plate. His main philosophy

was presenting food with beauty, style, and flair, but never losing sight of the main attraction: the maximization of the flavors that characterized each dish.

DEVELOPING MY OWN STYLE AS A COOK

Although the famous chefs played an enormous role in my appreciation for food, I found other ways to make my own cooking evolve. I loved to incorporate nuances from my family's background, to introduce flavors in a sort of geographic ode to the many cultural influences in my life. My grandparents were once the governor and governess of Martinique, so we had significant Caribbean rhythms pulsating through our family history. My father would combine the flavors of France with the foods of the Caribbean, and these flavors stayed with me over the years, like a deeply cherished heirloom. He always used to say, "The greatest food and the hottest music come from the people on the beaches of Caribbean islands." Those influences definitely carried over to me. I love great music and wonderful ethnic food. I now make new "concoctions," as my father would call them, using the ingredients from those food memories: rice, beans, roasted pork, and plantain. It also inspired me to pursue other authentic ethnic flavors in locations all over the world.

COOKING SECRETS

My greatest cooking secrets evolved out of necessity, when I knew for health reasons that I should be cooking with less fat and more nutrition. There are so many ways to reduce the health risks without sacrificing flavor in much of our daily cooking. You don't have to give up flavor to end up with healthy food. My tofu ice cream is a wonderful example of substituting things for fat, lactose, and sugar. Fruits add an enormous punch of flavor, particularly fruits with a lot of intensity such as strawberries and raspberries. Rich concentrations of fruit flavor add significant sweetness and depth to a dish, without a lot of additional sugar. Tofu is a wonderful replacement for the lactose in ice cream. It also acts as a carrier of flavor, due to its own neutral characteristics and its ability to absorb flavors of other foods with which it is combined. Tofu is also a clean, fresh food that doesn't leave an oily residue on the tongue.

There are other ways of increasing the nutrient density of foods without adding a lot of fat. Try combining a little fat-free sour cream with a small portion of cheese on top of freshly cooked broccoli. The flavor is immensely satisfying without overdoing the fat and calories. Reductions of stocks, wines, and sauces are also terrific in cooking because they intensify the flavors, again without adding fat. Use concentrated oils such as mandarin or lemon oil. All that is necessary is a drop or two, and you've maximized the flavor and minimized the fat. I even use oils in the barbecue sauce that I manufacture as a fund-raiser for the firefighters of America. Known as the Original Brand Firehouse Barbecue Sauce, one of its secrets is concentrated wild orange oil.

Make sure the herbs you use are as fresh as possible in order to bring out their most aromatic and flavorful qualities. Sometimes I like to roast the herbs first in order to begin to release some of their essential oils. Another option is to put some herbs in a blender with a little oil, blend it, and then let it sit in a bowl overnight in 3 or 4 layers of cheesecloth, allowing the concentrated oils to drip out. That is a beautiful way to bring out flavor.

Chutneys are also wonderfully concentrated sources of flavor. One of my favorites is a chutney with hot Scotch bonnet peppers boiled together with some red bell peppers and sugar. It results in astonishing flavor. Or try using sauces to add complexity. A marvelous combination is a lovely Caribbean ginger-lime marinade mixed with soy sauce and balsamic vinegar. The flavor is just out of this world.

THE ELEGANCE OF FRESH FLOWERS

When I think of beautiful food, one specific dish comes to mind. Called Crème Catalan, it gives me a wonderful stage to display the edible flowers from my herb garden. I grow them to ensure their freshness and purity. Crème Catalan is like crème brûlée, but it uses a lot of fruit such as strawberries, raspberries, and blueberries in the preparation, incorporated at their peak of freshness. After I put the brûlée-style coating of caramelized sugar on the top, I drape the dessert with edible flowers, allowing them to spill over the top and sides. It's a very romantic dish.

MY PHILOSOPHY OF COOKING

I believe in leaving the guest with a crescendo at the end of every meal, just like a great piece of music. When it comes to dessert, the flavor can't just drop off the edge and disappear at the end of the evening. The dessert has to keep with the cultural theme of the meal and it has to be as good as, if not better than, the courses that preceded it. For example, after a wonderful meal of Indian cuisine, I would offer something like a curry-pumpkin cheesecake with saffron ice cream. For other dinners, I'm a big fan of cheese. It's a splurge, so you have to eat it in moderation, but on special occasions it's wonderful. It's hard to leave a diner more impressed than when left with a gorgeous selection of outstanding and richly complex cheeses. But perhaps that is the European in me.

I am also committed to cooking as organically as possible with the freshest of ingredients. It not only is the best way to capture flavor, but also allows you to maximize the nutritional value of the food. At the same time it reduces the toxicity that invades our land through the corporate farming systems. We need to learn from the countries that live simply, eating good fresh food with real flavor. When you look closely, you'll find them living with less coronary heart disease, cancer, and osteoporosis. It's good for all of us to streamline.

FRITZ PASQUET

THE CHEF'S LESSON

STRAWBERRY TOFU ICE CREAM

(SERVES SIX)

Chef Pasquet brought this ice cream into our Nutrition class for everyone to sample. Even the most skeptical students were amazed by its strawberry flavor and silky texture. There was no hint that tofu was this recipe's secret ingredient. :: CWM

ICE CREAM INGREDIENTS

1, 16-ounce package Soft Tofu
1 cup Vanilla-Flavored Rice Milk
4 teaspoons Pure Vanilla Extract
1/4 cup Vegetable Oil
1 cup Sugar or Sweetener Substitute to taste
1, 16-ounce package Frozen Strawberries

ICE/SALTWATER BATH INGREDIENTS

1 quart Cold Water
1 cup Rock Salt
1 cup Ice Cubes

:: Chef's Note

Students invariably ask, "How can you retain great flavor, mouth feel, and satisfaction from anything that is low fat, low sugar, or salt-free?" My tofu ice cream is a great answer. It is also lactose-free for those who have an intolerance to milk products.

PROCEDURE

1. Put all the ice cream ingredients into a large bowl. Stir well.

2. Place approximately 2 cups of the mixture in the blender. Blend until it has a smooth consistency. Due to the rice milk in the recipe, be sure to pulse the blender initially to ensure that the mixture does not force off the lid. Once the ingredients have begun to incorporate, you can leave the blender on without further pulsing.

3. Repeat with the rest of the mixture until all ingredients are blended smoothly.

4. Put the ice cream mixture into an ice cream maker and follow the manufacturer's directions for freezing.

5. If you do not have an ice cream maker, it is possible to freeze this in your freezer, although it will have a noticeably different texture. Pour the mixture into a freezer-safe container with relatively high edges, then place the container into a pan of the same height but with ample room on the sides. Carefully pour a mixture of the water, rock salt, and ice cubes into the bottom container. Add as much of the salt water as you can and place in the freezer. Stir the ice cream frequently and carefully throughout the freezing process to reduce the amount of crystallization. Freeze overnight.

6. Approximately 10–15 minutes before serving, place the ice cream in the refrigerator to soften slightly.

ZUPPA DI ZUCCA (PUREED ZUCCHINI SOUP WITH FRESH THYME)

(SERVES SIX)

Soups are a wonderful way to incorporate vegetables and nutrient-dense dishes into a family's diet. Pureed soups are completely versatile and can be served as a main dish for lunch, or as a first course to accompany an elegant dinner. If you enjoy a little more body in your soup, add some leftover rice before pureeing to act as a thickening agent. :: CWM

PROCEDURE

1. Heat a saucepan. Add the clarified butter and allow it to get hot. Add the zucchini, chili flakes, and thyme. Sauté the zucchini until it just starts to brown.

2. Turn off the heat, stir in the garlic, and let it stand for approximately 10 minutes.

3. Put some of the zucchini mixture in the blender with enough warm chicken stock to make the blender spin easily. Pulse initially to allow some of the liquid to incorporate. Puree until the mixture has a smooth consistency. Pour the contents of the blender into a new saucepan.

4. Repeat this process until the entire mixture is blended smoothly and is fully incorporated.

5. Reheat the soup over a low flame. Stir occasionally. Carefully season with salt; remember to taste twice and season once. Also keep in mind that if cheese is used to garnish the soup, it will add a degree of saltiness.

6. Ladle the spoon into serving bowls, garnishing with cheese and/or a sprig of fresh thyme.

INGREDIENTS

3/4 cup Butter, clarified (or less, for a
   lower-fat soup)
1 1/2 pounds Zucchini, medium diced
1/4 teaspoon Red Chili Flakes
2 tablespoons Thyme, fresh, chopped
1 tablespoon Garlic, chopped
3 cups Chicken Stock, warmed
Kosher Salt

ACCOMPANIMENTS

Parmigiano-Reggiano, Romano, or Asiago
   Cheese, for garnish
Sprigs of Fresh Thyme, for optional garnish

:: Chef's Note

This multigenerational "old country" Italian recipe was handed down to me from my father. Arguably, the French methods of classical cooking began when Italy's own Caterina de' Medici left her home in Florence and married the dauphin of France, bringing her Italian chefs and culinary traditions with her. It makes sense that Italian recipes also made their way into my father's own classical repertoire.

NOTES ON ICE CREAM:

· If the consistency of the ice cream is slushy even after the freezing process, check the sugar and/or alcohol levels in the recipe. If these levels are too high, the ice cream won't freeze properly. Try reducing these products and increasing the other ingredients to result in a firmer dessert.

· To keep the leftover ice cream fresh, cover the surface of the ice cream with plastic wrap or waxed paper, then place the whole container in a plastic bag before placing it back in the freezer. This helps to keep the ice cream from absorbing other flavors from the freezer as well as maintaining the creamy texture.

· Make sure not to overfill the ice cream freezer when beginning the freezing process. The volume of the ice cream increases by 50% by the time it has finished freezing.

TOFU:

· Tofu is derived from soybeans, which are the legumes that contain the most protein. When tofu freezes, the texture becomes chewier and actually becomes more porous, allowing it to take on more liquid flavorings such as the strawberry juice in this recipe.

· Tofu can act as a healthy substitute in many different recipes: for example, in place of mayonnaise in salad dressings, in place of ricotta cheese in lasagna, and if blended, in place of some of the cream in some soups.

ZUPPA DI ZUCCA:

· Literally this translates to "zuppa" meaning a soup, usually served with bread, and "zucca," meaning a squash, winter squash, or pumpkin. So this zucchini soup is one that would be lovely with a beautifully chewy loaf of Italian bread. If the bread is dunked in the soup instead of slathered with oil or butter, this reduces fat and calories.

· The browning of the zucchini in this recipe is due to a process known as the "maillard reaction." This browning happens when higher temperatures are applied to foods that are not primarily sugar. Simply put, the carbohydrate unit reacts with the amino acid, which results in color and flavor changes because of the by-products that are produced. The reason this happens in the zuppa di zucca is because the zucchini is cooked first in the butter without liquids present. This allows the temperature in the pan to rise above 212°F and closer to 312° or 320°F, which is necessary for this browning reaction to occur.

THE USE OF FRESH HERBS:

· Fresh herbs are best if picked immediately before using. In the absence of an herb garden, store them in a closed plastic bag along with a slightly damp paper towel in the refrigerator, or place the fresh herbs in a small container with enough water to cover the stems. Fresh herbs are best used within five days.

· The addition of fresh thyme early in this recipe allows the flavors to mellow and blend with the dish.

· If using dried thyme instead of fresh, substitute one-third as much (about 2 teaspoons for this recipe).

THE CHEF AS TEACHER

TEACHING AND MASLOW'S HIERARCHY

It means everything to me to be a teacher. In management class we talk about Maslow's Hierarchy of Needs and the attainment of self-actualization, or, in other words, becoming the person you can potentially be. I was meant to teach. I know my enthusiasm comes from finding such a lovely niche. It's particularly meaningful to me when students I've instructed in nutrition come back to visit me after they're through with school. They specifically come to ask for good nutritional choices they can put on their menus. I'm completely touched to have that continued connection with my students. It's a great sense of satisfaction.

NUTRITION AND FLAVOR ARE NOT MUTUALLY EXCLUSIVE

When it comes to meeting needs, the need to provide balanced nutritional meals for our customers should rank high on our list. But unfortunately, it doesn't always work out that way. When restaurant owners put the little red flag by a menu item to indicate that the entrée is a "heart healthy choice," it's like hammering a death nail into that food item: It will never sell. People don't go out to eat to be good: They go out to celebrate. They don't necessarily want "healthy" food: They want choices of food that they can't or won't make at home. So when students come to me for advice of what to put on their menu, I tell them how to make healthy food with fabulous flavor, rather than focusing on how to reword a menu. People want results. If they can get healthy food that tastes phenomenal, there's no reason to tell them that it also happens to be good for them.

A PERSONAL VIEW OF NUTRITION

One project that I have my students complete in nutrition class is a self-analysis of their daily dietary intake. It's an amazingly enlightening exercise that has students record every food item they ingest over a five-day period. The information gets logged into a computer program, and each person's daily habits are revealed. Food pyramids are drawn based on their own personal food choices. When people see that their "pyramid" looks more like an hourglass or a martini glass, they do a

double take and reassess their own food choices. That is the whole point of the exercise: We have to know how to make our bodies healthy with foods we enjoy ourselves before we can, as chefs, try to do that for other people.

THE TESTING KITCHENS

It's a boost to your cooking if you can take time to experiment in the kitchen with healthy products. It doesn't mean you have to find the best way to brunoise tofu, just try different flavor combinations without the use of butter, heavy cream, and salt. Combine fruit juices in new ways, experiment with concentrated oil infusions, or try out an essence of a new flower. Good nutrition doesn't have to be boring.

PATIENCE AND THE SENSE OF URGENCY

In school you are pressured to do things quickly. Although it seems like a contradiction in terms, you really do need to be patient with yourself to get faster. Learn things in the kitchen the right way first, or your progress toward efficiency will be compromised and it will end up taking you longer in the end. Even though you are expected in most cases in this industry to hit the ground running when you leave school, the time to be patient is early on in your career. Do it correctly now, and the speed will come later.

ADDITIONAL RECIPES

GOLDEN POPOVERS

From Chef Joel Brookstein

(SERVES FOUR)

A side dish that would work well with Zuppa di Zucca is this version of the classic popover. Popovers are a comforting addition to meals. They are fabulous for breakfast, but go equally well with soups or stews. Try blending in 2 ounces of blue cheese to give these a wonderful savory flavor. :: **CWM**

INGREDIENTS

Vegetable Oil, for pan preparation
1 cup Milk, room temperature
5 ounces (1¼ cups) All-Purpose Flour, sifted
¼ teaspoon Salt
½ ounce (1 tablespoon) Butter, melted
3 Eggs, room temperature
1 ounce (2 tablespoons) Butter, clarified

:: Chef's Note

The purpose of blending the mixture is to ensure that air is incorporated into the batter. As a result, when the popovers bake in a very hot oven, the batter essentially blisters into a pocket of trapped air that is locked in by the surrounding batter. The result is a beautiful, hollow product with a delicate exterior. Be sure to use clarified butter where it is called for, or the popovers will burn.

PROCEDURE

1. Preheat the oven to 450°F. Rub the bottoms of a 12-mold muffin or popover pan with oil.

2. In a blender, combine the milk, flour, salt, and melted butter. Blend, then add the eggs 1 at a time through the lid while the blender is still running. Continue blending until the batter is fully incorporated and has the consistency of heavy cream.

3. Preheat the muffin or popover pan in the oven for 3 minutes, then remove it and quickly drizzle the 2 tablespoons of clarified butter evenly into the bottoms of its molds.

4. Immediately fill the molds with batter until each is two-thirds of the way full. Do not overfill or the popovers will not pop.

5. Bake at 450°F for 15 minutes. Without opening the oven door, reduce the oven temperature to 350° and bake for an additional 10 minutes, or until the popovers are a beautiful golden brown.

6. Serve warm with butter, jam, or whatever accompaniments you desire to complement your entrée.

BRAISED CHICKEN À LA FUSCO

From Chef Jackie Kerrigan

(SERVES FOUR)

In earlier times the chickens on Italian farms were so valued for their egg production that they were rarely slaughtered for their meat. Families were lucky to have them once a week. As a result, in comparison to other types of recipes, there are relatively few chicken recipes in old Italian cooking. :: **CWM**

PROCEDURE

1. Finely chop the parsley and garlic together. Set aside.

2. Season the chicken with salt and pepper.

3. Heat 2 large cast-iron Dutch ovens or deep skillets on the stove. Add olive oil to each until it is 1/8" deep. Heat the oil until it sizzles when the chicken is added in order to ensure proper browning. If the chicken does not sizzle, remove it and heat the oil more. Be certain to lay the chicken skin-side down in the pan of hot oil.

4. Do not move the chicken pieces until the skin is golden brown. Turn and repeat the browning procedure for all sides of the chicken.

5. Add the parsley, garlic, and oregano. Turn the chicken in the herbs to coat completely.

6. Continue to cook the chicken with the flavorings for approximately 1 minute. Do not allow the garlic to brown.

7. Add the wine and stock or broth by pouring it in the side of the pan, not over the top of the chicken. Cover, then simmer the chicken until the meat is fork-tender, approximately 45 minutes.

8. Season with salt and pepper and serve over freshly made farfalle or bow tie pasta.

INGREDIENTS

1 bunch Italian Parsley, leaves only
8 cloves Garlic, fresh, peeled
2, 3-4-pound Free-Range Spring Chickens, cut into serving pieces
Kosher Salt and freshly ground Black Pepper
Olive Oil
2 teaspoons Oregano, dried
1 cup Dry White Wine
1 1/2 cups Chicken Stock or Low-Sodium Chicken Broth

:: Chef's Note

Since Dutch ovens are generally made of heavy cast iron, they retain heat and distribute it evenly throughout the cooking process. The size and structure of the oven allow the chicken to cook slowly and evenly, resulting in a tender product.

catering and garde manger

INSTRUCTOR: CHEF TIM FIELDS

AS I CONTEMPLATED THE PRINCIPLES OF HOW I WOULD RUN A KITCHEN, MANY OF MY IDEALS LOOKED TO THE TEACHINGS OF CHEF FIELDS AND THE ATTITUDE HE EMBODIED IN HIS COURSE.

His standards as an Executive Chef are high, his technique is superior, and his ease with his chefs nurtures their best assets. His ease with people is an exemplary quality, one that lends itself particularly well to the world of catering, where the focus is on meeting the needs of a diverse clientele. A need for flexibility and an ability to adapt are also positive attributes, as catering includes everything from the reconnaissance of a remote kitchen to the budgeting of costs, from the development of a theme for the cuisine to all of the preparations and timing needed to pull off a major event. The field of catering readies chefs for anything—hors d'oeuvres, canapés, aspics, chaud froid, ice carvings, or a full-course dinner gracing the lengths of the dinner tables—there is an endless variety of choices in entertaining. I learned much from Chef Fields in this class, including the value of respect in a kitchen. As important, he grounded me with the idea that ethnic, regional cuisine is not only about the flavors of the world beyond America's borders; but that ethnicity is about American cooking as well. Coming home to celebrate the freshest in local produce puts new meaning on the concept of roots, supports the livelihoods of our micro farmers, and encourages well-tended gardens that provide living food. :: **CWM**

REFLECTIONS OF A CHEF

COOKING AS AN AMERICAN CHEF

I grew up with all the flavors of the Heartland, visiting Grandma on the farm with peaches and cream for breakfast, freshly picked corn for lunch, and typical homemade dinners on Thanksgiving Day. But American cuisine is so much more than that. The richness that makes up American regional cooking is in a class by itself, with a depth that goes far beyond what most people envision as our national foods.

The United States is the melting pot of all cuisines, not just people. Being exposed to the flavors of the world affords us the depth of understanding of these global ingredients and allows us to fuse them into new creations with more wisdom and meaning. It allows us to marry flavors like wasabi-mashed potatoes whose ingredients harmonize beautifully, simply, elegantly. What is American about American cuisine is the perpetual movement and change that happen to our food as well as the constant encouragement of new thought in the kitchen. It's thinking outside of the box and not being afraid to take that calculated risk.

REGIONAL INFLUENCES

I believe it's very important to start with a solid understanding of classical cuisine, no matter what type of cuisine you intend to focus on in the future. Learning the basic techniques and classical dishes helps you concentrate on the essentials of good cooking and serves you well no matter which direction in the world you plan to concentrate your attention. For example, I am completely inspired by local ingredients. Having spent a significant part of my career in Tucson, it was only natural that I started to include the southwestern indigenous products in my cooking. Chiles, local greens, squash blossoms, roasted red peppers, cilantro, jicama, and blue corn are regularly incorporated into my dishes using French techniques. Nopalito paddles, prickly pear, rattlesnake, and elk make their appearances as well, again using classical techniques to bring out their best characteristics. I love rattlesnake gumbo served in a hollowed-out acorn squash with grilled nopalito paddles.

One of my greatest influences in the Tucson area was Janos Wilder, who owns Janos', one of the very best restaurants in the region. His house-cured salmon carpaccio is unforgettable: Pounded lightly with a sprinkling of pico de gallo, it is finished with a red chili aioli and a lime aioli drizzled over the top in a crisscross pattern as if the fish had been caught in this delicious net, with tiny baby greens and fresh currant tomatoes.

Another chef's signature dish, Duck YaYa Soup, fascinated the entire cooking elite of the region. Jonathon Landeen created this duck soup with a brown roux, then would add julienne peeled Pippin apples. Just before service, we would take the apples out. Chefs would come from miles around to try to figure out what that essence was. There was even a certified master chef who used to stop by to try to guess what was in that soup.

THE IMPACT OF WASHINGTON

In 1983 I worked in Washington with Roberto Donna at the Galileo restaurant and later with Jean-Louis Palladin at the Watergate. The Galileo was a small place just down the street from the White House, and was one of President Reagan's favorite restaurants. Roberto was a trendsetter. He would make these amazing little beet raviolis that would turn you to butter. He would simply boil the beets, puree them, then he would insert some of the pureed beet inside of the raviolis. Then he would poach them in a little of the reserved beet water and it would turn the pasta slightly pink. The little pink raviolis would be topped with chive butter and extraordinary beluga caviar. After he made these, you would walk into what seemed every restaurant in Washington for the next two years and see beet raviolis on their menu.

I worked with Jean-Louis Palladin at the Watergate from 1985 to 1986, but I didn't see much of him because he was working on the first draft of his *Cooking with the Seasons* cookbook. His sous-chef and I would bake brioche every day and work on desserts and sorbets. His pastry chef did a plum soup with a wild berry sorbet that just blew me away. Each table at Jean-Louis's would get a tiered amuse with a toasted circle of brioche on the bottom with a quail egg cracked in the center and then salamandered, or broiled, until the egg was nicely poached. It was then topped with caviar. It was beautiful. He had a theater menu with three prix fixe menus to choose from that ranged at that time $75-150 per person. But some days he would come in at 5 P.M. and throw us a new menu and we would open at 5:30 or 6 so we'd have to scramble. It was very, very intense because he demanded a lot from everyone he worked with. His cooking was based upon simplicity to bring out the best in the food, but his presentation was astonishing. He could make split pea soup look fantastic.

STAYING OPEN TO INSPIRING FORCES

I'm also inspired by people who are not famous, like José Landa Verde—the best butcher I have ever seen. He could break down a piece of meat or chicken in nothing flat. You can learn lessons from everyone from the dishwashers to the sous-chefs. It's all important.

IMPORTING AN ITALIAN CONSCIOUSNESS

In recent years I have become completely enamored by Tuscan food and the Italian way of life. Spending time in Italy touched me in ways I will never forget. The Italians' ability to weave their culture through their food leaves me breathless. Watching every doctor, barber, and silversmith close their shops to linger over a two- to three-hour lunch, then celebrate the end of each evening laughing and waxing rhapsodic about joys of the day with family and friends during a luxuriously long dinner, is to me the essence of quality of life. They celebrate food in all of its beauty: where it came from, who nurtured it, and, the king of all discussions, how it was prepared to make its way onto the table. You watch individual farmers arrive at the kitchen doorstep every afternoon with beautiful red, ripe tomatoes heaving with freshness. Or marvel as the mushroom man shows up with armloads of porcini mushrooms that he just gathered on the neighboring hills. You can feel the people living with a relaxed contentment, surrounded by the best things in life: dear friends, adoring family, and magnificent food. That is living. It's also

something very lacking in the American way of doing things, hell-bent on living life in the fast lane. We miss the greatest moments that way.

I've tried to incorporate as much as I can from that lifestyle into my daily routines here in my kitchens. At the Mirabel Club where I am the executive chef, we have been nurturing relationships with as many little micro farms as we can. Everything from shrimp farmers to sausage producers to sources of beautiful fresh herbs—we have a bounty of wonderful small farmers to choose from to provide the freshest, highest-quality food we can find. I even tried incorporating the lessons from Italy into the family meals we have for my cooks. As a culinary educator, in our school during family meal, we provided only nourishment for our young chefs. We need to improve that to include the true appreciation of fine dining, not just fine cooking. In Italy the meal for the kitchen help goes way beyond nourishment, as they sit down every day with bottles of wine to eat the same food that is served to the guests. The time in the kitchens is not only our job, it is our life, it is time we need to enjoy life to the fullest. Those moments in complete celebration of great food really do bring people closer together: They make lives richer; they make cooks better chefs.

REVELATIONS FROM THE GREATEST ARTISTS IN THE WORLD

When I was in Italy I also had the opportunity to drink in some of the world's greatest art. To hear about Michelangelo's David is

TIM FIELDS

one thing. To go there and stand right next to that breathtaking statue is another. To feel the blood, sweat, tears, and devotion that went into the beauty of that sculpture is extraordinary. It inspired me to go beyond even my own idea of my limitations, to research and dig deeply for my own greatest insights of incorporating art into what I do. Seeing other works of art throughout Italy such as the Gates of Heaven, The Birth of Venus, and other monumental works moved me to put more elements of artwork into my own designs. I work to put flow, strong lines, different textures, height, and color into every plate that comes out of my kitchen doors. I am committed to creating dishes where your eyes flow across the plate like a beautiful work of art.

Frank Lloyd Wright's designs also made an enormous impact on my work. His influence surrounds me daily since the Mirabel Club is based on his designs. It translates into my cooking when I combine the rustic with the simple elements of food to bring out the essential beauty in each dish.

Even the energy of Cirque de Soleil inspires me since it captures the rhythms of the kitchen on a busy Saturday night. The movements, the resonating colors, the strong lines, the flow and balance of the designs, even the artfulness of the bodies in motion— all these elements work together to enhance the whole picture. That choreography is just as necessary in the kitchen. By working in balance, every aspect of the entire piece is accentuated and works to bring the whole piece together. When things are really working in the kitchen, that's how I feel, it's our own Cirque de Soleil.

COOKING SECRETS

"The dish of patience" is the descriptive phrase that captures the nature of great risotto. Preparing it perfectly is one of the most lovely secrets I know. Risotto should never be prepared ahead of time; it has to be prepared immediately upon the time it is ordered. It takes constant attention for 15-20 minutes, so state right on your menu that the

diner's patience will be appreciated because risotto done properly is worth the wait. Start by incorporating the deep rich stock by ladling it in to cover the rice, then stir constantly until the liquid is absorbed, followed by adding another ladleful of stock. Repeat the process, without stopping the stirring, until the risotto is tender but still has an al dente bite in the center of the kernel. The consistency around the kernels should be rich, smooth, and creamy, not globbing the kernels together in clumps. The seasonings and finishing touches are up to you. The best secret is to cook it from your heart. If you cook with passion, you will always be successful.

I was once told by Billy Joel that I had cooked him the best white truffle risotto he'd ever had in his life, even though he had brought in the white truffles himself. When he came in to my restaurant he called me to his table, reached in his pocket, pulled out the truffles, and said with a twinkle in his eye, "Here, could you make me some risotto?" It was beautiful to be requested to make it because it is absolutely one of my favorite things to make in the kitchen. I was pleased that he savored it, too.

I've cooked for a variety of well-known people, but cooking for celebrities is no more or less important than any other cooking you do. Your food should come out as your best no matter who is sitting at the table.

THE CHEF'S LESSON

TOMATO CROSTINI

(SERVES SIX)

Chef Fields's recipe provides a good lesson on the effects of salt upon the moisture content of food. The technique of salting the tomatoes before draining helps draw out the moisture from inside the tomato, resulting in less water and a more concentrated flavor. Drier tomatoes also help keep the toast from becoming soggy. These tomato crostini are perfect for catered occasions, either as appetizers circulated to the guests or served as a first course to diners at the table. :: **CWM**

INGREDIENTS

3 ripe Roma Tomatoes, peeled, seeded, small
   diced
Kosher Salt, to taste
2 tablespoons Basil, fresh, chopped
2 tablespoons Italian Parsley, fresh, chopped
¼ cup + 2 tablespoons Extra-Virgin Olive Oil
Kosher Salt and Red Pepper Flakes, to taste
6 slices Country-Style Bread, Pugliese or
   Ciabatta
2 cloves Garlic
4 ounces (1 cup) Fresh Mozzarella, sliced thinly

:: Chef's Note

This crostini recipe can easily be turned into a bruschetta by substituting a few of the ingredients. Replace the Roma tomatoes with 1 pound fresh heirloom tomatoes and substitute 1 tablespoon oregano for the 2 tablespoons Italian parsley. Allow the tomatoes to marinate in the herbs for 2 hours and eliminate the fresh mozzarella. Presto! You have Fresh Heirloom Tomato Bruschetta.

PROCEDURE

1. To prepare the tomatoes, begin by scoring a small X in the top of each. Blanch them in boiling water for about 10 seconds, then plunge them immediately into an ice bath. After a minute or so, you can easily peel and seed them before dicing them in ¼" x ¼" cubes.

2. Salt the diced tomatoes and let them drain in a colander over a bowl or sink.

3. Roughly chop the basil and parsley leaves, then mix them with ¼ cup of the oil. Season to taste with salt and red pepper flakes.

4. Toast the bread on a grill or toaster. Slice the garlic cloves in half and rub the exposed sides on each piece of bread. Brush the remaining 2 tablespoons oil onto the bread.

5. Just before serving, cover the top of each slice of bread with the tomato mixture and the sliced mozzarella, then warm in the oven until the cheese just begins to melt. Serve immediately.

PAN-SEARED SEA BASS PUTTANESCA

(SERVES SIX)

In catering it is important to understand how to adjust a theme to fit the preference of the customer. Some customers may want a strictly literal translation of old traditions centered on a theme; others may want a more contemporary interpretation of a meal, fusing flavors across cultural lines. Here Chef Fields offers a fabulous sort of Tuscan-Tucson fusion that reinterprets traditional Italian favorites with fresh local ingredients. :: CWM

SAUCE INGREDIENTS

1 Red Bell Pepper
1 Yellow Bell Pepper
2 tablespoons Extra-Virgin Olive Oil
1/2 White Onion, small diced
1/2 cup Kalamata Olives, chopped
2 tablespoons Capers, drained
1 tablespoon Crushed Red Pepper
2 tablespoons Italian Parsley, leaves only, chopped
2 tablespoons Oregano, fresh, chopped

SEA BASS INGREDIENTS

6, 3-ounce portions Chilean Sea Bass
Salt and Pepper
1/4 cup + 2 tablespoons All-Purpose Flour
2 tablespoons Olive Oil

ACCOMPANIMENT

Creamy Parmigiano Risotto (recipe follows)

:: Chef's Notes

Some recipes for puttanesca sauce include tomatoes and anchovies. This version is wonderfully flavorful on its own and does not need the additional pungency. The kalamata olives bring the necessary saltiness, and the roasted peppers add the robust flavor generally offered by tomatoes.

Larousse Gastronomique states: "When only cheese or saffron is added [to risotto], it is served as an accompaniment to meat, eggs or even fish." This puttanesca is exquisite with Creamy Parmigiano Risotto.

PROCEDURE

1. Place the red and yellow peppers directly on top of the flame of a gas burner on the stove. Rotate the peppers over the flame until the skin is evenly blackened. If you don't have a gas stove, you may do this directly on the oven rack under a hot broiler for 5-10 minutes.

2. Remove the peppers from the heat and immediately put them into a plastic bag. Let them rest for at least 10 minutes to allow the skin to loosen. One at a time, remove the peppers from the bag to peel. Reserve the flesh, but peel and discard the skin, stem, and seeds. Do not wash the flesh of the pepper, which would diminish the roasted flavor.

3. Cut the flesh into cubes or diamond shapes that are 1/4" x 1/4". Set aside in a large bowl.

4. Heat a sauté pan and add the oil. After the oil is hot, sauté the white onion until it just begins to turn translucent. Add to the peppers in the bowl.

5. Add the remaining ingredients, mix, and allow the flavors to blend together at room temperature for at least 30 minutes, but no longer than 1 hour.

6. Wash the sea bass and pat it dry with a paper towel. Salt and pepper both sides of the fish. Just before searing, dredge each portion in flour and pat off the excess coating.

7. Heat a sauté pan, then add the oil. When the oil is hot, lay the fish down from the front to the back, to avoid oil splatters. Allow the fish to sear in the pan without moving until it forms a golden-brown crust, about 3 minutes per side. Plate by placing the fish against a scoop of risotto and spooning the puttanesca sauce in stripes over it.

CREAMY PARMIGIANO RISOTTO

(SERVES SIX)

This is a very traditional method of making risotto. Its time-honored lessons are still practiced because the resulting dish has such a beautiful texture and creaminess. The addition of the butter and Parmesan at the end of the recipe is so beloved, it actually has its own name in Italian: It's called mantecato, which literally means "creamed." :: CWM

PROCEDURE

1. Put the chicken stock in a saucepan over medium-high heat and bring it to a boil. Reduce the heat and keep the stock simmering throughout the risotto-making process.

2. Heat a large saucepan over medium-high heat. Add the oil and allow it to get hot.

3. Sauté the onion in the oil until translucent.

4. Add the rice and stir to coat it with the oil.

5. Increase the heat to high and add the warm chicken stock ½ cup at a time. Stir constantly until the rice absorbs the liquid.

6. Repeat the process until the chicken stock is completely incorporated. Make certain you are stirring continuously. This process takes approximately 20–30 minutes.

7. The risotto is done when the consistency is creamy, but the rice kernels still have an al dente bite in the middle. Finish by gently stirring in the butter and cheese. Be sure to adjust seasonings with salt and pepper after you add the cheese. Serve immediately.

INGREDIENTS

4 cups Chicken Stock, warmed
2 tablespoons Extra-Virgin Olive Oil
1 small Onion, small diced
1 cup Arborio Rice
2 tablespoons Butter
¼ cup + 2 tablespoons Parmigiano-Reggiano Cheese, freshly grated
Salt and Pepper

:: Chef's Note

Risotto is very adaptable to different flavor profiles. Porcini mushrooms are one of my favorite additions. However, you can marry almost any vegetable with risotto and end up with a flavorful combination. Be certain to prepare it just prior to service to ensure superior quality.

HOW TO MAKE FRESH MOZZARELLA:

· Start with fresh curd (which you can find at a helpful local Italian deli). You can assume that this curd was actually derived from a starter culture that began as the whey from previous cheesemaking. This whey was left out at room temperature to sour naturally, then calf's rennet was added, resulting in a semi-soft curd.

BRINGING THE CURD TO TEMPERATURE:

· Take 3 pounds of mozzarella curd and cut it into 1" cubes. Put these cubes into a very large stainless steel bowl that can accommodate 3 pounds of cheese plus 1 gallon of water.

· Heat 1 gallon of water to about 100°F and pour this over the mozzarella to cover. After about 20 minutes, check the temperature of the water. It should be around 80°F.

· Measure out a second gallon of water into another pot; add 1 cup of Kosher salt. Put this on the stove and allow it to come up to 170°F. When the salted water is 170°F and the curd is 80°F, pour off the first gallon of water and pour the salted 170°F water into the bowl with the curd. Let this sit for a maximum of 1 to 2 minutes.

<u>THE PROCESS OF MOZZATURA</u>:

· ("Mozzatura" means "chopping" or "cutting off," which is where this cheese gets its name.)

· Put on two pairs of thin rubber or latex gloves to help temper the heat for your hands. Have a bowl of ice water nearby to occasionally dunk your hands in to cool them off.

· Submerse your hands in the 170° water and gently squeeze the curds together, without any stretching motions.

· When the cheese begins to melt slightly, choose about a 1-cup portion to work with. Work with this piece of cheese underwater by gently stroking it across the top with your thumbs while cupping the lump of cheese with your fingers underneath. This creates an arched, tunnel-like log shape.

· When the cheese begins to look smooth and is free of lumps, remove it from the bowl and wrap it in a piece of plastic wrap. Twist the two ends of the wrap simultaneously by holding the ends and twirling the cheese in front of you. The resulting shape is a log about 4" long and 2" thick. Store in a bowl of milk or whey.

· Repeat with the remaining curd and consume as soon as possible.

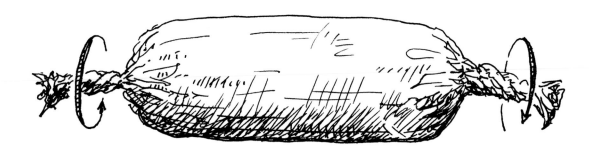

THE CHEF AS TEACHER

A SNAPSHOT OF THE CLASSROOM

I love thinking about the sights and sounds of the classroom kitchens in culinary school. There's always lots of excitement, lots of noise. Pots and pans clattering. As people prepare to work, there are discussions and laughter about what happened the night before. Some people are animated, others focused on the preparation of their mise-en-place. Some students have no problem asking questions, but I seek out the ones who do have a fear, to help draw them out. It's all a part of school: sharing visions, sharing information, sharing lives. It's also fertile ground to experiment, to push yourself, to make mistakes, and to find out why those mistakes happened. The days are filled with learning about teamwork and bonding with the people in your kitchen. They're filled with going deep inside your own thoughts to bring forth your most inspired creations. It's about learning to re-create dishes perfectly as well as inventing dishes on your own. It's being careful with every detail and yet feeling the constant pressure of the clock to develop your sense of urgency and get the job done on time.

As a teacher I spend much of my time listening to students before I respond. I need to get inside their thinking first to see where they want their education to take them, and to understand how they as individuals need to grow. You can only motivate people if you really come to understand their needs. It's important for teachers and students to know how to listen. It's like Einstein said, "I never learn a damn thing when I'm talking."

TEACHING AND PARENTING

There are amazing parallels between parenting and teaching because they really are synonymous in many ways: A parent is a teacher, and sometimes a teacher needs to act in a parental capacity as well. It's helpful for teachers to apply good principles of teaching that parallel good principles of parenting: Be patient, be firm, be fair, be flexible sometimes and persistent in other situations. You have to hold consistency, fairness, and truth on the same pedestal, and give every person what he or she needs to grow. That may differ from time to time and person

to person, but if you're fair about your actions, people will know why you've chosen your individual response.

Just as with parenting, it's a huge responsibility to know that I'm teaching others. I must always be on my best behavior. It means I must inspire not only through my thoughts and mannerisms, but through my food. I let my food do the talking, and my demeanor is there to back it up.

ONE OF MY MOST MEANINGFUL MOMENTS OF TEACHING

Jamie was a young student of mine who was making she-crab soup, a famous creamy crab soup from South Carolina. He made a beautiful soup and topped it with a little shell of puff pastry to garnish it with a couple of chives coming out from under it. The flavor was wonderful. All I did was tell him his soup was awesome, but the response I got from him was what hit me. He didn't say anything at the time, he just beamed and then came up to me at the end of class and handed me a handwritten note. It said, "Chef Tim, Thanks for giving me some confidence." Not a lot of confidence, just some. That little praise that I offered meant so much to him: He just needed that little boost to believe in himself. If people believe they can do good work, they'll strive for that mark in the future.

ADDITIONAL RECIPES

TOAST POINTS WITH MEDITERRANEAN ARTICHOKE MOUSSE

From Chef Skip O'Neill

(SERVES SIX)

The use of artichokes in cooking originated in Sicily, but in France they were first revered for their medicinal assets. They were thought to be an aphrodisiac, and women were forbidden to eat them. The globe artichoke's botanical name, *Cynara scolymus*, is derived from an ancient Roman fable about a little girl named Cynara who was turned into an artichoke. :: **CWM**

INGREDIENTS

1 Lemon, zest and juice only
4 Anchovy Fillets, drained, patted dry
2, 14-ounce cans Artichoke Hearts, drained
1/2 cup loosely packed Italian Parsley,
    fresh, leaves only
1/2 cup Parmigiano-Reggiano Cheese,
    freshly grated
1/2 cup Mayonnaise
1/2 cup Extra-Virgin Olive Oil
1 Sourdough Baguette, sliced into 1/4" ovals

:: Chef's Note

Artichokes are actually the flower bud of a large thistle. This explains why they open up when they are overripe: They are blooming. The hearts used in this recipe come from the center of the cluster of leaves. If you are cooking them fresh, not out of a can, you can speed up the trimming process by first smashing the artichoke top-down on top of a hard surface to loosen the leaves.

PROCEDURE

1. Grate and reserve 1 teaspoon lemon zest. Squeeze the lemon half and reserve 1 tablespoon of the juice.

2. Combine the zest, juice, anchovy fillets, artichoke hearts, parsley, cheese, and mayonnaise in a blender. Blend until the contents have an even, smooth consistency.

3. Then, as the blender is mixing, gradually add the oil in a constant, thin stream to properly emulsify the ingredients.

4. Transfer the artichoke mixture into a bowl and place it in the refrigerator to chill for at least 2 hours to allow the flavors to combine.

5. After chilling, remove the artichoke mixture and transfer it into a piping bag with a star tip.

6. Just before serving, make the toast points by placing the baguette slices on a sheet tray and toasting in the oven at 350° until they are a very light brown color, about 10 minutes.

7. When the toast points are ready, pipe the artichoke mousse into 1" rosettes on top of each toast point or, if you prefer, spread it on top with a knife. Garnish as desired.

OSSO BUCO IN VALPOLICELLA

From Chef Randy Foote

(SERVES EIGHT)

Meat that falls to its knees when lifted from the plate, marrow that moves me to dig endlessly to the farthest recesses of a hollow and hallowed bone, risotto that makes me swoon . . . what more is there? :: **CWM**

PROCEDURE

1. Season the veal shanks on both sides with salt and pepper. Dredge the shanks in flour and gently shake off the excess.

2. Heat a large stockpot on the stove. Add just enough oil to coat the bottom of the pot. Heat the oil until it is very hot, then add the veal shanks. Brown them on all sides.

3. Remove the veal shanks from the pot and set them aside.

4. Reduce the heat to low, then add the carrots, celery, onions, and garlic to the pot. Cover and allow them to sweat for 3–4 minutes.

5. Deglaze the pan by pouring in the wine while the pot is still hot. Stir the bottom of the pot to make sure any of the lovely browned bits that have formed there are incorporated into the wine. Allow the contents to reduce by three-quarters.

6. Add the remaining ingredients, plus a pinch of salt and pepper. Allow the shanks to simmer for 3–4 hours, or until the meat is fork-tender. If you would prefer to cook it in the oven, place it, covered, in a 275°F oven for the same length of time. Remove the meat, season it with salt and pepper, and set it aside in a warm location.

7. Remove the orange and lemon halves, but pour the rest of the liquid and vegetables into a food processor or blender. Puree the contents until smooth to make the sauce. Strain the sauce using a fine strainer or chinois.

8. Adjust the seasonings of the sauce with salt and pepper. Serve the osso buco next to a spoonful of Risotto alla Milanese with the sauce ladled in front of the shanks.

OSSO BUCO INGREDIENTS

8, 1-1½-pound Veal Shanks, bone in
Kosher Salt and freshly ground Black Pepper
Flour for dredging
Oil for searing
¾ cup Carrots, peeled, medium diced
¾ cup Celery, medium diced
1½ cups Onions, medium diced
1 tablespoon Garlic, minced
1 cup Valpolicella Wine
2 cups Mushrooms, cut in half
2 Oranges, cut in half
1 Lemon, cut in half
5 cups Veal Stock or Low-Sodium Beef Broth
2 teaspoons Basil, fresh, minced
2 sprigs Thyme

ACCOMPANIMENT

Risotto alla Milanese (recipe follows)

:: Chef's Note

Osso buco literally means "bone with a hole." The marrow that occupies this hole is known as midollo in Italian and moelle in French. It is such a coveted delicacy that it is sometimes served with a special little silver spoon to capture every last bit. In Italian this little spoon is called an escatorre, which translates to "tax collector." Osso buco is traditionally served with Risotto alla Milanese, but its hearty flavor pairs well with many different side dishes.

RISOTTO ALLA MILANESE

(SERVES EIGHT)

There are many different theories as to why Risotto alla Milanese is colored and flavored with saffron. One tale depicts an artist at the Duomo cathedral in Milan who was particularly proud of his work. He began stirring gold leaf into his risotto as a sort of bragging right, exploiting his good fortune. Later, perhaps in somewhat less pompous or more ravenous moments, he replaced the gold with saffron. :: **CWM**

INGREDIENTS

6 cups Veal Stock, warmed
2 ounces Beef Marrow
1½ tablespoons Extra-Virgin Olive Oil
4½ tablespoons Butter
1 small Yellow Onion, peeled, small diced
1½ cups Carnaroli or Arborio Rice
½ cup Pinot Grigio or Soave Wine
12-15 threads Saffron
⅓ cup Parmigiano-Reggiano Cheese, grated
Salt and Pepper

:: Chef's Note

Italian rice for risotto is sold in four different categories, based on the characteristics of the grain: commune (household rice), semifino (round grained), fino (medium grained), and superfine (superfine). Carnaroli comes from the superfine category and has long, thick grains that are shaped like a half spindle. If the package of rice also has "ai pestilli" written on it, that is good news for cooks who love risotto. The words refer to a hulling process that leaves an extra-powdery starch on the rice, which translates into even creamier risotto. Although Arborio rice will produce fine risotto, Carnaroli is traditionally used by Milanese chefs.

PROCEDURE

1. Bring the veal stock just to a boil, then reduce the heat and keep the stock simmering throughout the risotto-making process.

2. Heat a second large saucepot over medium heat. Add the marrow, oil, and 2½ tablespoons of the butter to the pot and allow them to melt.

3. Add the onion to the marrow mixture and stir until translucent, 5-6 minutes. Do not allow the onion to brown.

4. Add the rice and stir to coat the kernels with fat. Add the wine and stir constantly until the wine is reduced to au sec, or almost dry.

5. Ladle ½ cup warm stock into the pot. Stir constantly until the rice absorbs most of the liquid. When the rice is no longer runny, add the next ½ cup and repeat the process.

6. When a little over half of the stock has been incorporated into the risotto, bring the stock in the saucepan back up to a boil, then pour 1 cup of it into a small separate bowl. Add the saffron threads and cover the bowl immediately with plastic wrap. Allow the saffron to steep for 5 minutes: The cover traps the beautiful aromatics releasing from the saffron.

7. Continue stirring and adding stock. Save the saffron solution for the last addition of stock to the risotto and stir until the rice kernels are tender, yet retain a slight firmness in the center The total cooking time of the risotto from start to finish is approximately 20 minutes.

8. Finish by stirring in the remaining butter and the cheese. Adjust the seasonings with salt and pepper. Serve immediately alongside the osso buco.

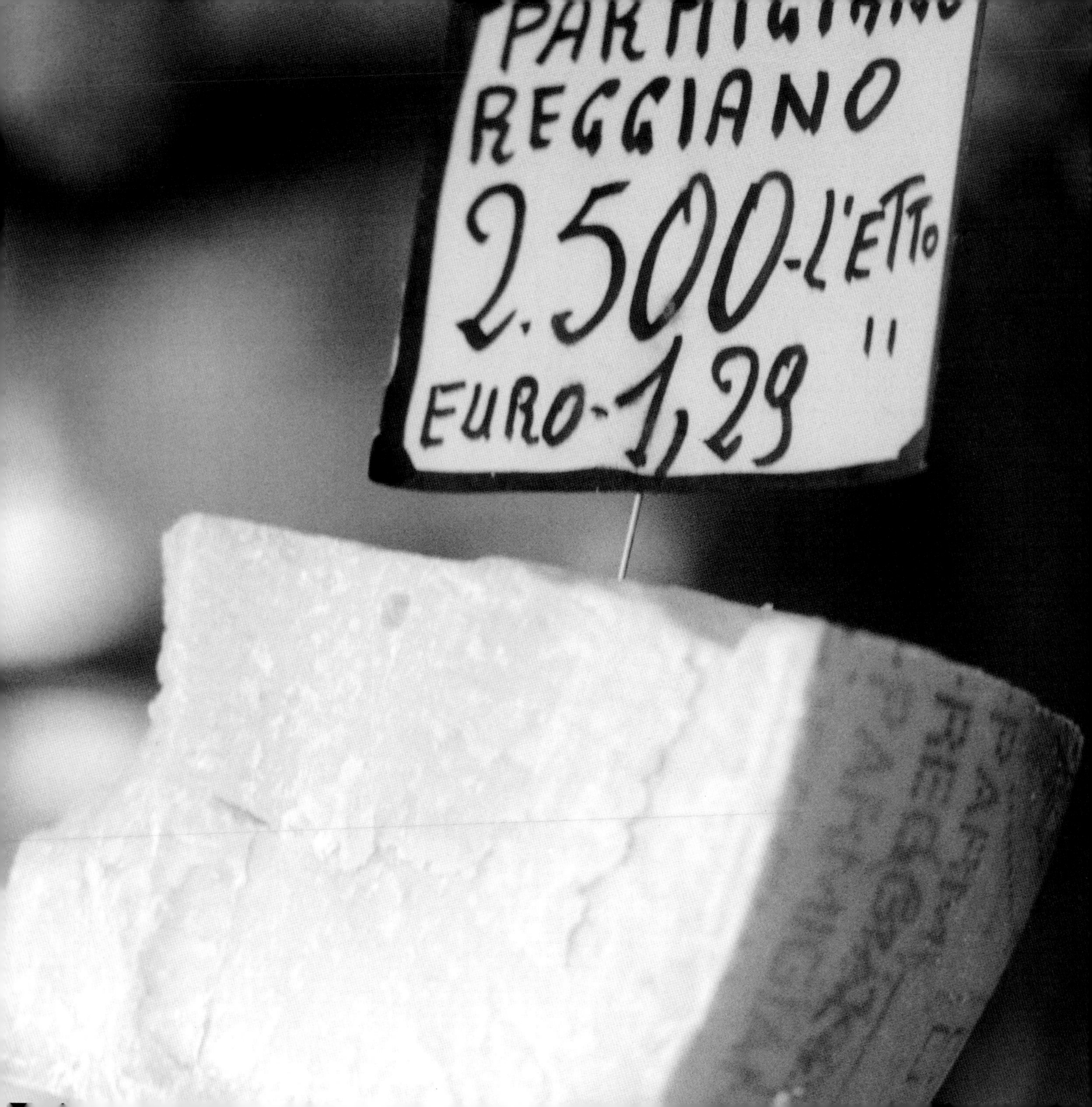
REGGIANO
2.500-L'ETTO
EURO-1,29

basic baking I

INSTRUCTOR: CHEF RICHARD EXLEY

IT IS TRUE THAT THE PRINCIPLES OF SCIENCE BELONG
TO THE ENTIRE KITCHEN OF COOKS, BUT BAKERS WOULD ARGUE
THAT THEY CAN CLAIM FIRST RIGHTS TO THIS EXPERTISE.

All students of Basic Baking learn to calculate the loft and holding power of meringue, identify the physical characteristics of flours, adjust the speed of leavening, monitor the precision of measurement, and understand the process of gluten development as we produce our daily breads, desserts, and pastries. However, as I talked with Chef Exley about his influences as a chef, it was the lessons he learned as a builder that inspired me to rethink my own philosophy of baking. His experience with physics and architecture revealed how delicate food can be built with a strong foundation: "When I build height into my plate, I have in mind the shapes and structures of buildings I have made with my own hands. I am amazed by the notion of structures with stories to tell. I speak through design." His ideas on vertical food designs also helped me use time and space in the design of food. Textures and flavors unfold in sequence as the fork cuts down through the layers, and the diner enjoys the contrasts that distinguish one layer from the next, changing as time passes. A sorbet on a baked dessert is served on a plate drizzled with caramelized sugar. The sorbet drips down over the dessert and sugar, changing the intensity of the flavor as it melts. Suddenly the possibilities for construction became endlessly intoxicating. :: **CWM**

REFLECTIONS OF A CHEF

A BUILDER'S VIEW OF THE WORLD

The design of structures all over the world fascinates me, from the ancient ruins in Peru to the Guggenheim in New York. Bridges kidnap my imagination. Frank Lloyd Wright's work that surrounds us in Phoenix is particularly fascinating to me because it represents a time when building was more thoughtful, more reflective than the fast pace of building in the city now. Old buildings just fascinate me. I'm struck by how the building survived over time; I marvel at the hands that have touched it, the lives that have been changed within the walls. Even in Denver, a relatively young town by worldly standards, the old Cosmopolitan Hotel was being torn down. I walked through it just before it was demolished. I could hear the history as I walked down the hallways toward the kitchen in the basement. I could feel the memories as I ran my hand down the countertops because so much had happened in that building over the years. I love how a structure can have so much to say.

I go through life looking at shapes. The shape of an object captivates me even more than the object itself. I've been known to go shopping with my wife when she may be drawn to an object for sale, but I'm drawn to the shelf it's sitting on.

I use those daily lessons of the structures around me to become better in all aspects of design. When I am creating in the kitchen, even though I'm concentrating on design, I start with the flavors first and think through how and when I want to combine them as the dessert is eaten. Then I move into the structure itself and concentrate on which actual products I can use to physically carry out the design I have in mind. Finally I look at the colors and how those will balance the design on the plate. I sketch it out first so that I can more carefully think through each of those components before I bake it.

THE GRACE OF GREAT THINGS

My background in carpentry is particularly helpful in understanding the physics of

structures. The stability of the design is critical because although it is lovely to build a creation in the kitchen, the servers must still be able to carry the dish to the customer and have it arrive in one piece, even in a rush. It needs to hold its shape even if it sits on the table for quite a while. Even though the presentation is fabulous, you still need to create a dish that can be eaten with ease. It's all part of the enjoyment. Smoothness is not just about the surface of a dish, it is also your goal for the entire eating process. The fork should glide through a dessert, not be stopped by a tough crust. Your food should allow your guest to dance through the consumption with graceful, flowing movements. You have to think of it from start to finish. The ultimate responsibility is to satisfy your guest. From the first bite to the last, it has to be fabulous for the entire performance. It's their last memory of a breathtaking meal and it all has to come together to leave the diner with a blissful memory.

PLAYING IN THE KITCHEN

Experimenting with flavors or textures that aren't traditionally meant to go together characterizes my playtime in the kitchen. Lately I've been dreaming about the delicate sweetness of sweet pea blossoms. When they come in season, I'd like to create a sorbet or an ice cream out of sweet peas. I'd also love to do more with goat milk out of the Hispanic traditions. Hibiscus flowers are wonderful to experiment with: The organic flowers give a gorgeous color, a lovely aroma, and a very natural sweetness when you steep them and use the essence in the water to make sorbets or crème brûlée. Different products bring out different characteristics of the flower. I love finding out which ones do it best.

Besides my fascination with floral accents, I also experiment with flavors and products from world markets, particularly incorporating Asian influences into my desserts. From the influences of the Southwest, it is wonderful to combine sweet and spice. One

RICHARD EXLEY

of my favorite creations is a flourless chocolate chili torte with a sarsaparilla mascarpone mousse on the side. I used a mixture of European chocolates with a combination of Mexican cayenne pepper and a touch of habanero to create the nice bite in the back of your mouth after you taste the chocolate. In a way, it was a recipe that was a bit autobiographical since it combined my experiences as a chef: the influence of Europe from my apprenticeships and the inspiration of my life in the Southwest.

THE APPRENTICE SYSTEM; OR, LIFE AS BONDED LABOR

When the time came, I was completely ready to begin working in an apprentice system: anything to escape my mother's cooking. My memories of eating as a kid involve Swanson's TV dinners and cruises through McDonald's. Hamburger Helper was a familiar name around our household. My mom was not a big cook. I actually never knew meat was supposed to be pink until I began working at my first job at a country club. My mom's idea of a roast was a piece of meat in a 375°F oven for at least 3 hours. Dry didn't begin to describe that meal. I wanted to get into cooking as soon as possible.

When I was about 15 years old a French man came into the country club where I was working. He let the cooks know he was opening up a French pastry shop with one of the high-end catering businesses in town. Since he had just come over from France, he was interested in finding an apprentice–i.e., a grunt–

to help him with his pastries. For me, at the time, it was a great opportunity. I'll never forget the first moment I walked into his shop and saw the glaze on the strawberry tarts. It was done with such perfection that I was captivated and wanted to learn everything there was to know about baking pastries. I've been enamored with baking ever since.

The European apprenticeship system is set up so that you are at the beck and call of your chef. You need to anticipate his or her every move and be ready, in advance, to meet every need. That takes a special mental mise-en-place to be able to forecast the needs of a truly innovative chef. You have to stop, look, and listen without talking to get into the mind and movements of another cook. By doing that you also learn the love and traditions that are carried on to produce that particular food. Learning at that level allows you to feel and understand food differently; it allows you to experience it in a context other than just something that you eat. You see the connections of food in society and realize how it is the lifeblood of the world around you. Apprenticeships help you involve yourself completely in the work and progress of another chef. You just have to be certain that the food and the culture the chef teaches you are the food and culture you want to learn; otherwise learn somewhere else.

FOSTERING A WORLDVIEW

I really enjoy artists who experiment with new techniques. I don't like popular, trendy ideas; I like true innovation. I'm also a big fan of contemporary Indian art. I have a small collection of kachina dolls, Native American sculptures, even welded creations that I look to for inspiration.

That appreciation for other cultures is important to me to portray in my own artwork. It's equally as important for me to bring that appreciation into my teaching. I feel a need to bring a deeper respect for other cultures into my classroom in order to move my students out of their American mind-set. It's immensely important to help them grow in their worldliness and be able to adopt different points of view. Since the kitchen tends to be a very diverse place, it's crucial to stay flexible in your thinking. My hope is that their view becomes broad enough to be open to every source of inspiration.

A LOVE FOR TRADITIONAL TECHNIQUES

At one point in my career I became part of a team of cooks that presented showpiece work at food shows. The food was designed to highlight the offerings of different venues in the city. It was for the purpose of display only; it was never intended to be eaten. I will never forget the energy in that kitchen as we worked 24-48 hours straight preparing for this big event. We'd use the old-style techniques of covering food in aspic gelatin and creating chaud-froid centerpieces. But the most fascinating part was watching the creativity that flowed from this group of chefs as we stayed up all night cooking together.

One of the methods that is not often seen anymore is one of my favorite techniques in the kitchen: cocoa painting. Even though I also adore pulled and blown sugar, cocoa painting is a medium that I can just get lost in forever. The procedure starts out with a pastillage backdrop, which consists of a hard candy canvas, so to speak. Then you take cocoa and mix it with either a clear alcohol such as vodka for a more watercolorlike effect, or oil for more of an oil-paint finish. You can use different cocoas to create different shades and textures. Then you use the cocoa mixture to actually paint a painting on the pastillage canvas. When you're finished, you can spray it with food glaze or, if it's not consumed, even hair spray to coat it. The result can be very intricate with its deep brown-and-white contrast.

THE ATTRACTION OF BAKING

I love the finesse that's necessary to bake well. It's wonderful to watch when the human body and the human mind work together to move on a level of complete precision and flow. I also love the endless possibilities just waiting to be discovered and incorporated into your next creation. There is no grand finale, no pièce de résistance; there's always more to invent.

THE CHEF'S LESSON

PASSION FRUIT CRÈME BRÛLÉE

(SERVES TEN)

Caramelizing sugar is not as difficult as it looks, but you do have to be very careful. Make sure the top of the brûlée does not get too dark. Light brown caramelized sugar is rich, deep, and pungent. If it becomes too dark, the flavor becomes bitter. The name of the dessert acts as a constant reminder to be careful on this step: Crème brûlée translates to "burned cream." :: **CWM**

PUREE INGREDIENTS

6 Passion Fruit, yellow pulp and seeds only
2 ounces (¼ cup) Sugar
¼ cup + 2 tablespoons Water

BRÛLÉE INGREDIENTS

3 pints Heavy Cream
12 Egg Yolks
6 ounces (⅔ cup + 2 tablespoons) Sugar
1 cup Passion Fruit Puree (see above)
2 teaspoons Pure Vanilla Extract
¾ teaspoon Salt
Superfine Sugar

ACCOMPANIMENTS

Fresh Berries, to garnish
Reserved Passion Fruit Seeds (optional),
    to garnish

:: Chef's Note

Add the water for your water bath to the pan just before sliding it into the oven. This prevents the water from spilling into the brûlées. Since the brûlées will be served in the ramekins they are baked in, also be sure to clean off the rims before they begin to bake.

PROCEDURE

1. Preheat the oven to 350°F.

2. Combine the passion fruit pulp and seeds, sugar, and water in a saucepan. Heat just to a simmer, then turn off the heat.

3. With a small hand blender, puree the mixture until it is smooth. The seeds will only separate from the pulp; they will not blend in.

4. Pass the puree through a chinois or a fine strainer and allow it to cool. Reserve a few of the seeds for garnishing the finished brûlée.

5. Bring the cream to a scald. When it just begins to froth, turn off the heat. Allow it to cool slightly.

6. Mix together the egg yolks and sugar until they are evenly distributed. Keep this mixture in motion until you stir in the puree, or the sugar will actually curdle the eggs.

7. Stir in the passion fruit puree.

8. Take a small portion of the warm cream and mix it into the egg mixture to temper, or gently warm, the ingredients and help ensure that they do not curdle.

9. Then gradually stir the warm cream into the egg/passion fruit mixture a little at a time. Be patient with this step: A hurried incorporation will end up scrambling the eggs.

10. Add the vanilla and salt. Pour the mixture through a fine strainer into a container that allows for easy pouring.

11. Put 10 ramekins in a hotel pan or 2 cake pans. Fill the ramekins to a height no lower than ⅛" from the top. The custard will settle when baking, so pour the brûlée mixture as close to the top of each ramekin as you can.

12. Bake in a water bath until the custard is set, approximately 25 minutes.

13. Remove from the oven and take the ramekins out of the water bath. Cool on the countertop. When cool to the touch, transfer to the refrigerator.

14. Just before serving, sprinkle the top of each ramekin with superfine sugar. Do not sprinkle on too much or the crust will be too hard. In contrast, the spoon should be able to cut right through the warm crust to reach the cool custard below. Brush off any sugar on the rims.

15. Caramelize the sugar using a small kitchen blowtorch, or place the pan of ramekins under the broiler. Watch carefully, as these burn easily. Garnish with a few washed, reserved passion fruit seeds or fresh berries.

ABOUT PASSION FRUIT:

- Romance is the notion that comes to mind when passion fruit is mentioned. However, the "passion" in the name comes instead from Spanish traditions comparing the passion fruit blossoms to symbolism representing the crucifixion.

- To get the juice out of a passionfruit, simply cut it open and strain the seeds out using a strainer. The shell-like skin is not eaten. (Passion fruit juice is also available commercially in small tubs.)

EGG WHITES-HOW THEY WORK:

- When beating egg whites, it is important to remember that their volume can increase up to eight times. Therefore, it is important to plan ahead with an appropriately-sized mixing bowl prior to whipping the whites.

- To maximize the volume of egg whites, follow these guidelines:

  1. Start with fresh eggs (the protein is stronger)

  2. Use egg whites that are at room temperature.

  3. Use a copper bowl if possible, since the copper stabilizes the foam and makes it harder to overbeat. In the absence of copper, a pinch of cream of tartar can add similar stability.

  4. Make sure the bowl is completely clean and and that the whites don't contain any bits of yolk or they won't whip.

  5. Don't use plastic bowls since they may contain a greasy film that would contaminate the whites.

WHIPPING STAGES OF EGG WHITES:

FOAMY

When looking into the bowl, the surface of the whites looks frothy "like the head of a beer."

SOFT PEAK

This foam will mound up to a curl, but won't hold its shape. (When lifting your spoon from the surface, the curl of the peak "closes its eye.") It is bright white, moist, and shiny.

MEDIUM PEAK

This forms dense peaks with curls that hold their shape in open curls with less drooping (the "eye" does not close).

FIRM/STIFF PEAK

This foam is at its maximum volume and holds stiff, upright peaks (comes to a point). It is not dry, however, and appears glossy on its surface.

GREAT CHOICES FOR DIFFERENT MERINGUE TYPES:

- COMMON MERINGUE is the most volatile form of meringue and is best used for soft desserts or for cake bases that will be cooked. It is used in the ladyfinger recipe because of this principle.

- SWISS MERINGUE uses a warm foaming method of production. It is a good choice to use for lemon meringue pie or baked Alaska since it browns well without dissolving.

- ITALIAN MERINGUE, a dense and stable meringue, is the best choice if the food item needs to rest before baking. It is a particularly good choice for buttercreams, icings, mousses, or this tiramisu.

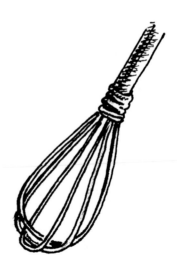

THE CHEF AS TEACHER

A BEAUTIFUL SURPRISE

I didn't expect to be so rewarded by teaching. It's brought such meaning to my work to see that my involvement can actually help others accomplish their dreams. At this stage in my life I enjoy the introspection that comes with teaching; I adore the research. But when I can put those inspirations together in a setting that catapults others' careers, it puts that much more meaning into the work I do. It's a way of giving back and feeling useful in this world. Discovering the world of teaching is like being awakened to a lovely gift. In fact, one year an Oriental student of mine made me a gift that completely touched me. It was simply a small origami swan that she had made and tucked inside a Christmas card to me. Those small beautiful gestures mean more to me than just about anything.

THE TELLTALE SPARK

I also appreciate it when students come up to discuss books that they've read or pastries that they've seen. They want to extract everything they possibly can from me. It's like watching potential embodied. Even during discussions, their eyes light up and there is a little smile in the corners of their mouth as they talk about new creations. When you see that kind of enthusiasm and wonder, you know you have a student in your classroom with potential.

EXPERIMENT WITH NEW FLAVORS

You have to be willing to taste everything before you will be able to invent something wonderful on your own. So it thrills me to help students to be brave, to try the obscure. Balut eggs from Malaysia which contain a partially-developed embryo, or the live octopus from Korea that attaches its tentacles to your face before you eat it, may be too extreme for most tastes, but the more food you can try, the more flavors you have in your back pocket to choose from. Look for combinations that make sense, but consider choosing them from uncommon places. The more you experiment with the flavors of the world, the more you can experience a little touch into how other people live their lives.

CHEFS WHO KNOW PASTRIES

Baking and pastry tend to demand more precision and science than cooking on the savory side of the kitchen. People tend to either love it or hate it. It's helpful for those who are less naturally drawn to pastries to learn from some of the best chefs in this country whose background and/or love for pastries has allowed them to create miracles in the kitchen. I've always admired Michael Richard because he started in baking and pastry before he moved into the world of executive chef. His expertise in all areas allows him to be such a completely well-rounded chef, with techniques available to him that chefs without his background avoid because they are not as comfortable incorporating them into their food. Hubert Keller, chef-owner of Fleur de Lys, one of the best restaurants in San Francisco, is another chef I admire. His ability to build an entrée plate just blows my mind because it is as precise, flowing, and flavorful as a dessert plate. The more you know about all cooking, the better executive chef you can become.

ADDITIONAL RECIPES

TROPICAL BAKED ALASKA

(SERVES EIGHT)

The juxtaposition of contrasting climates evident in its name perfectly captures the nature of this crowd-pleasing dessert: Although the drifts of meringue on the exterior imitate the snowfields of Alaska, they happen to be the warmer component of this dish. When you cut into the center to serve a slice, it exposes the other irony: The rainbow of tropical flavors layered inside supplies the icy-cold sensation. :: **CWM**

STEP ONE: THE PURE VANILLA POUND CAKE

(SERVES EIGHT IF MADE AS A SEPARATE DESSERT)

INGREDIENTS

1 pound (2 cups) Butter, unsalted, room
    temperature
8 Eggs, large, room temperature
2 tablespoons Butter, unsalted, melted
1 pound (3 3/4 cups) Cake Flour
2 teaspoons Pure Vanilla Extract
1 teaspoon Salt
1 pound (2 1/8 cups) Superfine Sugar

:: Chef's Note

Not all pound cakes have a pound each of butter, eggs, flour, and sugar. See the Citrus Sour Cream Rose Cake on page 175 to compare how other pound cakes can be proportioned. This recipe, however, is the old-fashioned version. The relatively firm density of the pound cake is required in the Tropical Baked Alaska recipe to hold up the layers of ice cream and keep its structure even when the ice cream melts on top.

PROCEDURE

1. Preheat the oven to 350°F. Prepare 2, 10" round cake pans by wiping the inside of the pans with the melted butter, then inserting a circle of parchment paper in the bottom of each pan.

2. Sift the flour and set aside.

3. In a small bowl, mix together the eggs, vanilla, and salt.

4. Using the paddle attachment to the mixer, mix the room-temperature butter for 2 minutes, then gradually add in the superfine sugar. Mix until the butter is fluffy, approximately 5 minutes.

5. Slowly add about 2 tablespoons of the egg mixture into the mixing bowl at a time, waiting for each addition to be incorporated before adding more.

6. Stop the mixer and scrape the bowl well.

7. Fold in the flour gradually, one-fourth of the flour at a time, until all of it is incorporated. Do not overmix.

8. Pour the batter into the 2 prepared pans and bake for approximately 1 hour, or until the cakes are golden brown and the centers spring back to the touch.

9. When the cakes are done, remove them from the oven and immediately run a sharp knife around the edges of the pans. Invert the cake pans, remove the cakes, and allow them to cool on a rack until they are room temperature.

10. Once the cakes are cooled, if you are using them to serve on their own, wrap them entirely in plastic wrap to keep soft until you are ready to serve. Or, if you are using them to build the Tropical Baked Alaska, wrap and place in them in the freezer.

(continued)

(Tropical Baked Alaska continued from page 146)

STEP TWO: THE MANGO/RASPBERRY/PASSION FRUIT ICE CREAMS

Although Chef Exley's Tropical Baked Alaska is a wonderful lesson in how to create luscious homemade ice creams, a shortcut can be used that saves a tremendous amount of time if you are in a hurry to make a spectacular dessert. Simply buy a quart of the highest-quality vanilla ice cream you can find, divide it into three equal parts, and mix in the three separate fruit purees with their respective citrus juices. Work quickly, then slip the ice cream back into the freezer to complete a process that cuts your preparation time in half. Just remember: If you have the time, nothing truly beats a product made from scratch. :: **CWM**

PROCEDURE

1. In a large saucepot, combine the milk, salt, and half of the sugar. Split the vanilla bean in half lengthwise and scrape the seeds into the bowl.

2. Heat the mixture to a scald, about 165°F.

3. Mix the egg yolks and other half of the sugar until light and fluffy.

4. Temper the egg mixture by taking out a small portion of the hot milk and pouring it into the bowl with the eggs, whisking constantly. Then gradually add the eggs into the hot milk mixture, again stirring constantly but being careful not to create air bubbles or foam. The tempering helps equalize the temperatures and reduce the chance for curdling.

5. Pour the mixture into a double boiler and stir continuously with a wooden spoon until it has a nappe consistency, approximately 180-185°.

6. Pour the nappe mixture equally into 3 separate containers. Add the mango puree and lime juice to the first container. Mix well.

7. Add the passion fruit puree to the second container. Mix well.

8. Add the raspberry puree and lemon juice to the last container. Mix well.

9. Freeze the ice creams according to the manufacturer's instructions.

INGREDIENTS

1 quart Milk
1 pinch Salt
12 ounces (1½ cups) Superfine Sugar
1 Vanilla Bean
12 Egg Yolks
1 pint Heavy Cream, cold
¾ cup Mango Puree
1 teaspoon Lime Juice, freshly squeezed
¾ cup Passion Fruit Puree
½ cup Raspberry Puree
1 teaspoon Lemon Juice, freshly squeezed

STEP THREE: THE SWISS MERINGUE

(ENOUGH TO FROST ONE BAKED ALASKA)

MERINGUE INGREDIENTS

5 Egg Whites, room temperature
4 ounces (1/2 cup + 1 tablespoon) Sugar

PROCEDURE

1. After forming the Baked Alaska in the mold (see below), warm a pot of water on the stove to approximately 140°F.

2. Place a mixing bowl (from your mixer) on top of the warm pot of water. Add the egg whites and sugar.

3. Using a wire whisk, whip the mixture continuously to combine and warm without coagulation. Beat until it's warm to the touch, approximately 120°.

4. Remove the bowl from the top of the pot and fasten it to the mixer. Whip the meringue on high speed until it forms stiff peaks and the bottom of the bowl feels cool to the touch.

STEP FOUR: FORMING THE BAKED ALASKA AND FINISHING WITH MERINGUE

INGREDIENTS

1/3 quart Mango Ice Cream
1/3 quart Raspberry Ice Cream
1/3 quart Passion Fruit Ice Cream
1, 10" Pure Vanilla Pound Cake
1 recipe Swiss Meringue
1 Eggshell, top 1/4 removed, washed
1 tablespoon High-Proof Alcohol
1 cup Coconut, flaked, lightly toasted

PROCEDURE

1. After the ice cream flavors are frozen, soften them slightly by placing them in the refrigerator for about 15 minutes in preparation for the layering process.

2. Begin by spooning the slightly softened mango ice cream in the bottom of a round metal bowl or bombe mold (see note). Smooth the surface evenly and quickly.

3. Repeat the process with the raspberry ice cream, and finally with the passion fruit ice cream, making smooth, distinct layers.

4. Return the mold to the freezer.

5. While the ice cream starts to firm, place one of the frozen pound cakes on a cake stand to facilitate even cutting. Using a serrated slicer, prepare the pound cake by slicing off the very top portion to smooth off its rough surface. Then place 4 toothpicks horizontally, 1/2" down from the surface of the cake around the exterior of the cake to use as guides to ensure that you make an even cut.

6. Place your slicer parallel to the cake stand on top of two of the toothpicks. Slice across the cake with smooth, even strokes from one side to the other to create an even 1/2" layer of pound cake. Remove the toothpicks.

7. Place the 1/2" pound cake layer on a cutting board. Use the scraps for another purpose.

8. Remove the bombe mold from the freezer and place it, open-side down, on top of the pound cake. Cut the cake around the shape of the mold and trim it so that it will fit perfectly into the mold. Clear away scraps and crumbs. Invert the mold to set it on the counter. Place the cake on top of the ice cream and wrap the entire product in plastic wrap.

9. Return the mold to the freezer while you prepare the Swiss Meringue. When the meringue is ready, transfer it into a large pastry bag fitted with a large star tip.

10. Remove the bombe mold from the freezer. Take off the plastic wrap and rewrap the bottom of the mold with a warm, wet towel to allow the ice cream to release from the sides. Invert the mold on top of a serving platter, shake, and let the molded ice cream cake gently slide out onto a serving platter.

11. Apply the meringue as quickly as possible. Be sure the air is removed from the piping bag by tightly twisting the bag closed right next to the meringue at the bag's end. Starting from the bottom outside of the ice cream cake, pipe meringue out carefully and evenly around the circumference. Hold the piping bag firmly and apply pressure evenly to ensure that the meringue is piped in even spirals.

12. Continue piping around the cake, laying the stripes right next to each other as you apply the meringue in a spiraling pattern. Completely encase the cake in meringue.

13. If you desire, you can quickly decorate the top by adding a few additional piped meringue shapes on top of the other meringue.

14. Finish by placing a washed and dried eggshell on top of the center of the cake and piping meringue around it. This will serve as a container to add the final touch to the cake.

15. Then, take a kitchen blowtorch and quickly sweep evenly back and forth across the meringue to lightly brown its textured surface. Turn off the blowtorch.

16. At this point, the Baked Alaska can be put into the freezer for anywhere from 5 minutes to a few hours to firm up before serving time.

17. At serving time, take the dessert to the dining table and fill the eggshell with a high-proof alcohol. Touch it with a lighted match and enjoy the flame as it flickers and disappears.

18. Remove the eggshell before cutting hearty slices of the Baked Alaska for each guest. Sprinkle each piece with a few flakes of the toasted coconut and serve.

:: Chef's Notes

Refine your piping skills by practicing first on an inverted metal bowl. This way you can perfect your method without ruining a finished product.

A bombe mold is an elliptical metal form that is shaped very much like a lobed bicycle helmet. It is specifically designed to layer ice cream, sorbet, or mousse desserts that highlight contrasting flavors and textures.

ROASTED BANANA TIRAMISU

(SERVES EIGHT)

The whipped ingredients in these ladyfingers call for urgency. Get the batter into the piping bag and the piped shapes into the oven as soon as you can after preparing, or else the structures will collapse and the cookies will not have the necessary spongelike consistency. To save time, ladyfingers may also be purchased at the store, but the taste and texture of your tiramisu will be noticeably different. :: **CWM**

LADYFINGER INGREDIENTS

11 Egg Yolks
4 ounces (1/2 cup + 1 tablespoon) Sugar
11 Egg Whites
5 ounces (1/2 cup + 3 tablespoons) Sugar
9 ounces (1 1/2 cups + 1/2 tablespoon) Bread
   Flour, sifted

TIRAMISU INGREDIENTS

6 Bananas, unpeeled
5 Egg Yolks
4 ounces (1/2 cup + 1 tablespoon) Sugar
3 tablespoons Brandy
1 pound (2 cups) Mascarpone Cheese
2 tablespoons Coffee Liqueur
1 cup Brewed Espresso
1 recipe Swiss Meringue (see page 150)
Ladyfingers
Cocoa Powder

PROCEDURE

1. Preheat the oven to 450°F.

2. In a mixer on high speed, whip the egg yolks and 4 ounces sugar until light and creamy. Reserve the yolk mixture in another bowl or, if possible, use a second mixer to prepare a common meringue. Ideally, you'll keep the yolk mixture in motion on low speed while you whip the egg whites.

3. In the new bowl, whip the egg whites and 2 1/2 ounces (1/4 cup + 1 1/2 tablespoons) sugar on high speed until it is foamy and has tripled in volume, approximately 2 minutes.

4. Then gradually add the remaining 2 1/2 ounces sugar to the egg whites while continuing to mix on high speed until the meringue forms stiff peaks.

5. Stop and take the bowl off the mixer. Using your hand, alternately fold one-third of the meringue, followed by one-third of the sifted flour, into the yolk mixture.

6. Fold in the remaining meringue, followed by the remaining flour. Be sure to fold carefully by hand. Do not overmix or the ladyfingers will not rise well in the oven.

7. Working quickly, put the batter in a pastry bag with a 10mm tip. Pipe the batter onto a Silpat or parchment-lined sheet pan, making strips 1 1/4" wide by 4" long.

8. Immediately place in the oven and bake for 7-10 minutes, or until light golden brown. Cool the ladyfingers on a wire rack. Turn the oven down to 400°.

9. To begin the other parts of the tiramisu, begin by roasting the bananas. Place them, unpeeled, on a baking sheet. Bake for 25 minutes or until the skin is blackened completely. Cool and peel.

10. Combine the egg yolks and sugar in a mixing bowl and whip on high speed until light and creamy.

11. In a separate bowl, mix 1 tablespoon of the brandy into the mascarpone. Then, using your hand, fold in the whipped yolks. Set aside.

12. Prepare the Swiss Meringue, then carefully fold it into the mascarpone mixture.

13. Mash the peeled, roasted bananas and fold them into the mixture.

14. Mix together the remaining 2 tablespoons brandy with the liqueur and espresso. Pour this mixture into a glass pie pan and dunk the ladyfingers in briefly to flavor them with the liquid.

15. Put one-third of the mascarpone mixture into a serving pan and put a layer of flavored ladyfingers on top. Repeat until the final layer of mascarpone mixture is on top.

16. Cover and chill overnight. When it is time to serve, put the cocoa powder in a small strainer and tap the sides, dusting the tiramisu.

:: Chef's Notes

Tiramisu gets its name from the effects of the espresso in the recipe—the name literally means "pick me up."

Hands are used in the folding process of the tiramisu because they are an efficient tool. The tactile cues you receive allow you to immediately identify when the mixture is thoroughly incorporated, which helps reduce the chance of overmixing. At the same time it preserves a traditional technique that intimately connects you to the food.

basic baking II

INSTRUCTOR: CHEF SCOTT MALLETT

WE CONTINUED TO MASTER THE BASICS AND IMPROVED OUR SKILLS
MEASURING, MIXING, SHAPING, AND FINISHING OUR
PRODUCTS WHILE INCREASING OUR SPEED AND CONSISTENCY.

As we advanced in our techniques, I began to look beyond the day-to-day production and started to consider how art is expressed through my food. A composer as well as a culinarian, Chef Mallett has significant experience making artistic statements. The production of music mirrors the process of cooking and just as a composer needs to practice musical scales before producing a powerful concerto, so, too, the basics of food preparation must be mastered before complexity can be successfully introduced. Refining your cooking and baking techniques gives you the freedom to put meaning and depth into your food. Food is first and foremost about flavor, color, and texture—all involved in the consumption of the food. Chef Mallet taught that those same qualities could be used in the art of the dessert. As I considered the range of possible messages I would project through my cooking, I learned something about myself: I would prefer to pay attention to what the food has to say first, rather than force my opinion upon it. The food has its own qualities to bring to the dish; my job is first and foremost to enhance those inherent characteristics. After that, I could add elements of surprise, contrast, passion, whatever I felt would complement it. In that way, the food became more a collaborator than an object to be manipulated. It's a matter of joy and respect. :: CWM

REFLECTIONS OF A CHEF

THE JOY OF COMPOSITION

Food is just as valid a medium to express emotion as clay, or oil paint, or musical notes. I don't know why there has ever been a controversy as to whether food is art or not. It is obvious to me that food is just another medium through which emotion can be expressed. No greater, no lesser choice than the media of artists who create in the more traditional art forms. We begin with emotion in our cooking; guests end with their own emotional response. Their interpretation of that dish is derived from whatever perspective they bring to the table. The transmission is that simple. The art is complete.

COOKING AS THE ULTIMATE ART FORM

The beauty of food as an art form lies in the number of ways it can be experienced. It can be seen, touched, smelled, tasted, and in some cases heard. What a delightful palette to choose from to say what it is we are trying to convey. Where else can you put the art itself into your body? It's completely intimate. The beauty to me lies in the tangibility of food. Emotions are intangible and elusive. Expressing yourself through food allows the luxury of moving beyond three-dimensional aspects and seeing that emotion embodied into something real, tangible, touchable, consumable. How better to totally involve yourself in the art than to put it inside you? How lovely to see something real personify your emotional state. It's very validating.

All art forms are an extension of yourself. So when you can have an art form that can be experienced on all levels by the human body, you're crazy if you don't use it as an extension of yourself, to put all of yourself into your cooking and hope that it elicits a response from every part of your guest.

ON PHILOSOPHY

I have a Taoist philosophy, allowing the dish to speak for itself. Once the plate is finished, it's done, leave it alone, don't push it beyond its natural elegance. You have to look at the natural capabilities of a product to ensure the design isn't forced. Let movement and naturalness work for you, not against you. If you have to dig for inspiration, you will probably end up with mediocrity. Let your ideas be inspired by opening up to what's around you. When composing a song, let your hand relax to move across the keyboard, let your pencil fly across the paper. When composing a dish, loosen your hand as you decorate with a bottle of sauce. Get your mind out of the way and allow your body to move for you.

WHAT I STRIVE FOR IN THE KITCHEN

If I have room to create, I try to use my emotional state in the kitchen as opposed to hiding what I'm feeling that day. It's honest to work from that place in your soul. I'd like to meet the guy who's going through a divorce and a foreclosure who can leave all that at the kitchen door. Use that emotion in your work to open up new sides of your creativity. If you have license to stretch in your designs, and you're angry, your desserts can reflect that anger and result in a design that surprises you with its dark beauty. A joyous day brings new colors, patterns, and movements to your plates and before you know it, you have desserts that represent the whole spectrum of your emotions.

PASTRIES AND ARTISTIC TRANSLATION

There's a lot more that you can create artistically in pastries than you can attempt to do on the hot side of the kitchen. It's hard to re-create the Mona Lisa using meat loaf. You can give it your best shot, but you can do more using chocolate as your medium. Joan Miró is one of my favorite painters of abstract surrealism. I once did a three-

SCOTT MALLETT

dimensional piece based on his work. I also did a couple of showpieces as an ode to Van Gogh. "Chair and Pipes" was a piece in chocolate with a wicker chair, pan flute, and a smoking pipe. I was inspired to make that piece in relief after seeing the cover of Paul McCartney's album *Pipes of Peace*, where they did it in chrome. So in that sense, classic rock influenced my sculpting, which in turn influenced my food.

A STUDY IN GRACE

I studied ballet at a little civic theater under the tutelage of a Broadway dancer for quite some time. Dance teaches you grace, control, and discipline to make your body move in flowing movements, which directly translates into eloquence in plating design.

THE BEST PLACE TO FIND PASTRY EQUIPMENT

Home Depot is the pastry chef's playground. When you walk to the counter with sponges, rollers, a Wagner spray-paint gun, and plastic fluorescent light panels, nine times out of ten, the cashier will look up and say, "So you're a pastry chef?"

THE THINGS OUR GUESTS DON'T KNOW

We had a party at the Ritz-Carlton with about 200 crème brûlée desserts and one working blowtorch. However, even that torch would work for only 3 minutes before it would overheat, need to be turned off, and then allowed to rest for half an hour before it worked again. We discovered this complete oversight in our mise-en-place 45 minutes before service. I had to drive 90 miles an hour from the Ritz to Home Depot and back in order to caramelize 200 desserts to be ready for service.

WHAT IT TAKES TO BE A GOOD PASTRY CHEF

The pastry chef needs the ability to master minutiae, to work on a very tiny scale to create beautiful designs. The adage that "hot-side chefs can't work in pastry" may be an arrogant position, but the definitive skills lie in the ability to physically master the intricate details required in pastry work. Movement needs to be completely precise. Measurements need to be absolutely exact. Not all cooks are cut out to operate that way. It does not mean people with big hands are automatically at a disadvantage. I remember one student who was a very big guy with huge hands. He made the most beautifully delicate butter roses I've ever seen. It's all a matter of coordination.

Pastry chefs and bakers work in the middle of the night. It takes a particular mind-set to live such an alternative lifestyle. But the nighttime hours, away from the frenzy of rush hour, allows you to tap into the deepest parts of your creativity. With choices of media to work with from tempered chocolate to pulled, blown, or spun sugar, to pastillage, and beyond, the possibilities are limited only by your imagination.

THE CHEF'S LESSON

DECADENT CHOCOLATE MOLTEN CAKES

(SERVES EIGHT)

This rich dessert, served in little ramekins, is a great ending to a meal as it is. If you really must add a garnish, just tap on a tiny bit of powdered sugar or cocoa, or the tiniest dollop of whipped cream with a few chocolate shavings, but don't cover up the whole beautiful crust. :: **CWM**

INGREDIENTS

9 ounces (2¼ cups) Dark Chocolate
9 ounces (2 sticks + 1 tablespoon) Butter
11 ounces (1½ cups) Sugar
6 Eggs

:: Chef's Note

When choosing a chocolate to use in this recipe, consider using Scharffen Berger brand for a luxuriously rich, dark chocolate flavor.

PROCEDURE

1. Preheat the oven to 325°F. Chop the chocolate into fine pieces and transfer it to a mixing bowl.

2. Melt the butter and pour it over the chocolate pieces. Mix it together with a paddle attachment on low speed until the chocolate is completely melted.

3. Add the sugar, then the eggs 1 at a time, while operating the paddle at medium speed. Mix until the sugar is dissolved and the eggs are incorporated.

4. Pour the contents into individual 4-ounce ramekins that have been brushed on the bottom with butter and placed in the bottom of a deep-sided sheet pan or cake pan. Fill the ramekins two-thirds full.

5. Take the pan to the oven before adding water to create a shallow water bath. Bake in a 325°F oven for approximately one-half hour, or until a sizable, rustic-looking crust forms on the top of the dessert and a wooden skewer inserted into the cake ⅛" in from the edge comes out relatively clean. The middle of each ramekin will have a crust over the top but the interior will still be soft after the baking is finished. A skewer inserted in the middle will still have chocolate clinging to it, so don't rely on the center of the cakes to show the typical signs of doneness.

6. Serve warm. The beauty of this dessert is in the deep chocolate flavor combined with a contrast of textures: the crusty top with the rich, soft interior.

CHOCOLATE PARALLEL MOUSSE CAKE

(SERVES EIGHT)

What makes this recipe so unique is that it is made up of a group of individual desserts that, when added together, become the mousse cake. :: CWM

STEP ONE: THE CHOCOLATE FLOURLESS BISCUIT

BISCUIT INGREDIENTS

5 Egg Whites, room temperature
5½ ounces (½ cup + 4 teaspoons) Sugar
5 Egg Yolks, room temperature
1¾ ounces (½ cup) Cocoa Powder

:: Chef's Note

Use Dutch-process cocoa for the best results in this biscuit. DUTCH PROCESS will appear on the label of the cocoa, and it refers to a method of treating the roasted cocoa beans or the chocolate liquor cake with alkali. The result is a softer flavor and a deep reddish brown color.

PROCEDURE

1. Preheat the oven to 425°F.

2. Using a thoroughly clean bowl, whip the egg whites to the medium-peak stage.

3. As the mixer continues to turn, slowly sprinkle in the sugar and continue to whip the egg whites until they reach the stiff-peak stage.

4. Add the yolks 1 at a time, whipping on low speed until each is just incorporated.

5. Remove the bowl from the mixer and gently fold in the sifted cocoa powder by hand.

6. Delicately spread the batter smoothly and evenly into a brownie pan prepared with sprayed parchment paper.

7. Bake until the cake just begins to release from the sides of the pan (only 4-5 minutes).

8. While the biscuit is baking, cut a piece of parchment to a size that extends 4" wider than the brownie pan on all sides. Position the parchment on top of a cooling rack.

9. As soon as the biscuit comes out of the oven, run a sharp knife around its edges. Then immediately invert the chocolate biscuit onto the parchment paper.

10. Remove any parchment paper on the top of the biscuit that is left from the brownie pan.

STEP TWO: THE CHOCOLATE SPREAD

PROCEDURE

1. Chop the dark chocolate into fine pieces.

2. Transfer the chocolate to the top of a double boiler (or just a bowl over simmering water) and stir until the pieces melt completely.

3. Immediately spread the melted chocolate evenly over the top of the cooled biscuit. Allow it to cool until hardened.

4. Once the chocolate is completely hardened, pick the biscuit up with your hand under the parchment paper and invert it into a clean, freshly prepared brownie pan with sprayed parchment paper on the bottom.

5. Peel the parchment paper off the new top of the chocolate biscuit. The hardened chocolate spread should now be at the bottom of the pan.

STEP THREE: THE CHOCOLATE MOUSSE

(SERVES EIGHT IF MADE AS SEPARATE DESSERT)

PROCEDURE

1. Finely chop the chocolate and transfer it to a stainless-steel bowl. Set aside.

2. Separate the eggs and reserve the yolks in a separate mixing bowl. Set aside. Discard the whites, or keep them in the refrigerator or freezer for another use.

3. Whip the cream with a mixer until it forms soft peaks. Set aside.

4. Combine the sugar and milk in a saucepan. Heat and stir the contents over medium heat until the milk just begins to boil. Reduce the heat to low.

5. Temper the egg yolks by first taking some of the milk out of the pan and mixing it in with the eggs, whisking constantly. Then pour the egg mixture a little at a time into the pan with the rest of the milk, again whisking continuously.

6. Continue cooking and stirring until the milk mixture thickens to a nappe consistency.

7. Immediately pour the mixture over the chocolate pieces and whip it vigorously until completely smooth.

8. Allow the chocolate to cool slightly, then gently fold in the whipped cream. Chill in the refrigerator.

9. After the mousse is thoroughly cool to the touch (45-60 minutes), remove it from the refrigerator and spread it evenly on top of the chocolate biscuit.

10. Transfer the biscuit to the freezer to allow the mousse to freeze firmly.

SPREAD INGREDIENTS

6 ounces (6 squares) Dark Chocolate

MOUSSE INGREDIENTS

10 ounces (10 squares) Dark Chocolate
8 Egg Yolks
2 3/4 cups Heavy Cream, cold
2 1/2 ounces (1/4 cup) Sugar
3/4 cup Milk

:: Chef's Note

If you are making this mousse (or the following white chocolate mousse recipe) for a separate dessert, pipe it into individual serving containers such as stemmed glasses before placing it in the refrigerator. The structure of a mousse is possible because of a protein in the eggs that causes the liquid foam to turn solid when heat is applied.

STEP FOUR: THE WHITE CHOCOLATE MOUSSE

(SERVES EIGHT IF MADE AS A SEPARATE DESSERT)

MOUSSE INGREDIENTS

14 1/2 ounces (1²/₃ cups) White Chocolate,
  finely chopped
1/4 ounce (2 1/4 teaspoons) Powdered Gelatin,
  unsweetened
1/4 cup Water
3 1/4 cups Heavy Cream

:: Chef's Note

White chocolate is not a true chocolate in
the sense that it does not contain chocolate
liquor. It does contain cocoa butter, along with
sugar, milk solids, vanilla, and lecithin, which
combine to create its characteristically rich
flavor.

PROCEDURE

1. Finely chop the white chocolate and transfer it to a stainless-steel bowl. Set aside.

2. Combine the gelatin and water in a small bowl and allow it to bloom: The gelatin will become soft and swell into a jellylike state.

3. Pour 2 1/4 cups of the cream into a mixing bowl. Whip until it forms soft peaks. Set aside.

4. Pour the remaining cream into a saucepan and bring it just to the boiling point. Turn off the heat and add the gelatin mixture.

5. Stir until the gelatin is completely dissolved. Immediately pour the mixture over the top of the chocolate pieces and whip it vigorously until the mousse is smooth.

6. Cool slightly, then carefully fold in the whipped cream. Chill in the refrigerator.

7. After the mousse is thoroughly cool to the touch (45-60 minutes), remove it from the refrigerator. Remove the mousse cake from the freezer and spread the white chocolate mousse evenly on top of the frozen chocolate mousse.

8. Transfer the biscuit to the freezer to allow the mousse to freeze firmly.

STEP FIVE: THE CHOCOLATE GANACHE

(YIELDS ENOUGH TO FROST ONE CAKE)

PROCEDURE

1. At least 1 hour before making the ganache, remove the mousse cake from the freezer to allow it to thaw partially.

2. Just before staring the ganache, remove the cake from the pan by running a knife around the edge of the pan, placing a plate or wire rack on top, and inverting the pan to release the cake. Remove any parchment paper that remains on the bottom of the cake.

3. Place a cake stand on a baking sheet to catch the excess ganache that will run off the cake. Invert the cake again onto the top of the stand so that the white chocolate mousse is again on top. The cake is now ready to be coated with the ganache.

4. Finely chop the dark chocolate and place it in a stainless-steel mixing bowl. Bring the heavy cream just to the boiling point and pour it immediately over the chocolate. Stir the mixture with a wooden spoon until it has a smooth consistency. Be sure to use ganache immediately, while it is still warm, to ensure that the coating is completely smooth.

5. Pour it over the top of the mousse cake and allow it to run completely down all sides. Do not use your offset spatula unless it is absolutely necessary to cover the rest of the cake. Any excess use of the spatula will result in a reduction in the sheen of the ganache coating.

6. Catch the excess ganache in the sheet pan underneath the cake stand. If necessary, this can be used to coat any parts of the cake that you missed with the first coating, but first it needs to be re-melted. Do so by placing the bowl of the excess ganache over a hot-water bath.

7. The mousse cake is ready to be garnished once the ganache has set.

GANACHE INGREDIENTS

10 ounces (10 squares) Dark Chocolate
1 1/4 cups Heavy Cream

:: Chef's Note

Ganache is one of the most versatile products in a baker's kitchen. It coats cakes, éclairs—anything that needs a glistening chocolate coating. If you'd like to use it for other recipes in more of a frosting consistency, whip it after the melting process until light and fluffy. Extra ganache can be kept in the freezer for several months.

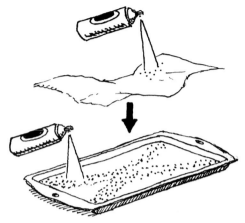

PREPARING A SHEET PAN:

· First spray an "X" of vegetable oil spray directly onto the pan.

· Next, place a piece of parchment paper, cut to fit the entire pan, over the top.

· Finally, spray the top of the parchment lightly. Don't allow the spray to build up; apply only a light coat.

TO ASSEMBLE THE PARALLEL MOUSSE CAKE:

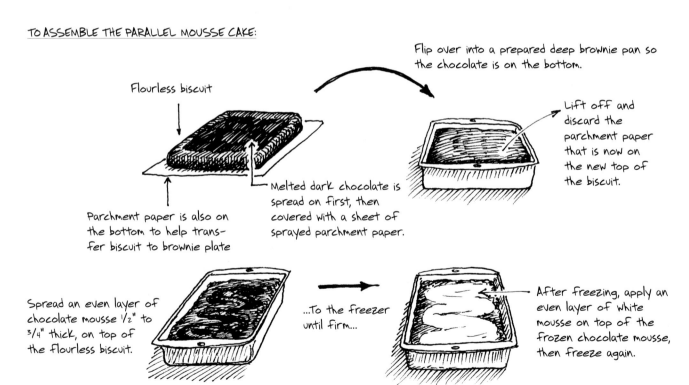

Flourless biscuit

Flip over into a prepared deep brownie pan so the chocolate is on the bottom.

Lift off and discard the parchment paper that is now on the new top of the biscuit.

Parchment paper is also on the bottom to help transfer biscuit to brownie plate

Melted dark chocolate is spread on first, then covered with a sheet of sprayed parchment paper.

Spread an even layer of chocolate mousse ½" to ¾" thick, on top of the flourless biscuit.

...To the freezer until firm...

After freezing, apply an even layer of white mousse on top of the frozen chocolate mousse, then freeze again.

TO ICE THE DESSERT:

· Pour warm ganache over the cake and allow it to slide evenly over the sides.

· Only use an offset spatula to assist the coating when it is absolutely necessary to cover the cake entirely.

· Try to catch the excess ganache on a tray below the turntable.

THE CHEF AS TEACHER

LEARNING TO MANAGE EFFECTIVELY

Early in my classes I try to elicit my students' perspectives on what it means to be a true professional in the food industry. It's interesting to me to see how many still view the consummate executive chef as one who manages from an old style of ranting and raving in the kitchen. To me that's more miserable than professional. To manage effectively you need to operate from a stronger base, one that can manage stress on a more even keel. Truly effective managers—who know when to be tough but also know when to laugh—are able to bring out the best in their cooks. If everyone in your kitchen is totally on edge, you're not going to bring out their best creativity. You need a balance in your kitchen: a strong work ethic, a commitment to excellence, but also the emotional freedom to do your work.

INSPIRATION FROM TOP PASTRY CHEFS

I particularly admire Norman Love as well as Ewald Notter for their abilities to turn any inspiration they have into a piece with actual form, color, and texture. I had the honor of taking a couple of classes with Ewald, and what struck me was his openness to new ideas. He learned from everyone in the classroom even though he is regarded as one of the best pastry chefs in the world. He would look over my shoulder and say, "Oh! What are you doing there?" He was constantly soaking in everything around him without any trace of an ego getting in the way. If I can nurture that continual fascination in a student of mine, I will have achieved great things.

DESSERTS THAT TELL STORIES

I actually have an exercise in my classroom where my students need to choose a particular feeling and translate that into a dessert. "Chocolate Rage" was a great example: It was a dark chocolate cake hit with splashes of raspberry and served with a chili powder ice cream and a jagged piece of tempered chocolate for the top. "Apple Jealousy" was another one of my favorites. A woman made a very tart, bitter green apple mousse cake topped with a green mirror (food glaze colored

with green food coloring) served with a lime reduction sauce. It worked well as a dessert and as an artistic statement. That is the key in cooking: You can make any statement you want, but the bottom line is the guest has to enjoy it.

"Gluttony and the Seven Deadly Sins" was another great plate. Lust was represented through a passion fruit mousse. Sloth was a big pile of chocolate and caramel with no purposeful form to the design whatsoever; it just sat on the plate. Envy was represented through tart flavors. Greed was a rich chocolate cake with gold leaf. Vanity was an extremely ornate piece with intricate piping. Wrath was depicted through a storm of strong, vibrant sauces, and gluttony was represented by the plate as a whole.

THE EASE OF CONFIDENCE

We talk at the end of the very first day in my classroom about the difference between confidence and ego. When you're constantly defending your ego, your mind is shut off to new possibilities. Confidence and creativity translate well in the kitchen. If people trust themselves enough to be creative, that's when the most inspired work takes place.

ADDITIONAL RECIPES

SATINY CHOCOLATE FROSTING

From Chef Karen Kleinknecht

(FROSTS ONE CAKE TEN INCHES IN DIAMETER)

This frosting has a caramel-like consistency that holds its shape, clings well to the surface of the cake, and maintains its shine. From chocolate cake to orange, this frosting would be a good choice for a range of flavors. Try it drizzled over the Citrus Sour Cream Rose Cake (page 175). :: **CWM**

FROSTING INGREDIENTS

2 tablespoons Butter, unsalted

4 ounces (4 squares) Unsweetened Chocolate, finely chopped

1, 14-ounce can Sweetened Condensed Milk

:: Chef's Note
To finely chop chocolate, it is helpful to use a serrated knife.

PROCEDURE

1. Melt the butter over very low heat.

2. Add the unsweetened chocolate. Stir until the chocolate is melted and blended with the butter.

3. Increase the heat to medium and slowly incorporate the sweetened condensed milk. Stir the frosting constantly until it starts to thicken. The proper consistency can be seen when holding up a spoonful of the frosting to see if it forms a slight mound in the middle of the spoon. Remove from the heat.

4. Use the frosting immediately, while still warm. Pour it on the cake and allow it to flow over the surface as much as possible. When necessary, use an offset spatula to finish covering any bare spots. Minimal use of the spatula will maintain the satiny sheen on the cake's surface.

basic baking II

CITRUS SOUR CREAM ROSE CAKE

From Chef Connie Jenkins

(SERVES EIGHT)

Citrus and sugar combine in this very moist version of a pound cake. We learned the secrets of making a delicate cake in Basic Baking: Use cake flour, as its low-gluten content will make the crumb tender; make sure your ingredients are at room temperature so they are lighter and mix well; and weigh your dry ingredients whenever possible, to keep the measurements exact. :: **CWM**

PROCEDURE

1. Preheat the oven to 325°F.

2. Prepare a 10" rose bundt pan by spraying it with vegetable nonstick spray, then dusting it with flour. Be firm when tapping out the excess flour: In a bundt pan, there are many places where flour can get trapped.

3. Sift together the flour, salt, and soda. Set aside.

4. In a mixer, cream together the sugar, butter, and vanilla until light and fluffy.

5. With the mixer on low, add the eggs 1 at a time, waiting for each egg to become incorporated before adding another egg to the bowl. Turn off the mixer and scrape the bowl well.

6. In a small bowl, mix the orange zest, sour cream, and orange juice together.

7. Put the mixing bowl back on the mixer and add a quarter of the dry ingredients. Start the mixer on low so that the ingredients do not fly out of the bowl. When the ingredients are just incorporated, add a third of the sour cream/orange mixture and mix until incorporated. Alternate adding the wet and dry ingredients in this pattern until all of the ingredients are just combined. During the last addition of the dry ingredients, add the dried cranberries if you are using them.

8. Pour the batter into the pan and bake for approximately 80 minutes, until the cake is golden brown and a long wooden skewer comes out clean when it is inserted halfway between the edge of the pan and the center hole.

9. Remove the cake immediately from the pan and cool on a wire rack. Finish with a dusting of powdered sugar or drizzle with your favorite glaze.

INGREDIENTS

16 ounces (3½ cups + 1 tablespoon) Cake Flour

½ teaspoon Salt

½ teaspoon Baking Soda

16 ounces (2 cups + 4½ tablespoons) Superfine Sugar

8 ounces (1 cup) Butter, unsalted, room temperature

1 teaspoon Vanilla

6 Eggs, large, room temperature

2 tablespoons Orange Zest

1 cup Sour Cream, room temperature

½ cup Orange Juice, navel, freshly squeezed

1½ cups Dried Cranberries, optional

:: Chef's Notes

This cake uses the creaming method to mix the ingredients. The fat and sugars are creamed together until light and fluffy; the eggs are added one at a time; and finally, the remaining dry and wet ingredients are added in an alternating method. The last stage always ends with the dry ingredients in order to absorb any remaining liquid in the bowl.

The heavy, rose-shaped pan makes a gorgeous cake. It can be found at specialty shops.

advanced baking

INSTRUCTOR: CHEF JUDY PALMER

I WAS READY FOR MORE. I COULD TASTE IT. I'D LEARNED MY BASIC
METHODS OF BAKING, AND NOW I WANTED TO BRING MY
DESSERTS AND PASTRIES TO A NEW LEVEL OF PROFESSIONALISM.

When Chef Palmer came to class on the first day of Advanced Baking and began to apply chocolate patterns on a jocande cake with a Wagner spray-paint gun, I knew I had come to the right place. But new toys are not the be-all and end-all for great technique in baking. It takes diligent memorization of recipes and a constant synthesis of information in order to think on your feet in a "real world" kitchen. In Advanced Baking, you learn the more intricate processes in the production of cakes, desserts, pastries, décor, and plate presentation. Suddenly, my baking had the potential for real style. The bar for professionalism had been raised and Chef Palmer was just the woman to raise it. Her technique is masterful. Her path to success was as straight as the bicycle path that leads her on her daily rides. Her bike rides free her thoughts and allow her a clarity of vision that helps her to see what needs to be accomplished in her kitchen. She encouraged all of us to find spectacular designs, to draw inspiration from bold sources, and to keep clean lines. Her work is born of intelligence and commitment to perfection. It became clear in Chef Palmer's class that to succeed as a pastry chef, you must set standards for yourself that will accept nothing less than absolute consistency. :: **CWM**

REFLECTIONS OF A CHEF

A WORLD OF PASTRY OPTIONS

Perhaps the most amazing cooking experiences come from my moments spent at the Cannes Film Festival, where I spend 10 days each year cooking for the stars as a part of the American pavilion. Cooking there may seem like a day at the beach, where all of the best elements come together: the food, the sun and sand, the celebrity chefs, the amazing people, the help from the students I take with me each year; it's in France, for God's sake. But the reality of that time is characterized by real drama.

The most memorable parts of these trips to the Riviera come from making something out of nothing. Despite the backdrop of magnificent moments in film, on my kitchen set, there is only ingenuity at its finest: I have only the barest of essentials to work with. There are no glorious kitchens, no cast of thousands, no trailers full of kitchen props. Because of the massive number of parties, galas, and soirees to feed the throngs of people at this event, everyone there scrambles to make the best out of any space. You have to use what you can find to work with. On top of it all, despite these Spartan arrangements, you have to churn out fabulous desserts that consistently blow people away. We produce food for 500 people a day, for some of the most discriminating palates in the world, and we begin our days with a hot plate, a bowl, and a spoon.

I start by looking out the window of the penthouse on top of the palais, past the red rooftops of southern France to breathe in the fresh salty air of the sea. Then, as if I am an outsider looking in, I stare vacantly down at the bowl of frangipane filling that I am stirring with my wooden spoon. There is no electric mixer, no electrical equipment of any kind in the room, and I say to myself, "What's wrong with this picture? In one of the most opulent settings in the world, why are my only pieces of equipment a bowl and a spoon?" Since we stay in the resident hotels to do our work, we have to beg, borrow, and steal any cookware that we can from the condo kitchens. I love working on that edge. Having to be so resourceful is part of the rush: It keeps you constantly on your toes and focuses your energy on the absolute basics of cooking, which is where the brilliance of great food always comes from. It's a complete wonder to make art happen out of nothing but your own inventiveness.

Because we use local ingredients in our desserts, we go first to the farmers' markets for produce, next to the boulangeries to gather any baked goods we need, and finally to the Monoprix supermarkets to collect the other products on our list. I only know a little French, so a trip to buy local wares is an adventure, to say the least. When I first started going to the festival, I remember needing chocolate pieces for my desserts. So, when I found a bag of chocolate in the local store, I did my best to read the side panel to be certain of the ingredients. After being confident I'd chosen the right type of chocolate, I brought armloads of these bags back to the penthouse kitchen. As we started cooking, my student assistants opened the bags to begin working with the chocolate. They were quiet for a moment, then looked up at me and said, "Uh, Judy? What do you want us to do with these?" I looked in the bag and found that each tiny piece of chocolate was individually wrapped in gold foil. We didn't have time to go back and exchange them, so we just pushed up our sleeves and frantically started unwrapping them, every countless piece. You just have to laugh in those situations. It's critical to keep a sense of humor in this business, it's what makes life wonderful.

There is a film called *Vatel* that comes the closest to capturing how the chefs feel about the pressures and responsibilities of handling major events in Cannes. Even though it's set in France in Victorian times, from a chef's perspective it's a great comparison. In the movie Gérard Depardieu plays Vatel, an executive chef who is in charge of the major events at the castle. As they prepare for a massive seafood banquet, Neptune's Tribute to Helios, the cooks are all working with only the tiniest rays of sunshine struggling in through the windows, enormous bread vats are being worked by hand, and fruits dipped in caramelized sugar are hanging to dry on lines around the yard like giant strings of glistening, dripping icicles. Massive ice carvings of Neptune rise up to welcome the boatloads of seafood that were to be delivered to feed the army of guests. When the movie cuts to two little fishermen unloading a cart with only a handful of disdainful fish slithering in the bottom, Vatel comes out to meet them. When he sees the paltry catch, the look on his face is one of complete resignation as he clearly sees his road to ruin. Our work may not be Vatel's creations for kings, but the onus feels the same. The chefs in the audience all shake their heads in complete empathy when they watch that scene.

BALANCING A SUCCESSFUL CAREER AND MOTHERHOOD
Given that my career has taken me all over the country as well as to different parts of the world, I have often been told that you can't be a chef and a mother. Well, I beg to

JUDY PALMER

differ. I've got two great kids and have had a completely satisfying career. My kids have come with me to television demos as well as traveling with me all over the country. They have had wonderfully unique experiences their entire lives. But it has not been easy. I worked until a week before each child was born and went back to work four weeks later. Because of the necessity of working nights as well as some weekends and holidays, I've missed out on a lot, too. Those parts of their lives I can never get back. You have to have a real love for this work to make those kind of sacrifices.

Before I started teaching, the bulk of my career was spent in five-star, five-diamond properties working in pastries: the Four Seasons, the Grand Hyatt, the Inn at Spanish Bay in Pebble Beach, the Princeville in Kauai, the Phoenician in Phoenix, and many other beautiful properties in between. But I made a move to a smaller setting when I began to start my own family: I worked at a wonderful family-owned Italian bakery in south Philadelphia. Whenever my abdomen got bigger, I would just tie my apron strings a little higher. The bakery had been there for-ever with the ovens in the basement and dumbwaiters installed to carry the products up and down between levels.

My job there was to decorate an enormous number of half-sheet cakes with pictures on them, made to order to the cus-tomers' request. Kids would come in with their parents to ask for birthday cakes with specific pictures on them and plead, "Could you make a cake with the New Kids on the Block on it, but only

with Joey and Johnny?" I made cakes with Cabbage Patch dolls with green eyes and purple polka dots; I even reproduced a photo on a cake that depicted a woman kayaking down the Colorado River. One day when an order came in I paused and thought, "I am a classically trained chef with all the experience in the world, and here I am making Mickey Mouse cakes." But it worked while I was pregnant, and besides, they did the best cannolis in town.

THE QUALITIES OF A SUCCESSFUL PASTRY CHEF

Before you can succeed in the pastry business, you first need to know the basics; that is obvious. Culinary school is a great place to learn the basics, but where you take it from there is up to you. You also have to clarify your own philosophy of cooking. To me great pastries are typified by simplicity. Clean lines. All the flavors need to be incredible on their own as well as have an unbelievable marriage with the other flavors on the plate. You also need to have a clear conception of what you feel represents an entire dessert menu. I feel it's important to bring a true range of choices to the diner. Look at all aspects: hot and cold, symmetrical and asymmetrical, a chocolate item and a fruit item, something with nuts, something without. You need to think about color and texture and consider all your choices before you can choose wisely. It's the variety that allows you to touch everywhere, to satisfy every need with your food.

Second, you have to be resourceful in the food industry. No matter where you work, you will never walk into a perfect kitchen with unbreakable equipment or the ideal working environment. You have to know how to fix things when something goes wrong at the last minute. You have to be the one who knows how to pull the kitchen together despite what's going on around you. When I worked at the Berkshire Palace in New York, they were in the process of building my pastry kitchen. I had to work in the back employee entrance with no heat in the middle of January: We were working in down jackets and gloves. I shared space with the butcher with all his raw protein, so we had to divide what little room we had completely in half. When my first day of presentations for the dessert menu arrived, I had all my desserts laid out when the air vents got turned on. It sprayed black soot over everything and I had to go back and redo it all. You just have to shrug, then get in there and fix the problems. There's never enough time to fall apart, you just have to know how to go on.

The opportunities for networking are endless. I also keep in touch with people not just for job opportunities, but because their work inspires me. A pastry chef in Hawaii built a room-sized kiln to make life-sized sculptures out of bread, making Renaissance-style angels with massive wingspans. He wants to retire one day to move to Greece and be surrounded by all the sculptures that inspire him.

ARTISTS WHO INSPIRE

I look at everything around me from an artistic perspective. I love Salvador Dalí. I love work that starts with a classical base and then twists it to create something new. I don't try to replicate fine art, but I definitely take references from great works of art and build them into my work. As with other art forms, you have to choose your medium to work with. In pastries that decision is based on several factors, including the purpose of the dessert and the cultural surroundings in which it is served. For example, you wouldn't necessarily present the same work in the desert of Arizona as you would on the island of Kauai. You need to take your milieu into consideration as well as contemplating the anticipated response to your work. Adding shadows, black-and-white contrasts, or varying textures on a plate adds subtle elegance. I love avante-garde designs that leave you with a contemporary statement of off-center balance. Whimsy is a great ingredient to use because the diner is left with a wonderful lightheartedness at the end of a perfect meal.

You do have to be careful, however, that your enthusiasm doesn't overtake your sense of good judgment. It's very difficult when your style of presentation differs from the ideas of the executive chef. You have to know how to mitigate those situations. While you are negotiating your compromise, you have to be ready to stand behind your creations and find a way to continue with what you feel is beautiful and innovative. Just because your style may be different doesn't mean that it is wrong.

IN LIEU OF DANCING

I've always had a love of dance. I have studied with teachers on Broadway and been a part of a ballet company, but I found that cooking called out for me too clearly. I definitely see dance in the kitchen, especially in pastries where rhythm is critical to the consistency of your products. Everything is choreographed; you have to have that kind of work flow in a kitchen. This is not an industry that showcases solo work; you have to be able to work with many people, often in tight quarters. If things are orchestrated the way they should be, there is a rhythm and integration of movement of arms, legs, and whole bodies, which even in the absence of music is undoubtedly dance. It's cooking a cappella.

THE CHEF'S LESSON

VANILLA BEAN PANNA COTTA

(SERVES SIX)

Gelatin sheets were one of my favorite products to discover in Advanced Baking class. Although they are used in moderation to balance texture and stability, they seem almost magical as they transform liquids into dependably congealed products. They can be found in specialty baking stores. If you can't get them in your area, try searching on the Internet for a convenient mail-order source. Another option is to substitute $2\frac{1}{2}$ teaspoons unflavored gelatin powder for the $2\frac{1}{2}$ sheets of gelatin called for in this recipe. :: **CWM**

INGREDIENTS

$2\frac{1}{2}$ sheets Gelatin
3 cups Heavy Cream
4 ounces ($\frac{1}{2}$ cup) Sugar
$\frac{1}{2}$ ounce (2 tablespoons) Dark Rum
1 Vanilla Bean, split

ACCOMPANIMENT

Fresh Fruit Salsa (see note)

:: Chef's Note

A fresh fruit salsa is completely refreshing over these panna cottas—and very easy to make. Combine 1 pint water with 1 pint sugar and bring to a boil. Take it off the heat and stir in 1 tablespoon balsamic vinegar. When the mixture is cool, pour it over fresh, ripe, sliced strawberries, mangoes, raspberries, and black-berries. Toss gently to distribute the flavors and spoon over the panna cottas just before serving. You can also puree some of the rasp-berries, put in a squirt bottle, and use to add complementary patterns on the plate.

PROCEDURE

1. Set up an ice bath in a container large enough to accommodate a saucepan. Prepare 6, 4-ounce ramekins by coating them lightly with nonstick spray. Bloom, or soften, the gelatin sheets in a bowl of ice water.

2. Meanwhile, pour the cream, sugar, and rum into a saucepan. Scrape the vanilla bean and add the seeds to the pan. Bring to a boil over medium-high heat, then reduce the heat to low and cook for about 5 minutes, stirring continuously.

3. Squeeze out the gelatin sheets and add them to the hot cream mixture while the stove is still on low. Stir until the gelatin has completely dissolved into the cream. Do not allow it to boil once the gelatin has been incorporated.

4. When the gelatin is completely dissolved, remove the saucepan from the stove and place it directly into the ice bath. Stir the cream constantly while it cools, being careful not to get water into the saucepan.

5. Pour the mixture into the prepared ramekins and refrigerate for at least 3 hours, preferably overnight. The panna cottas are ready when they are quite firm; remove them from the ramekins just before serving.

CHOCOLATE SILK PIE

(SERVES EIGHT)

This recipe for chocolate silk can be used for tarts or a pie. What I like most about it is the texture. Where commercial pie fillings are often thickened with cornstarch, this recipe uses butter to bind the mixture. No wonder the pie is absolute heaven! :: **CWM**

PROCEDURE

1. Roast the hazelnuts by placing them in a large, dry sauté pan, flipping them constantly until they just start to become lightly toasted. Remove the nuts from the heat. Allow them to cool and then crush them until they are finely ground.

2. Add the nuts to the sugar and butter. Combine well, and then press into a pie pan to form an even crust. Set aside.

3. Pour the semisweet chocolate into a metal bowl and place it over a pot of simmering water.

4. In a large mixing bowl, cream together the butter and sugar.

5. Add the eggs gradually, mixing well after each addition.

6. Add the melted chocolate next, followed by the cream and vanilla. Mix well.

7. Pour the chocolate filling into the piecrust and allow it to chill completely. The pie is ready for serving when it is cool and set.

8. Garnish with a small dollop of whipped cream or a decadent coating of ganache (see page 165).

CRUST INGREDIENTS

2 cups Hazelnuts
2²⁄₃ ounces (¹⁄₂ cup) Brown Sugar
²⁄₃ cup Butter, unsalted, melted

FILLING INGREDIENTS

1 pound, 4 ounces (20 squares) Semisweet Chocolate, high quality
8 ounces (1 cup) Butter
8 ounces (1 cup + 1 tablespoon) Sugar
8 Eggs
¹⁄₄ cup Heavy Cream
1 tablespoon Pure Vanilla Extract

:: Chef's Note

If you are concerned about salmonella, you can use pasteurized eggs in this recipe. The process of pasteurization heats the egg to a temperature of 140°F and holds it there for 2–3 minutes. This process does not scramble the egg because the coagulation process begins at about 180°F. Pasteurized eggs are available through specialty food stores.

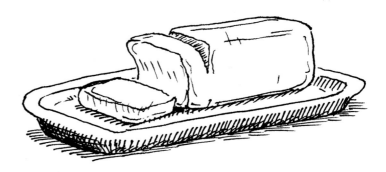

VANILLA: WAXING RHAPSODIC

"If some exquisite little goddess of gluttony were to exist, her name would surely be Vanilla, and she would be a delicate, slim, dark creature in a dress sparkling with tiny perfumed crystals."

—MAGUELONNE TOUSSAINT-SAMAT,
HISTORY OF FOOD

THE VANILLA PLANT:

· The beans begin as green pods that are picked, boiled and dried, resulting in the slender, glossy beans that add such a comforting dimension to food.

MY THOUGHTS ON VANILLA:

I've always loved the juxtaposition of food and flowers. They seem to bring out the most delicate qualities in each other. Perhaps that's why the notion of vanilla coming from a tropical orchid is so beautiful to me. The exotic origins of vanilla from central to South America add to the plant's organic mystery.

ORIGINS OF PANNA COTTA:

· Panna cotta began in the Piedmont region of Northern Italy. Even though its name means "cooked cream," the dish is only warmed to the boiling point to dissolve the sugar and enhance the flavoring agents.

DISSOLVING OF GELATIN SHEETS FOR PANNA COTTA:

· Gelatin sheets look like transparent lasagna noodles. As they are placed one by one into any icy liquid they quickly "melt" into the bowl. Like lasagna noodles, if added individually, they won't clump together and will result in the desired consistency.

UNMOLDING THE PANNA COTTA:

· At the time of service, it's possible to unmold the panna cotta either by very gently warming the bottoms and sides of the ramekins with a kitchen torch . . .

. . . or by briefly warming the ramekin in hot water, being careful not to allow any water over the edges.

THE CHEF AS TEACHER

SEIZING THE MOMENT

As an educator your whole repertoire has to be engaging or you will lose the interest of your students. But it's particularly helpful to start out on the right foot the first day of class. You have to grab their attention the minute they walk through your door. If they are bored throughout the introduction to your class, you've lost the majority of your students, you've missed a wonderful opportunity. I love to start out with something novel to capture their enthusiasm, like using the Wagner spray gun to paint chocolate patterns on to a jocande cake or some other product. I can see the excitement in their faces with new toys. Once you've captured their attention they are much more open to the rest of the information you have to offer.

LEARNING FROM YOUR MISTAKES

A day in Advanced Baking is set up so that the students receive their assignments as well as specific points they need to watch out for in the process of production. This is followed by the actual production in the kitchen where, except on testing days, the students are allowed and encouraged to ask questions about any and all techniques. This is where the deepest learning occurs, the hands-on trial and error to grasp the concepts behind new techniques. Questions naturally arise more often during the experiential part of class, when people are literally up to their armpits in making a product. This is also where the spotlight shines on those who are truly motivated in class. The ones who ask real questions, who think deeply about the process behind the techniques, are the ones who usually end up with real success. They don't just go through the motions, they work to challenge themselves every day in the kitchen and take it upon themselves to seek out what it is that they don't understand.

The days when things don't go right can actually end up being the best learning experiences. I've shared a story with my students that is designed to let people know that mistakes happen, even to the best of us. The tale is from a day early in my career when I worked as assistant pastry chef at the Parker House in

Boston, home of the Parker House rolls. When I arrived at work my head just wasn't in the ball game. My job that morning was to make four, 60-pound batches of rolls. When I put out my first batch of rolls, the dough looked really liquidy, so I added flour but they still didn't turn out right, so I threw them in the trash. The next batch I made turned out fine, but the third batch was also too thin. I thought, "What is going on here?" as I threw that in the trash as well. So at that point I had 120 pounds of dough in the trash can and it started to proof. The steward came in, took one look at the trash can, and refused to empty it. It looked like something that was about to devour Boston. It was then that I realized what I had neglected to do. The 60-quart mixers we used had to be hand cranked up to meet the dough hook or it wouldn't reach the bottom of the bowl. I was leaving three-quarters of my dry ingredients in the bottom of the mixing bowl. When the pastry chef came in, he looked at the trash can and said, "Go home. Just go home." It's okay to make mistakes once in a while, just don't do it often, and learn from it when you do.

ADDITIONAL RECIPES

LAYERED PECAN RAISIN CARROT CAKE WITH VANILLA CREAM FROSTING

From Chef Melissa BonTempt

(SERVES EIGHT)

Just as hazelnuts pair perfectly with the chocolate silk, in my opinion, pecans and carrot cake are also meant to share the same plate. Many people are allergic to nuts, however, so they are optional in this recipe. When buying fresh pecans in the shell, be sure to shake them: If you feel them rattle, they are old. Store the nuts tightly wrapped in the pantry, the refrigerator, or even in the freezer. :: **CWM**

CAKE INGREDIENTS

1 pound, 2 ounces (3½ cups + 2 tablespoons)
   Bread Flour
¼ teaspoon Cloves, ground
¼ teaspoon Allspice
2 tablespoons Cinnamon, ground
1½ teaspoons Baking Soda
½ teaspoon Baking Powder
8 Eggs
1½ cups Vegetable Oil
1 pound, 12 ounces (4 cups) Sugar
1 teaspoon Salt
2 pounds Carrots, peeled, shredded
4 ounces (1 cup) Golden Raisins
5 ounces (1¼ cup) Pecans, crushed, optional

:: Chef's Note

Remember that the accuracy that comes with weighing the dry ingredients is what allows baked products to come out the same every time. Accuracy is critical in baking, and recipes should be followed with as much precision as possible. Purchasing a kitchen scale can be the one change in your kitchen that improves your baking abilities exponentially.

PROCEDURE

1. Preheat the oven to 350°F. Oil and flour 2, 10" cake pans, tapping them lightly to get rid of any excess flour.

2. Sift together the flour, cloves, allspice, cinnamon, soda, and baking powder. Set aside.

3. Put the eggs in a mixer and whip them on high until they become light and airy.

4. Reduce the speed on the mixer to low and add the oil very slowly, allowing it to incorporate before adding any more to the bowl.

5. Leave the mixer on low and add the sugar and salt until the ingredients are just combined.

6. Slowly add the sifted flour mixture to the wet ingredients while the mixer continues to run on low.

7. Remove the mixing bowl from the mixer and fold in the carrots, golden raisins, and pecans (if using).

8. Pour the batter into the prepared cake pans and bake about 50 minutes or until the surface of each cake springs back when touched. Remove the cakes from the oven and allow them to cool before frosting.

(continued)

(Layered Pecan Raisin Carrot Cake continued from page 194)

VANILLA CREAM FROSTING

(FROSTS TWO, TEN-INCH CAKES OR ONE LAYERED CAKE)

PROCEDURE

1. Using a mixer with a paddle attachment, whip the cream cheese on medium until completely smooth and fluffy. Stop the mixer, lower the bowl, and scrape its sides.

2. Return the bowl to its fixed position and start the mixer on low. Add all the sugar by slowly pouring it down the edge of the bowl. Mix until the ingredients are completely incorporated.

3. Keeping the mixer on low, slowly add the vanilla, then the cream. Add only enough cream to create the consistency you desire. Then gradually increase the speed of the mixer until the frosting is light and fluffy. Stop and scrape again to ensure that the ingredients have all been incorporated.

4. Stack the cakes on top of each other with $1/4$" of frosting in between to achieve a tall, layered version of this cake, or use to frost the layers separately for two cakes.

FROSTING INGREDIENTS

2 pounds (4 cups) Cream Cheese
$3/4$ pound ($2 3/4$ cups) Powdered Sugar, sifted
2 tablespoons Pure Vanilla Extract
$1 1/2$ cups Heavy Cream

international cuisine

INSTRUCTOR: CHEF SANTOS VILLARICO

I HAVE TWO DAUGHTERS, BOTH OF WHOM I HOPE WILL HAVE A DEEP APPRECIATION FOR THE WAYS OF THE WORLD.

I want them to grow up knowing that every culture's customs are worth exploring, every individual's perspective is worth considering, every work of art is worth contemplating. Food is no different. After they taste it all, they can identify what they, themselves, appreciate, believe in, and hold dear to their hearts. My desire to learn about culture and food stems not only from a commitment to personal evolution, but to that of my children. International Cuisine gave me a chance to indulge in lessons of custom, tradition, and flavor as it connects to a multitude of new perspectives expressed through the techniques and patterns in cooking and living. Chef Santos gave me not only lessons to learn, but lessons to teach as well. It's easy to see why Chef Santos almost became a priest before he decided to pursue life as a chef. His humility is sincere, coupled with a brilliance in the kitchen. He's willing to open himself to inspiration: "I hear my palate whispering to me in the morning when I wake up, telling me to try a specific combination of colors or textures or to try a dish with a particular balance of flavors." His reverence for cultural diversity is clear; he fills the classroom with ancient traditions as well as the people who maintain them. I left the course determined to preserve artisan methods of cooking and food production, as well as to keep my eyes open to new ways of living and cooking. :: **CWM**

REFLECTIONS OF A CHEF

A CHILDHOOD IN THE PHILIPPINES

I grew up in a fishing and farming village in the Philippines. The games the kids played were old games that imitated what happened in our village. So we played "Let's Go Fishing!" instead of the hide-and-seek and basketball that are more typical today. My family had their own area to fish that had been passed down through the generations: A river led out to the mouth of the ocean, and a small stream led to a pond. At high tide we would let the water in, using the small dike at the mouth of the stream. At low tide we would catch the fish. We would feed them by planting water moss and water plants to nurture them in the pond.

During our "game" we would grab our fishing poles and go out to the bank of the river. We would catch milk fish first. Then we'd go after the tilapia, shrimp, crab, and mudfish. Sometimes we would catch them with our hands or with a net, or spear them with a handmade spear. We'd go diving for oysters and mussels during the night and load them up in our own baskets made from woven bamboo leaves. When all the fish and shellfish were caught in our fishing game, my father would tell me we could go after the eels. After we cornered them in their burrows, we'd put them in our baskets and take them home to Grandma. It was my favorite game.

We would fish for lunch, then we'd fish for dinner. We'd catch only what we needed. If we happened to get a big catch, we would preserve them by salting and drying them, or cooking them in vinegar for later meals. We'd only have meat, usually pork, on Sundays. It was a big treat. Meat was hard to come by.

TRADITIONS OF ASIAN COOKING

Asian women in the Philippines take great pride in their cooking. Their recipes are passed down from great-grandmother to grandmother and sometimes to a friend. Recipes are guarded with jealousy, even though variations of the same dishes show up everywhere. The national dish called adobo (foods cooked in vinegar and garlic), Filipino menudo (a pork stew), and nilaga (a type of boiled dinner) are on nearly every menu. My favorite dish is one called sinigang that is a green tamarind boil with vegetables and fish. A dish cooked similarly is an entrée with milk fish in a broth of tomato and tamarind or kamias—a green fruit in the carambola, or star fruit, family.

Food is always simple and rustic. There is always rice on the table—it's the foundation of our meal. Without rice in Asia, there is no meal. Breakfast rice was usually left over from the night before. If there were no leftovers, we would steam rice and top it with fish boiled in tamarind or tomato, or just plain salted fish. Then we would dip the fish in a fish sauce with lemon or kalamansi, a fruit the size of a kumquat but very tart, somewhat like a cross between a lemon and an orange. We would also mash kamias that had been precooked, to turn the fruit into a dip for the fish. If those ingredients weren't available for breakfast, we would just make fried fish with rice and vinegar, chili and garlic.

With the influence of the Spaniards in the Philippines, there was also bread and coffee at times in our morning diets. Pan de sal is a salted bread in the shape of a French roll. It's wonderful freshly made by hand overnight. It is available in a commercial version in Oriental markets but it's not nearly as tasty.

HOW I EMERGED AS A COOK

We didn't have television in our home, so I would watch my mother, grandmother, and aunts cook. I especially loved watching them get ready for the different festivals during the year. Each town or barrio would have its own huge festivals to honor the Catholic saints. The Philippines is the only nation in Asia that is predominantly Catholic. The festivals were known for their parades, music, and nonstop feasting.

I did have an uncle who liked to cook during the festival times. He would make very elaborate dishes with a lot of braising and stewing over an enormous cauldron of fire. He would make kaldareta, which is a dish made out of chicken, beef, or, in our culture, out of dog. Other dishes that he would make included a Spanish dish called matambre, which is a rolled beef with corn, egg, and spinach. The Filipinos have a similar dish called morcon, where the beef is butterflied, filled, and rolled. The recipe was actually passed down from the Jesuit missionaries. Another wonderful entrée was bodiffarius, another dish from Spain. My mother always called it embotido in our language. The way it was made was to roll a piece of meat in a piece of burlap bag or in a banana leaf to let it steam as it cooked.

The first time I attempted to cook on my own was just before I left the house for basketball practice when I was 17 or 18 years old. My mother was busy when I asked her what was for lunch. She told me I was welcome to cook if I wanted something to eat. She volunteered to walk me through the steps, but I would have to cook it. She told me to chop onions, garlic, ginger, and squash to make a dish called upo sikaw. I knew what she was leading me through, I'd seen it so many times. So I prepped the vegetables and went on to also clean some frogs. She was teaching me to make frog soup. I sautéed the vegetables, added the cleaned frogs, some water, and vet-sin, or MSG, and let it simmer on the stove. It all seemed so natural to me, as if I'd already done it a thousand times. Ever since that afternoon, I would help my mother with the meals. I loved those days cooking with my mother, but when I turned 25 I decided it was time to make a go of it on my own. I decided to emigrate to the United States.

A VISION FROM A STREET VENDOR

The summer before I moved to the United States, I went on a five-country tour of Asia. The last stop was in Bangkok during the Khratong River Festival. We stayed at the Oriental Hotel right on the river and were fascinated with all the children taking part in the festival. We watched as they readied their little banana blossom boats that were tenuously loaded with tiny candles and bhat, or Thai coins, and lingered as they set their boats in the water to sail down the river. The boats were sent as good wishes for the gods to help with bountiful harvests for the year. Everything was in celebration of the New Year. Ceremonies depicted the retirement of the old and the coming of the new.

We were on our way to dinner one night during the festival when I became captivated by all the street vendors who exhibited their creations on the sidewalk. There were two food artisans who really caught my eye. One was a little man who was carving incredible sculptures out of watermelon, cabbage, taro root, and potatoes. They were all different shapes and sizes. He would turn these vegetables and fruits into eagles, monkeys, fish, cranes, anything you could imagine. But all he had to work with was a little run-down butcher knife. I said to myself, "One of these days, before I die, I want to be able to do that." The other chef I saw was making amazing creations out of sweetened mung bean paste. She would shape them into the most unbelievable re-creations of mangoes, peaches, bananas, and clusters of grapes. Instead of using artificial food colorings, she used pastes with

SANTOS VILLARICO

natural colors and flavors. When she was done molding the shapes, she would dip each piece in melted sugar, then in agar agar solution to keep the moisture from penetrating. If she hadn't done the final coating, it would have melted in the hot, humid streets of Bangkok. I was so moved by their resourcefulness, creativity, and grace.

THE DECISION TO ATTEND CULINARY SCHOOL

In one of my first jobs in the food industry, I worked at a little Italian restaurant in Colorado. During my breaks I would read *Gourmet* magazine and drool over the plates that were so pretty and placed so delicately on the elaborate buffet tables with their ornate watermelon and ice carvings soaring up in the middle of the food. It made me dream about the food vendors back in Bangkok. I reminded myself that someday I wanted to be able to do that work. I took myself seriously and decided then to enroll in culinary school.

In school I began to synthesize everything in an entirely different context. I was able to take the lessons from my childhood and put them together with information from an international perspective. That juxtaposition of old and new thought helped me discover things about my own culture that I'd never realized before. My life began to come full circle as I started to understand what I'd been witnessing in my home kitchen all those years. I realized that the basic techniques of sautéing and the use of a sofregit (onion, garlic, and tomatoes) in my stewing really formed the foundations of my cuisine. Another example was understanding the use of panada in a recipe such as meat loaf. Panada, which is a paste of white bread crumbs mixed with milk, is known for its ability to bind meat together. However, I also realized why it was used so much in my home: Like the use of stews and soups, panada stretched out the meal by providing filling ingredients without depending on a lot of expensive items. We always needed to make the food go as far as possible. My learning exploded as I put the lessons from the program together with my experiences from the past.

THE SACRIFICES OF A CHEF

I worked my way through many positions in wonderful restaurants. But as I found out, being a chef demands an enormous amount of sacrifice. In many ways you are forced to give up a family life. Whenever your family needs you, that is when they need you at work: Thanksgiving, Christmas, Easter. It was yesterday that my daughter was 10 years old and now she is fully grown. My son is taller than I am and I wonder where all those years went. It seemed whenever we were about to do something as a family, the phone would ring and my wife would say, "Don't answer that." But she knew me, I had to answer, and it always meant that I had to go in to work. What started as a promise to work two hours turned into four, then six, then eight. But in those days, I had to make that choice in order to make ends meet. I'll never forget one Christmas when my son said to me, "Daddy, why do you have to go in to work on Christmas?" And I pointed to each of the presents lying around the room and said softly, "So that I can buy you that, that, that, and that." He answered with a little "Oh," and I went off to work.

COOKING SECRETS

Through all of my years of cooking, the most important thing I have learned about food is to share it. It's the best ingredient. It always makes your cooking taste better.
It's also helpful to know techniques that give you ways to shorten processes in the kitchen without compromising the flavor of a dish. For example, learning to braise on the stovetop with the lid on as opposed to braising in the oven can save an enormous amount of time without diminishing your product. There are knife techniques to learn that allow you to cut faster. There are tools in the kitchen such as Suzy Wongs, or food mills, or other equipment that exponentially shortens your cooking time without taking away from the end result of your cooking. Learn to cook wisely instead of laboriously.

THE CHEF'S LESSON

SINIGANG NA ULANG
(FRESHWATER BLUE PRAWNS AND ASSORTED VEGETABLES IN A GREEN TAMARIND BROTH)

(SERVES SIX)

In International Cuisine class we would follow this recipe exactly as written to experience the full Filipino flavor. I loved the opportunity to try it in its original form, but I did find the heads of the prawns too intensely flavored for my Westernized palate. To result in a less-fishy flavor, cook the heads of the prawns separately and set them aside to use as a garnish. The addition of reduced coconut cream also brings a milder flavor to this dish. :: **CWM**

SINIGANG INGREDIENTS

1 gallon Water
1 large Onion, quartered
2 Roma Tomatoes, large diced
$1/2$ pound Green Tamarind, fresh, whole
2 medium Taro Roots, peeled, large diced
1, 14-ounce can Coconut Cream, optional
2 pounds Head-On Blue Prawns
$3/4$ cup Long Beans, cut into 4" pieces
$3/4$ cup Labanos (Daikon), peeled,
    cut in $1/4$" rounds
$3/4$ cup Talong (Chinese Eggplant),
    bias cut in $1/4$" ovals
2 Banana Chile Peppers, fresh, seeded,
    small diced
1 cup Kang Kong (Water Spinach),
    cut into 4" pieces
1 teaspoon Patis (Fish Sauce), or to taste
Kosher Salt and freshly ground Black Pepper

ACCOMPANIMENT

Steamed Rice

:: Chef's Note

You may substitute any seafood or fish for the prawns; lemons or green mangoes for the tamarind; habaneros for the banana chiles; and regular eggplant, spinach, and beans for the Asian varieties, although the dish will differ slightly in taste and texture.

PROCEDURE

1. In a large stockpot, bring the water, onion, tomatoes, and tamarind pods to a fast simmer. Once the water begins to simmer, cook for 3-4 more minutes.

2. Add the taro roots and simmer for 2-3 more minutes.

3. Turn the heat off under the vegetables. Pull all the tamarind pods out of the pot and allow them to cool slightly.

4. If you are using the coconut cream, pour it into a saucepan and reduce it by half, stirring constantly to make sure it doesn't scorch.

5. Meanwhile, place a sturdy strainer over the top of another stockpot. Peel the pods off the tamarind and scrape off any adhering pulp. Discard the pods and place the reserved pulp into the strainer.

6. To release the seeds from the pulp, press it against the sides of the strainer. Then pour some of the cooking liquid over the top of the seeds to rinse the remaining pulp into the stockpot. Discard the seeds in the strainer and reserve the dissolved pulp in the stockpot.

7. Add the prawns, long beans, daikon, eggplant, and peppers to the tamarind mixture. Using a slotted spoon, transfer the taro, tomatoes, and onion from the first pot to the tamarind/prawn mixture. Then pour in just enough of the vegetable cooking liquid to cover the vegetables and prawns. Set the remaining cooking liquid aside in case you need to thin your sauce later. Add the reduced coconut cream if you are using it. Simmer the mixture until the prawns are pink and the vegetables are almost al dente, about 3 minutes.

8. Add the spinach and simmer for 1 more minute.

9. Season to taste with the fish sauce. Use this sparingly, as it is very strong. Adjust the seasonings with salt and pepper and serve hot over steamed rice.

ACHARA AND ADOBONG KANDURO (CHICKEN ADOBO WITH GREEN PAPAYA RELISH)

(SERVES SIX)

Adobo, or adobong, is the national dish of the Philippines. Although its name is derived from the Spanish adobado, the flavor remains uniquely Filipino. Adobo is actually a method of preparation in which chicken or pork is stewed in vinegar and garlic, as well as soy sauce, bay leaves, and peppercorns. The method is also adaptable to quail, shrimp, or any other available protein, because cooking in the Philippines revolves around whatever has been caught that day. :: **CWM**

RELISH INGREDIENTS

1 Green Papaya, peeled and julienned
1/2 teaspoon Salt
2 cups Water Palm or Rice Vinegar
1 1/2 cups Sugar
1 tablespoon Kosher Salt
Black Pepper, freshly ground
1 Red Bell Pepper, seeded, julienned
1 Yellow Bell Pepper, seeded, julienned
1 Green Bell Pepper, seeded, julienned
1 Carrot, peeled, julienned
3 Shallots, peeled, thinly sliced
1 teaspoon Ginger, fresh, grated
1/2 cup Raisins, optional

CHICKEN INGREDIENTS

1 cup Soy Sauce, low sodium
2 cups Water Palm or Rice Vinegar
1 tablespoon Garlic, chopped
3 Bay Leaves
4 teaspoon Black Peppercorns
2 Fresh Young Free-Range Chickens, cut into
    serving pieces
Lard or Olive Oil, as needed
Salt and Pepper

ACCOMPANIMENT

6 cups Steamed White Rice

PROCEDURE

1. Make the relish the day ahead or at least 2 hours before you prepare the chicken. Begin by rubbing the julienned papaya with 1/2 teaspoon salt.

2. Place the salted papaya in a colander, cover the top with a piece of parchment or waxed paper, then weight it down with a heavy pan for 1-1 1/2 hours to draw out excess moisture.

3. Rinse the papaya with cold water and squeeze out as much moisture as possible. Repeat the rinsing process 2 or 3 times.

4. Combine the vinegar, sugar, kosher salt, and pepper to taste in a saucepan to make the pickling solution. Bring the solution to a boil. Reduce the heat and simmer for 3-4 minutes. Adjust the seasonings.

5. Pour the pickling solution in a large mixing bowl with a pouring lip. Allow it to cool.

6. Add the papaya, peppers, carrot, shallots, ginger, and raisins to the cooled pickling solution. Mix well, then adjust the seasonings again with salt, pepper, and sugar to taste.

7. Using tongs or just your hands, lift the papaya and vegetables out of the pickling solution and place them into very clean, large glass jars. Make sure the ingredients are evenly distributed among the jars. Then pour all of the pickling solution evenly into the jars over the top of the vegetable/papaya mixture. Cover and store in the refrigerator for at least 2 hours, or preferably overnight.

8. To prepare the chicken, begin by combining the soy sauce, vinegar, garlic, bay leaves, and peppercorns in a nonreactive bowl.

9. Marinate the chicken in the mixture for at least 20-30 minutes, but no more than 4 hours.

10. Preheat a large rondeaux, or roasting pan, on top of the stove. When the pan is hot, add enough lard or olive oil to coat the bottom.

11. When the fat is hot, lift the chicken pieces out of the marinade and place them in a single layer in the pan. Reserve the marinade. Sear the chicken on high heat until it is evenly browned on all sides.

12. Reduce the heat and add the reserved marinade by pouring it next to, not over, the chicken in the pan. Allow the marinade to come to a boil without disturbing the chicken. Then reduce the heat, cover, and simmer for approximately 1 hour, until the chicken is fork-tender and reaches an internal temperature of 165°F. Remove the cover near the end of the cooking period to allow the liquid to reduce to nappe. If the sauce reduces too quickly before the chicken is done, add some lard or olive oil to return it to a nappe consistency.

13. Adjust the seasonings with salt and pepper to taste. To serve, place a cup of hot, steamed rice on each plate, arranging the chicken next to the rice with a scoop of relish on the side and the sauce drizzled in front.

:: Chef's Notes

Although green or half-ripe papayas are common items in Oriental markets, if you can't find them, you can substitute 2 cups julienned Granny Smith apples tossed in lime juice to prevent discoloration. For a sweeter relish, replace the vinegar with the same amount of apple juice and replace the black pepper with 1 tablespoon finely chopped garlic. Finally, add 1 cup fresh mango, julienned, to the relish when the vegetables are added to the pickling solution.

This is one of those dishes that does well when I heed my grandmother's advice: I don't disturb the chicken as it cooks in the vinegar-based marinade until it comes to a boil. It's all about respecting your heritage in the kitchen, especially when the traditions improve the dish.

TURON DE SAGING
(CRISPY FRIED BANANA AND JACKFRUIT SPRING ROLLS)

(SERVES SIX)

This dish can be served as an appetizer but is equally as lovely served for dessert with vanilla ice cream and a mango coulis. For the coulis, simply combine ripe mango and a few drops of lime juice in the blender and puree until smooth. Pour the coulis into a squirt bottle to drizzle on the plates and spring rolls. :: **CWM**

PROCEDURE

1. Cut each banana exactly in half lengthwise.

2. In a small pan, mix the cornstarch and water to a pastelike consistency. Heat the mixture very gently over low heat for about 30 seconds, just until warm to the touch. Remove from the heat and set aside.

3. Lay the lumpia wrappers on the countertop with the bottom corners facing your stomach.

4. Lay 1 banana half and approximately 1 tablespoon diced jackfruit in the middle of each wrapper. Sprinkle each roll with 1 teaspoon brown sugar.

5. Fold the corner of the wrapper closest to you on top of the filling.

6. Fold in the left and right corners to the middle of the filling, then roll the wrapper up like a burrito to encase the fruit. Roll from the folded bottom corner first and end with the unfolded corner.

7. Just before you reach the unfolded corner, dab a little of the cornstarch paste on it. This way, when you finish the roll, the final corner will create a seal that keeps the wrapper in place while it cooks. Pinch the ends to tighten the seal.

8. Repeat this process until all the banana halves are rolled.

9. Heat a large skillet, then add oil until it is deep enough to submerge the spring rolls. Heat the oil to 350°F or until it sizzles when a tiny piece of wrapper or fruit is placed in it.

10. Fry the spring rolls a few at a time. Do not crowd them; if you do, the temperature of the oil will decrease, and the rolls will absorb grease and become soggy. Fry the rolls until they are light brown and crispy on all sides. Remove and place on a rack to drain and keep crispy. Serve immediately.

INGREDIENTS

6 Bananas, firm but ripe, peeled
1 tablespoon Cornstarch
Water, as needed
12 Lumpia or Spring Roll Wrappers
8 ounces (1 cup) fresh or canned Jackfruit, drained, diced
1/4 cup Brown Sugar
Peanut Oil for frying

:: Chef's Note

The taste of a jackfruit is somewhat like a cross between a banana and a mango. It is available in Oriental markets in cans, as well as fresh when it is in season. If you are buying fresh jackfruit, be sure it's ripe: The skin should be stretched, with each spike standing distinctly separated from the others. If the jackfruit has an odor, it is already overripe. If it's unavailable, you can substitute mango.

INGREDIENTS FROM FILIPINO DISHES:

· The food of the Philippines has influences from a variety of different cultures. China, Spain, Mexico, and the United States all made significant impacts on Filipino history and consequently left their marks on the culinary traditions of the country.

· All of the following ingredients may be found in Thai, Chinese, and other Oriental markets, as well as in some Indian markets.

HEAD-ON BLUE PRAWNS:

· The heads of these prawns offer not only intense flavor, they also add tremendously to the eye appeal of any dish they're in.

LONG BEANS:

· These extremely long beans are almost 1½–2 feet long. They should be firm when they are at the peak of freshness.

TAMARIND:

· This pod has a very sour pulp (similar to Tom Yam in Thai cooking). If it is unavailable, substitute twice the amount of lemon juice.

DAIKON:

· Also known as labanos or giant white radishes, they are eaten either raw or cooked.

TARO ROOT:

- The brown skin is peeled, and the white, spotted flesh is boiled for use in savory dishes or candied for desserts. The leaves are also edible but must be cooked before consuming.

WATER SPINACH (KANG KONG):

- Also known as "water convovulus" and "swamp cabbage." Its leaves are heart-shaped. If you eat it on its own, sauté it in garlic to bring out its beautiful characteristics.

CHINESE EGGPLANT (TALONG):

- This eggplant is delicious grilled, baked, stuffed, or sautéed. It is longer, lighter in color, and narrower than the deep purple eggplants.

JACKFRUIT:

- This spiny oblong product is actually a relative of the breadfruit. When it's ripe, its flavor is bland and sweet. It can grow to be up to 100 pounds.

THE CHEF AS TEACHER

TAKING THE KITCHEN SERIOUSLY

The ability to adapt is critical in the kitchen. If you can't adapt to new situations, the kitchen is not the place for you. The kitchen is a very hostile environment with chances to cut, burn, or mangle your body parts at any time. You have to be constantly aware of everything around you. Always be prepared for the worst to happen at any time.

But if you have common sense, grace, and the ability to adapt, it will make everything feel easy.

TRUSTING TRADITION

To me the most important lesson in International Cuisine is respect for another way of doing things. If you aren't prepared to learn that, then you have no business cooking in a cuisine other than that of your own culture. Cultures follow certain techniques and traditions that bring authenticity to their food and allow them to pass on a heritage. There was an Italian woman about 78 or 80 years old whom I met cooking in a restaurant in Aspen. She was making polenta when she needed help stirring and asked a young cook to step in for a moment. The next thing I knew she was screaming "Bloody Mary" because the cook was stirring in the wrong direction. Who can say if it matters which way you stir?—the importance lies in the respect for her traditions.

My grandmother always told me when you add vinegar to a pot that's cooking on the stove, you should never stir it or the vinegar will not cook. Do I believe that? From a Western perspective, maybe not, but I still do it her way because it works.

EXPANDING YOUR REPERTOIRE

If you are unfamiliar with a certain dish from a different cuisine—for instance, if you're making paella for the first time—I suggest you follow the authentic recipe from a book exactly as it is written. Although I am not a big proponent of recipes, in these cases they are extremely helpful. By following every word, you gain a basic understanding of what the food was intended to taste like. Then if you make

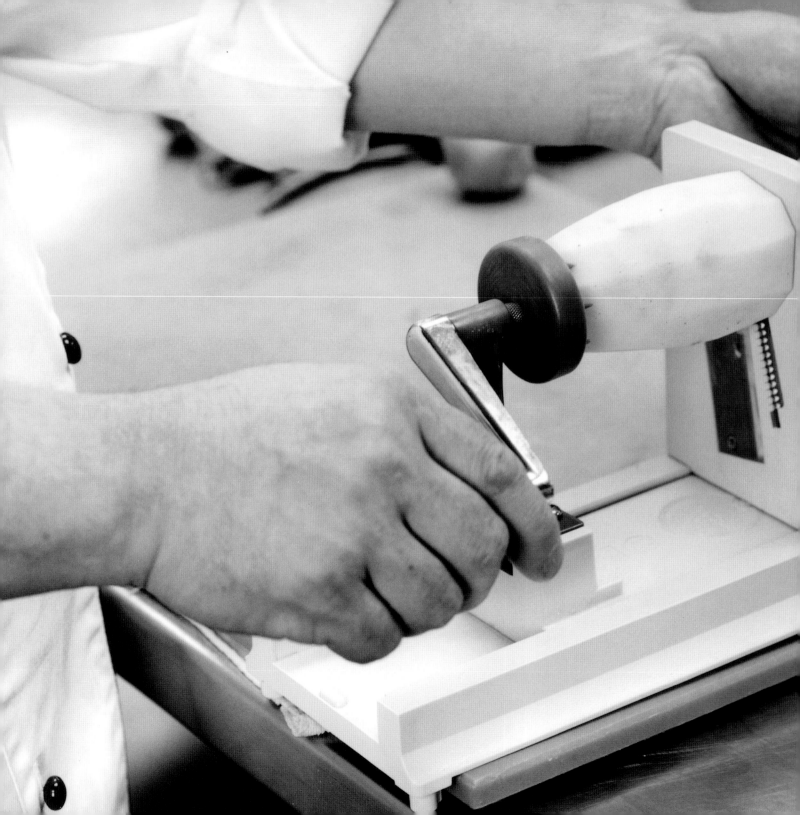

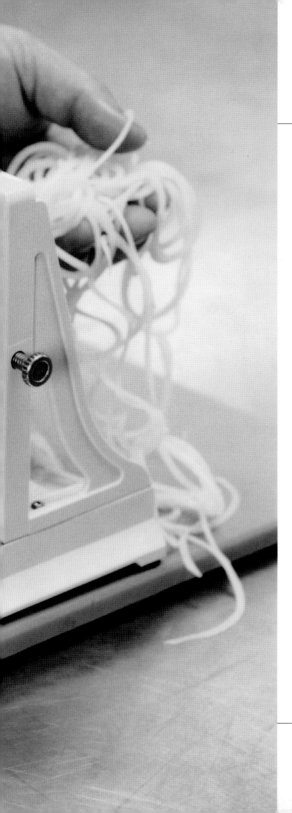

the dish again and you see a shortcut, try it out, but taste to see if it really does turn out the same in the end. Don't improvise until you have a full understanding of what the traditional dish is supposed to taste like. Follow the traditions first so that you understand why and how you made the dish differently later on.

TAKE CARE OF THE EARTH

We have to be careful with our world—its resources are our greatest ally. It's like the words to one of my favorite old Filipino songs: "When our kids grow up, will there be any more rivers to swim, or trees to bear fruit, or fields to harvest wheat or corn?" It's very beautiful in my language. We have to be better about taking care of it all.

ADDITIONAL RECIPES

KOBE BEEF WITH TOKO KOMOTO PANCAKES

From Chef Bryan Elliott

(SERVES FOUR)

These pancakes are like Asian versions of a potato pancake—only instead of potatoes, they use a combination of cabbage and radish. If you'd prefer to use another type of beef to accompany this traditional combination, choose a well-marbled New York strip or rib eye. :: **CWM**

PANCAKE INGREDIENTS

1/2 head Cabbage, cut in a chiffonade or
    thinly shredded
4 Eggs, beaten
1 cup Radish, grated
1/2 cup All-Purpose Flour
1/4 cup Water
Kosher Salt and White Pepper
Vegetable Oil

BEEF INGREDIENTS

4, 4-ounce portions Kobe Beef, room
    temperature
Kosher Salt and Black Pepper, freshly cracked
Olive Oil

:: Chef's Note

Kobe beef comes from a breed of cattle called Wagyu that originated on the mainland of Asia. They were exported to Japan, where they thrived in the Kobe region. Living a very pampered life, these cattle are not exercised; instead they are literally massaged, allowing them to grow with a high percentage of fatty marbling in their connective tissues. The result is an extremely tender and intensely flavored meat that is considered by most chefs to be the world's best beef.

PROCEDURE

1. Mix the cabbage, eggs, and radish together in a bowl. In a separate small bowl, add the flour and enough water to create a slurry with a pastelike consistency.

2. Add the slurry to the cabbage mixture a little at a time, stopping when the mixture is able to hold a patty shape when pressed together.

3. Add salt and pepper to taste.

4. Form the cabbage mixture into patties that are 1/4" thick and 3" in diameter. Set aside.

5. Preheat the oven to 450°F. Dry-rub both sides of each Kobe steak with salt and pepper.

6. Heat a cast-iron skillet on the stove for several minutes until it is very hot. Pour olive oil to just cover the bottom. Allow the oil to get hot, then place the steaks in the pan to sear for 2 minutes on each side.

7. Place the skillet directly in the preheated oven to finish bringing the meat to temperature. Allow 2 minutes for medium rare, 3 1/2–4 minutes for medium.

8. Remove the meat from the oven and place it on a plate to rest.

9. Use a paper towel to wipe out the skillet. Add 1 tablespoon vegetable oil to the preheated pan and set it over medium-high heat. Allow the oil to get hot, then fry the cabbage patties until golden brown on both sides.

10. Slice the meat and fan on the plate with the cabbage patties. Garnish as desired.

TENDER BRAISED GREENS WITH BACON

From Chef Robert McCullough

(SERVES SIX)

Another side dish that complements Asian food is this slowly braised accompaniment. Look for the greens to be best in the fall, winter, and early spring. Typically they are full of sand and grit, but resist washing them until you are ready to cook them so they will remain fresh and crisp. Keep them stored in the refrigerator in a perforated plastic bag. Then, when you are ready, fill a very large bowl or tub with water; add the greens, swirl them in the water, and lift them out of the bowl, leaving the dirt submerged below. :: **CWM**

PROCEDURE

1. Heat a rondeaux or large stockpot. Add the butter and allow it to melt.

2. Add the diced, uncooked bacon and thoroughly render out the fat. Remove the bacon and set aside, but leave the bacon fat in the pan.

3. Add the onion and sauté until translucent.

4. Deglaze the pan with white wine.

5. Add the greens and vinegar. Cook for 5 minutes, uncovered.

6. Add the chicken stock. Turn down the heat, cover, and braise the dish for 1 hour. Check intermittently to ensure there is sufficient moisture. If it is dry, add more chicken stock.

7. When all the greens are tender, season to taste with salt and pepper. Serve warm.

INGREDIENTS

½ pound (1 cup) Butter
1 pound Bacon, uncooked, diced
1 Yellow Onion, peeled, small diced
¾ cup White Wine
1½ pounds Turnip Greens, stemmed, washed
1½ pounds Mustard Greens, stemmed, washed
1½ pounds Swiss Chard, stemmed, washed
¼ cup Red Wine Vinegar
2 quarts Chicken Stock
Kosher Salt and White Pepper

:: Chef's Note

The secret to this dish is the use of the pork fat from the bacon to give it a beautiful, slight smokiness and to result in the best flavor combination with the greens.

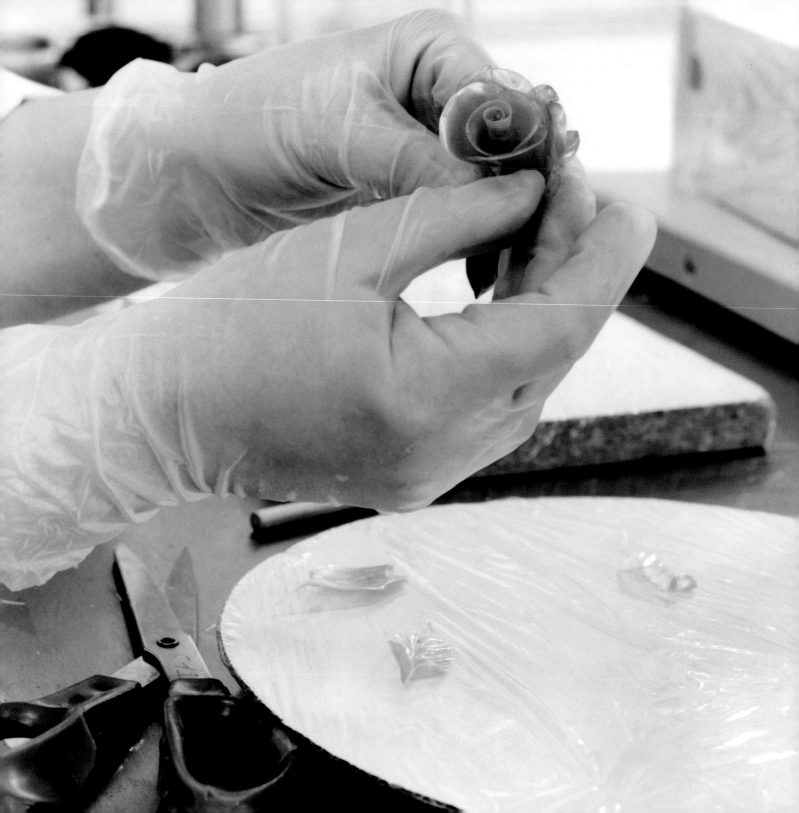

confectionery showpieces I

INSTRUCTOR: CHEF TRACY FLOWERS

MY PARENTS CAME TO MIND AS I CREATED MY FONDANT CAKES AND SUGAR SCULPTURES IN CONFECTIONERY SHOWPIECES.

They were florists by trade and though I had never consciously paid attention to the details of their work as they turned cut flowers into gorgeous three-dimensional creations, dozens of years later I found myself yearning for their input as I brought sugar, chocolate, frostings, and doughs to life in my own edible centerpieces. In wedding cake design, we applied tiny basket weaves of frosting, followed by delicate, intricate decorations made by our own hands. I found myself reaching for shades of peach and light yellow to color my fondant roses; they were the same hues of the real Peace Roses my mother had loved so much. I placed my father's designs squarely in the forefront of my thoughts as I built towering sculptures made of tempered chocolate or sugar that had been pulled, blown, spun, bubbled, or otherwise manipulated into dozens of new forms. I thought of his use of different planes for perspective, his use of color, his eye for detail. Because my parents are no longer living, I had to depend instead on Chef Flowers for guidance. She taught me the flow of movement so crucial in the advanced methods of decoration—she glides through as if the skill comes straight from her soul. Her life is in balance and it shows in the joy that pulses through her kitchen. She illustrated how precision, especially in baking, can act as a release. The knowledge that you've measured precisely allows your work to be consistent, freeing your thoughts to move on to the more artistic final touches. :: **CWM**

REFLECTIONS OF A CHEF

REVELATIONS OF A BAKER'S LIFE

It was Paris! Under the night sky I floated, not walked, down the Champs-Elysées and drifted past the Eiffel Tower after the most incredible dining experience of my life at La Tour d'Argent. I was walking on air. It was not just the delirium from the restaurant we had reluctantly removed ourselves from; there was more to the evening's bliss. Sure, I had been dazzled by the swirl of waiters as they surrounded our table with 12 domed plates of edible art, creating an intoxicatingly aromatic breeze as they lifted the domes in unison. Yes, I had been impressed by the freshly folded swan napkins that kept reappearing at our table, and lulled into a trance savoring such spectacular food as Notre Dame stood blessing our dinner with its awesome presence outside our window. But despite a completely euphoric meal that undoubtedly captivated every sense in my body, I was walking on air because of my own revelation. I had seen my future, and it was to become a chef.

To make the career choice of my life in a city like Paris, even though there is no city like Paris, was unbelievably romantic. It was like taking a slice of France home with me to know that my life's ambitions were to create food as beautifully as they do in that part of the world. To see the French people's passion for food, in the land of Escoffier, helped me understand Auguste's philosophy of classical cuisine from the perspective of simplicity. Later it became clear to me that the proper application of classical techniques is what allows you to master any other cuisine in the world. The theories behind a mother sauce, the techniques of braising, sautéing, and roasting, or the methods used in French pastries all provide a foundation of skills that are beautiful on their own, but are also immediately applicable when cooking in cuisines that are not specifically French. The secret to all classical cuisine is choosing the correct method of cooking and executing it perfectly and consistently.

Strolling the streets of Paris was a literal walk through those lessons. I was traveling with the owners of a bake shop where I'd first learned the basics of baking. We had come to Paris to attend a food show, to sample the cutting edge of pastry work from a baker's perspective, the definitive examples of haute cuisine. As we meandered our way to and from the show, we'd pass boulangerie after café after boulangerie after café and stop to compare every baguette and pastry we found, noting the elegant simplicity and marveling at the superiority of technique. We lingered over every display: loaves of bread woven into ladders, swans out of sugar, staircases of fruit tarts stepping over each other to reach the top of the next shelf. The metaphor of having revelations as I ingested éclairs was not wasted on me, as their name dates back to the days of the Renaissance and translates to mean "a flash of light." Certainly I was experiencing my own enlightenment.

BAKING BIG

I will never forget my first assignment in my first bakery job back home. It was cheese-cake, tons and tons of cheesecake. I had the recipe memorized, but I couldn't re-create just one cheesecake in my own home—I only knew how to make 300 at a time. I would make them in mixers that were so large I nearly had to climb inside to scrape the bottom of the bowl. Swiss buttercream, chocolate cake, chocolate chip cookies, tuile cookies, we made them daily. I still have my notebook from those days, completely torn but readable.

THE MAKINGS OF A BAKER

Although I didn't define my path in the culinary world until later, I did have moments in my childhood that, in hindsight, started my journey of becoming a chef. My fascination with baking correctly goes as far back as my first memories of learning to count. I distinctly remember learning to count to 50, since I had to stir the batter 50 times according to the directions of my recipe. My overwhelming desire to be accurate was prophetic

as I meticulously followed the directions on the back of the box of brownie mix: It forecast my later devotion to the precision of measurement that is imperative to have as a baker. Making brownies from a mix doesn't seem to require a lot of accurate measurement, but to me at the time, it was important to do it exactly right.

As a kid, I also loved projects that kept me absorbed in my work. Now I am fascinated by all kinds of intricate techniques: Making roses out of pulled sugar and decorating wedding cakes keeps me engaged for hours.

As an instructor of Confectionery Showpieces I need a fundamental understanding of the physics of design, since we build three-dimensional centerpieces out of an array of products. As a child growing up, I learned those lessons from hours and hours spent in the basement, building various projects out of wood with my father's gentle guidance. I am certain that the lessons in basic architecture from those magical moments with my father translated directly into understanding the basis of the creations I do now in the kitchen.

VISIONS FROM MY BLIND FATHER

Being able to see is relative. In my father's case, although he was blinded in the 1940s by a disease called uveitis, contracted by drinking contaminated cow milk, he was able to "see" the world in his own beautifully unique way. Not only did he teach me how to live a life with complete attention to detail–which is imperative in a household with a blind family member–but he also helped me see life from an entirely new perspective that embraced the natural rhythms of life, listened to the patterns inherent in daily living, and savored the joys of life without being caught up in misfortunes. He taught me grace.

All those lessons now serve me well as an educator and a pastry chef. His guidance in rhythm stemmed from his love for music. He studied conducting at Juilliard, so naturally his musical passions would fill our home. Music was an underlying pattern in the fabric of our lives. As a pastry chef those rhythms in my psyche are important. I draw upon them to create repetitive movement as I pipe on designs, or repeat other shapes in my work. A rhythm makes you consistent; it gives you flow.

Identifying patterns became a game in my household. Every Sunday after church, we would go for a drive to get ice cream. The activity we played on the drive was called the "Take a New Route in the Car Every Time and Get as Lost as You Possibly Can" game. We all tried desperately to remember how to get home, but it was always my blind father who knew how to direct us back. To him it was simple: two lefts, one right, three lefts. It's the same way a blind person navigates on a walk with a cane. He saw the patterns; the rest of us were caught up in our visual dependence. He taught me to free my mind and let the natural patterns inform me: how to turn mathematics into music in my head and how to let my movements respond without the clutter of extraneous detail.

Connecting your movements in a way that doesn't depend on a totally cerebral form of concentration frees your mind to move on to other things as you pipe basket weave after basket weave onto yet another wedding cake. Drawing upon lessons of rhythm, patterns, and musical flow allows you to bring symmetry and shape to a lovely design. They enhance your ability to elicit grace.

COOKING SECRETS

The secret of great piping begins with how you construct your parchment piping bag. When curling the parchment-paper triangle into the funnel shape, make sure all the seams line up so that when your piping line comes out of the bag, it is smooth and continuous. Then, when you start piping, lift the bag up high enough to make sure you have a string of icing to work with. Since you are manipulating a short string of icing as you pipe, you actually maneuver the icing slightly ahead of where it's landing on the cake. This is due to the slight delay that occurs while the line of icing drifts into place. The movement of the string comes from above the string rather than close to the cake. The result is a more flowing line to the design that is much more graceful.

CHEMISTRY IN THE KITCHEN

I learned a lot about flavor by watching my husband, Ivan Flowers, who is a phenomenal executive chef. I fell in love with his cooking as well as the man in the chef's coat. He has a natural gift in the kitchen that results in food that leaves you breathless. One of my favorites is his lobster bisque; it is so luxuriously rich, with a sensuous velvety texture that leaves you weeping in your napkin as you hesitantly wipe away the spots of soup left on your chin. He is a genius behind the stove as he combines flavors with a deep complexity and beauty that reflect his level of creativity and unfaltering commitment to brilliant food. Even though my world is baking, we both bring inspiration to the other's work. Our shared love of great food enriches our life and our cooking.

THE CHEF'S LESSON

CLASSIC TUILE COOKIES

(MAKES THIRTY-TWO COOKIES; SERVES EIGHT)

Tuile is the French word for "tile." These extremely thin, elegant cookies are classic additions to panna cotta, sorbets—anywhere you wish to add a delicate crunch to the textures on the plate. Here they are matched with a granita recipe. They are beautiful when fragrant petals such as lavender are added to the batter, or tapped onto the surface as the cookies are baking. :: **CWM**

INGREDIENTS

8 ounces (2 cups) Pastry Flour
8 ounces (1 cup + 1 tablespoon) Sugar
7 Egg Whites, room temperature
8 ounces (1 cup) Butter, unsalted, melted

:: Chef's Note

Because these cookies are thin, they bake and harden quickly. Therefore, you have to be ready with any supports you may want to use to help shape the cookies while they are warm. They can be draped over small bowls or muffin tins, wound around dowels, woven between pegs—indeed, any prop you desire can be used in the shaping process.

PROCEDURE

1. Preheat the oven to 350°F.

2. In a bowl, combine the flour and sugar. Whisk in the egg whites until the batter is well blended. Finally, whisk in the melted butter.

3. Spread the batter thinly and evenly over the top of the prepared template directly on a nonstick cookie pan (see the illustration page 233).

4. Bake until the cookies are a very light golden brown, approximately 5 minutes. Watch carefully, as they can overbrown quite easily.

5. When the cookies just start to become golden, open the oven door and slide the tray out to the edge. Being careful not to burn yourself, form each cookie into a three-dimensional shape to add height and interest. This must be done while the cookies are still warm, since they harden very quickly.

6. Allow the cookies to cool. Once cooled, they may be stored in airtight containers; they keep very well.

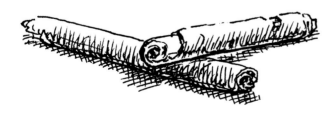

BLACK MUSCAT GRANITA

(SERVES EIGHT)

What a lovely thing to be able to serve iced desserts even if you don't own an ice cream maker. The Chinese invented the first ice cream freezer: They poured a combination of saltpeter (potassium nitrate) and snow over the top of syrup-filled containers in order to freeze the contents. When Marco Polo saw this in China, he rushed home to Italy with the idea. :: CWM

PROCEDURE

1. Combine all the ingredients in a hotel pan or shallow bowl and mix until the sugar is completely dissolved.

2. Put the bowl or pan in the freezer. Once the granité forms a rim of ice around the edge, stir by scraping the ice from the outside of the pan into the middle. Repeat every hour for the first 3-4 hours.

3. Freeze overnight without any additional stirring.

4. Just before serving, scrape the ice from top to bottom, and stir gently to incorporate any settled juices from the bottom of the pan. Serve in a stemmed glass with a tuile cookie on the side.

INGREDIENTS

3 cups Black Muscat Wine, Quady
  Elysium brand
1¼ cups Lemon Juice
1¼ cups + 2 tablespoons Orange Juice
¾ cup Sugar
4¾ cups Water

:: Chef's Note

When a product is frozen, the intensity of the flavors and the amount of sweetness both decrease. Too much sugar, however, will lower the freezing temperature of the granita. Therefore, you have to balance the flavor and the freezing capacity when adjusting the sugar content in a frozen recipe.

DIFFERENCES BETWEEN SORBETS, SHERBETS, AND GRANITAS:

· <u>GRANITAS</u> consist of flavorings of juices, sugar, and water in a mixture that is 4 parts liquid to 1 part sugar. Granitas are frozen in a method that results in soft, flaky ice shavings similar to the consistency of a snow cone.

· <u>SORBETS</u> are made with fruit puree, fruit juice, sugar, and other flavorings (such as champagne) but never with milk. They are smoother than granitas because they are made in ice cream freezers rather than raked with a fork. Their texture is also softer than that of sherbets.

· <u>SHERBETS</u> are very similar to sorbets since they are also made with an ice cream freezer. However, they may be creamier due to the optional addition of a dairy product (such as milk, cream, or eggs) and sometimes gelatin.

BLACK MUSCAT WINE:

· The wine in this granita has a sweet, musky flavor. The grapes used to make Muscat are actually so sweet they are also used to make raisins. They are grown throughout Europe as well as in California.

MAKING TUILE COOKIES:

· You can make your own template for the tuile batter by starting with a piece of sturdy plastic, such as the lid from an oatmeal box or sour cream container. Cut the lip off the lid first to get a flat surface, then cut the lid into a teardrop shape in order to provide a handle to lift the template off the dough.

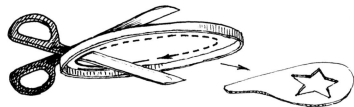

· Next, place a cookie cutter on top of the plastic. Trace and cut around the outside of the cookie cutter pattern to create the desired shape.

· When using the template, place it on top of a silpat (a nonstick baking mat made of flexible glass fiber and food-grade silicone), or, if you don't have a silpat, on a lightly greased and floured sheet pan. (Be sure to tip off the extra flour on the pan before using the template.)

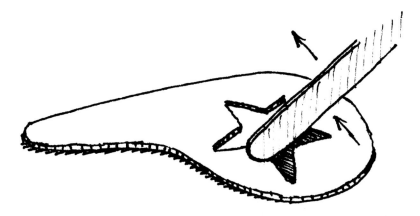

· Spread the batter smoothly across the template using an offset spatula. Make sure the batter is evenly spread across the template.

Lift up here while holding down the spatula on the other side.

· To remove the template, hold down one edge of the plastic with your spatula and lift off the template, using the handle from the opposite side. This allows the batter to remain undisturbed.

THE CHEF AS TEACHER

THE OPPORTUNITY TO TEACH

In addition to learning the joys of cooking early in my life, the joys of teaching made their impact on me during my childhood years. When I was eight or nine years old, I would make "appointments" with my mother to sit down and "teach her everything she ever knew about piano." Sitting there on the piano bench together, I not only realized how good it felt to be wearing the teacher's hat, but also felt the warmth of my mother's encouragement. She knew just how to motivate me and allow me to grow on my own terms. She was a wonderful mentor.

Much later in my life when I was working as a caterer, I had many opportunities to train people when I realized again how naturally that role came to me. I really enjoyed passing on information to other people, being a source of information. The ironic part is that despite the opportunities to teach, I am the one who is constantly learning. From my students, from my reading, from my co-workers, there is always more to pick up, more to experiment with, more to master. That endless growth is one of the most fascinating parts of this field. There is always more to learn.

Another reason I enjoy teaching is because of the differences that are inherent in the students. I have lectures prepared ahead of time, but if a student has a particular question, that lecture will take on a whole new direction. You have to be able to draw upon a whole breadth and depth of knowledge to be able to take your students wherever they need to go.

KITCHEN WISDOMS

I find that many of my students have difficulty making sponge cakes. There are some general concepts to know that will make your own sponge cake recipe more successful: Be sure to sift the flour three or four times first to make it light as air, otherwise you will end up overfolding your cake (unsifted flour is heavy, and heavier flour takes heavier stirring to combine); also, gently warm the egg whites first, so they whip up bigger, better, faster, and stronger. To properly mix the ingredients in the recipe, first take a couple of handfuls of cake batter and mix in

TRACY FLOWERS

any melted butter called for in the recipe. This mixing tempers the hot butter and creates a sort of slurry. Then slowly incorporate the slurry into the batter. This allows the melted butter to fold in easily instead of sinking to the bottom. It also reduces the chance of overfolding the cake batter. Overfolding makes the whole sponge cake collapse. Then, if you are working in a commercial kitchen with enormous pots, use the empty pot that was used to hold the butter as a pivot to place the mixing bowl on so that when you need to pour the batter, it's not a drippy mess.

CULINARY SCHOOL TIMES TWO

I went to culinary school twice: the first time for my culinary degree at the Culinary Institute of America, and the second time for my baking certificate. When I first came out of school, I wanted to do it all: be a chef, a restaurant owner, and a pastry chef. I wanted to achieve on every level. But the world of cuisine is too big; you have to choose. Without a focus, you're a jack of all trades and master of none. When I finally realized that my greatest passion was baking, I realized that I only knew how to bake, not why things worked in the oven. So I went back to school and became the kind of student that some teachers love and others dread. I had endless streams of questions that would come to mind. I questioned everything; I wanted to know it all.

A COMMITMENT TO THE WHOLE STUDENT

To cook well is only half the equation of becoming a great chef: Students also need to be able to nurture their best personal self. Regardless of your profession, it is generally your people skills that help you advance in your career, so it's important to help students nurture this part of their lives as well. Opportunities for responsibility, honesty, integrity, dependability, and reliability have to be incorporated into your classroom on a daily basis. To hold students to a lower level of standards is to do them an injustice. You need good people to create great food. Without a real foundation ultimately both will fail; with a good foundation the sky's the limit.

ADDITIONAL RECIPE

GRANNY SMITH SWEET ROLLS WITH CINNAMON BUTTER SAUCE

From Chef Connie Jenkins

(SERVES SIX)

In my opinion, there is no better way to start a weekend morning than with the smell of these rolls drifting out of my kitchen. They are best eaten immediately, but I appreciate a dish like this that can also keep a day or two. That way when I get up to go to school at 5:45 every morning, I have something wonderful to take along with my morning coffee. :: **CWM**

SWEET ROLL INGREDIENTS

3 1/2 cups Milk
1 1/2 ounces (6 packets) Active Dry Yeast
8 ounces (1 cup) Sugar, superfine
About 1 cup Butter, unsalted, softened
1 1/2 teaspoons Salt
2 Eggs
14 ounces (3 cups) Bread Flour
6 ounces (1 1/4 cups) Pastry Flour
1/2 tablespoon Cinnamon, ground
3 1/2 cups Granny Smith Apples, peeled,
    cored, medium diced

CINNAMON BUTTER SAUCE INGREDIENTS

4 cups Apple Juice
16 ounces (2 cups) Sugar, superfine
2 tablespoons Butter, unsalted
1 teaspoon Cinnamon, ground
1 teaspoon Nutmeg, freshly grated

PROCEDURE

1. Butter a 9" cake pan.

2. Measure all the ingredients and set them aside in individual containers. Sift together the bread and pastry flours and set aside.

3. In a small saucepan, scald the milk. Turn off the heat as soon as it starts to froth. Cool to lukewarm.

4. When the milk has cooled, dissolve the yeast in the milk along with 1 tablespoon of the sugar.

5. Put 1/2 cup butter, 1/2 cup sugar, and salt in a mixing bowl and mix on low with the paddle attachment until creamy.

6. Add the eggs 1 at a time and mix until incorporated.

7. Add the flour and liquid ingredients all at once and mix on medium speed for 4 minutes.

8. Grease a bowl with about 1 teaspoon butter, then put in the dough and turn once. Cover with a moist, clean towel and allow it to rise until double in size, approximately 1 1/4 hours.

9. When the dough has doubled, punch it down and turn it out onto a floured countertop. Knead for 10 minutes until the dough is smooth and elastic.

10. Roll out the dough to form a rectangle 14" x 9".

11. Brush 2 tablespoons of butter evenly over the center surface of the dough. Leave a border of 1" unbuttered around the edge.

12. Sprinkle the surface of the dough with a mixture of 1/2 cup superfine sugar and 1/2 tablespoon cinnamon.

13. Evenly spread out the diced apples over the surface of the dough. Do not put apples within a 2" border around the edge of the dough.

14. Roll the dough from one long edge to the other over the apples to create a spiraled log. To seal, pinch the edge closed along the entire length of the log.

15. Using a piece of strong thread, slide it under the dough about $1\frac{1}{2}$" from the end. Lift, crisscross the thread, and pull tightly to slice off a $1\frac{1}{2}$" piece from the apple roll.

16. Place the rolls in the prepared pan with the most recently cut side facing down. Space the rolls evenly in the pan.

17. Cover the rolls with a damp, clean towel and let them rise in a warm place until doubled, about 45 minutes.

18. About 25 minutes after the rolls are covered with the towel, preheat the oven to 375°F. Combine the sauce ingredients in a saucepan. Turn the heat on medium-low and reduce the mixture by half, until it has the consistency of a very light syrup, approximately 15 minutes. Do not allow the sauce to cook beyond this stage or it will harden when it is baked.

19. Turn off the heat and allow the sauce to cool slightly, approximately 1 minute.

20. Pour the sauce over the rolls in the pan and place them in the oven.

21. Bake until the rolls are golden brown, the dough is baked through, and the apples are tender, approximately 30 minutes.

22. When the rolls first come out of the oven, rub about $1\frac{1}{2}$ tablespoons of butter over the tops and allow it to melt over the surface. Serve immediately.

:: Chef's Note

This recipe calls for active dry yeast, which is the type that comes in the little packages. Fresh yeast that is sold in cakes can also be used. In place of the $1\frac{3}{5}$ ounces active dry yeast, use 6, $\frac{3}{5}$-ounce cakes fresh yeast.

confectionery showpieces II

INSTRUCTOR: CHEF ALLISON SCHROEDER

THERE ARE FEW PLACES IN LIFE WHERE THE EXTREMES OF CREATIVE THOUGHT ARE TRANSLATED INTO A PHYSICAL FORM.

In Confectionery Showpieces II, this was not just a possibility but a mandate. As we worked to refine our techniques in sculpting, molding, and shaping edible masterpieces, some students tempered chocolate with ease and twirled their parchment piping bags as if they had used them every day of their lives. Others struggled with the intricacies, swearing at the effort and yearning for the savory side of the kitchen. Chef Schroeder inspired all of us—pushing us and herself, creating next to us in the kitchen, continually prompting new thought. She discovered inspiration everywhere, especially in the endless possibilities available through her computer. Her understanding of the intricate techniques involved in Confectionery Showpieces helped us to see ourselves as sculptors; manipulating sugar, chocolate, doughs, and frostings as if they were clay, to result in projects with stunning appeal. Her love for detail encouraged me to ask every question as my proficiency began to advance: "How do you spin sugar evenly?" "What does cooked sugar look like when it's pulled enough?" "How do you add structural integrity to long threads of pulled sugar?" Chef Schroeder reinforced my conviction that to be a great chef, you must constantly be connected to some source of new thought. Whether it is literary, human, or electronic, each form of communication has its own merits; what is important is to pursue a constant evolution of ideas in order to continue producing food products that are consistently fresh. :: CWM

REFLECTIONS OF A CHEF

A WINDOW TO THE WORLD

Food provides a framework in which I can constantly pursue new information. It inspires me to learn; it invites me to explore the myriad perspectives on what constitutes a wonderful quality of life. Food is the thread that pulls all the information together and gives meaningful direction to every new discovery.

When I create confectionery showpieces, it's the same feeling. The sense of freedom is overwhelming in the kitchen because I can build any creation that comes to mind. The only thing more fascinating is watching what creations come out of my students' imaginations. One day their showpieces may be made out of pulled, blown, and spun sugar showcasing a journey beneath the sea; the next day it may be tempered chocolate in an ode to Janis Joplin. When it comes to confectionery showpieces, no journey is too fantastic; no idea is out of reach.

A WALK ON THE WILD SIDE

Ten servers, a manager, and me running the entire line: that was my initiation into cooking at a seafood restaurant when I was just out of high school. Even though I'm in pastries now, I did have my days on the hot side of busy kitchens. We'd serve 100 dinners a day; I was alone and completely slammed. I loved it. If people tried to help me, I'd scream at them to get out of my way because they would slow me down. I knew where everything was: the food, the pans, the garnishes. I knew when things needed to be put on the heat and when they needed to be taken off. It was all

right there in my head. I loved having enormous responsibility and layer upon layer of duties to do because it kept me from getting bored. I would go out of my mind on slow shifts. The major high comes from moments when the tickets are flying, the servers are screaming, the steaks are spitting out juices that crackle in the heat of the grill, the pasta water's heaving over the sides of the vat, the crusty sauté pans are stacked a mile high, and I'm a blur of nonstop motion behind the line. It's such a rush and a feeling of accomplishment.

THE TRANSITION TO BAKING

As much fun as I had on the line, I fell in love with baking when I went to culinary school. I was drawn to the tactile side of the work: rolling out the warm dough and feeling my body melt as the yeast smell took over my senses. Punching down the soft billowing bread dough and feeling it ease its hold on my arm as it sank to the bottom of the bowl. The sensory part of baking was attraction enough to hook me, but it was the "whys" of baking that kept me coming back: why the creaming method is used, why eggs coagulate in the bowl, why cream of tartar helps egg whites hold their volume. I wanted to know it all.

I am constantly hungry for deeper knowledge when it comes to food. Even historical facts about baking fascinate me, like the story about salt dough creations. Salt dough is like an extremely salty bread dough that is intended only for decorative purposes. It's a very versatile and forgiving product for students to work with. The sculptures formed from the dough are very slowly dried so that the surface stays smooth and unbroken. After they dry the surfaces can be painted or decorated, resulting in a sculpture that will last as a centerpiece almost indefinitely.

Since salt was extremely expensive in early times, it was considered particularly extravagant to offer a gift of a salt dough sculpture because, by its very nature, it wasn't consumed. To use salt in a way that didn't involve consumption was considered very lavish. That connotation of lavishness continued to characterize salt dough creations over time and, as a result, they are coveted even today. I love sharing stories like that with my students to put their work in context and allow them to feel the historical significance of the work that they do.

COOKING SECRETS

Everyone has a container of cream of tartar in their cupboards, but no one knows what it is. Out of habit, they just shake it into their egg whites and hope for the best. Cream of tartar contains tartaric crutar, which is an acid. Tartaric acid. What does an acid do? When it interacts with a protein, it causes coagulation. When you add an acid to meringue as it's whipping and thereby coagulate that protein with a low amount of acid, you're not truly cooking it—instead you're making it stable. Once it's stable, it won't collapse. So when you do actually cook it, the proteins won't shrink and extrude moisture onto your meringue pies. The acid also enhances the white color; the clear albumen in the egg coagulates and turns white. The result is beautifully white, nonweeping meringue, or snowy white marshmallows. I could go on and on about coagulation. I love coagulation.

But if you're cooking sugar, you won't want to reach for cream of tartar to help reduce crystallization. Cream of tartar also contains cornstarch, an anticaking agent that promotes crystallization. So when you need to add an acid to melted sugar to help with stabilization and coagulation, it has to be pure tartaric acid.

MORE COOKING SECRETS

When you're making buttercream rosettes with a piping bag, as you build the edges imagine how a roller coaster banks its curves. As your tip goes around in a circle, keep it angled like the cars on a roller coaster in order to keep the inertia flowing inward and to keep the rosette intact.

THE POSSIBILITIES OF FOOD

I love opportunities to turn mundane tasks into something fascinating. I see a trip to the grocery store as my dream time. When I look at food in the aisles, it's not just a piece of pork, or a head of broccoli, or a pile of pears; it's an idea. I don't just see things, I can smell, taste, and combine those ingredients in my head until I have the perfect combination to accentuate the main ingredient of the meal. Grocery stores to me are places of creativity and possibility.

APPRECIATING THE CIRCLE OF LIFE

My appreciation for food started on the farm. I grew up in Iowa, one of the most bountiful places in our country. Having a genuine understanding of the life cycles of animals and plants is one of the greatest benefits of growing up on a farm. When you've raised pigs from birth to slaughter, you realize what it means to put aside your love for that animal when it's time to give its life a new purpose as food. You know what it means to cross all your fingers and toes so that your harvest thrives despite the wind, rain, or hail that beats down on your fields. Your love and your respect for your food is automatic, it's ingrained in who you are. As you hold food, it feels different when all those memories are also in your hands.

THE DEATH OF A KITCHEN

Lessons that deepened my knowledge of the food industry came from even the most unexpected circumstances. My respect for small businesses grew immensely when I actually worked with a bakery that was about to go under. I found the job just as I was finishing culinary school. At the time I was unaware of what dire straits the business was in; I was just completely fascinated with German culture, and this little Bavarian shop seemed to fit the bill. They used authentic ingredients and German techniques to turn out products from scratch: beautiful handmade cookies, pastries, and Danishes that made you hear Wagner as you nibbled on each one. I learned from two wonderful women, one German, one Jewish, who worked together to create gorgeous wedding cakes.

Unfortunately, this little bakery was losing money hand over fist. When I learned of the situation, I tried to help my boss by working with his food costs, since he was operating at a whopping 60 percent. I also showed him how to limit his selections in the bakery case so that at the end of each day he wouldn't lose money due to waste. But it was too late; it was clear this business was going down. I thought, "I'm bound to

ALLISON SCHROEDER

learn from this situation, so it's better to learn from if it's not my own business." So I offered to work for the owner for free. It was such a feeling of family there, I just couldn't let this man meet his demise on his own. I had to be there for him.

There came a time that he had to let most of his other employees go, and we ran the shop at a bare-bones level. He would be out delivering baked goods and I would be back at the shop answering phones, running the retail, and do the baking all at the same time. One morning I had an unbelievably busy rush hour. The phone was ringing, people were in the storefront asking question after question, the kitchen was a mess, and I had 24 pumpkin pies baking in the oven. As I dealt with the storefront area, I knew I needed to get the pies out of the oven. I could feel them baking longer and longer, but I just couldn't get away from the counter. Just as the last person left, I ran back to the kitchen. There were ingredients everywhere, the pies were completely burned, all 24 of them, and my boss walked in the door. He took one look at the kitchen, walked to his office, pulled out a bottle of Jack Daniels, and cried. The emotion of that day will be etched in my memory forever.

THE CHEF'S LESSON

STILTON PEAR TART WITH SUGAR CAGE GARNISHES

(SERVES SIX)

In this recipe the classic combination of pear and Stilton cheese is interpreted in a new way, and the results are absolutely mouthwatering. Although the tart is delicious on its own, the optional sugar cage garnishes allow you to add true drama to your plate. :: **CWM**

STEP ONE: THE TART SHELL

TART SHELL INGREDIENTS

6½ ounces (1¼ cups) Bread Flour
1½ ounces (3 tablespoons) Sugar
⅛ teaspoon Pure Vanilla Extract
¼ cup Thyme, fresh, leaves only, chopped
4 ounces (½ cup) Butter, unsalted, cold
2 tablespoons Ice Water

:: Chef's Note

With this recipe, you don't actually have to go through all of the motions of cooling all of your utensils and ingredients, as some pie dough recipes ask you to do. If you start with cold butter and water and work quickly enough, the dough will come out just fine.

PROCEDURE

1. In a medium bowl, combine the flour, sugar, vanilla, and thyme. Using a pastry blender, cut in the cold butter until the dough's texture resembles cornmeal.

2. Sprinkle on 1 tablespoon of the cold water. Work quickly to form the dough into a ball, adding a few more drops of cold water if the dough needs more moisture to hold together. Manipulate the dough as little as possible to keep it from warming significantly, which would toughen it after it is baked.

3. Wrap the dough in plastic wrap and put it into the refrigerator. Allow it to chill for at least 1 hour or as long as a day or two.

4. Put the dough on a lightly floured countertop or pastry cloth and roll it out into a circle at least 14" in diameter and approximately ¼" thick.

5. Then, to transport the dough to the 10" tart pan, place a rolling pin on top of one edge and gently roll the dough onto the pin. Lift the rolling pin over to the edge of the tart pan and carefully unroll it across the top of the pan.

6. Gently press the dough down into the shell. Then use the rolling pin to cut the edges to fit the pan by rolling it back and forth across the top. The rough edges will drop off; the result will be a tart shell that fits the pan perfectly.

7. Smooth the top edges of the dough if necessary. Carefully cover the top of the tart shell with plastic wrap and refrigerate until needed.

(continued)

(Stilton Pear Tart continued from page 248)

STEP TWO: THE TART AND SAUCE

TART INGREDIENTS

24 ounces (3 cups) Sugar
7 1/2 ounces (1 cup - 1 tablespoon) Water
1 stick Cinnamon
2 Whole Cloves
6 green Bartlett Pears, cored, peeled,
    sliced 1/8" thick
1/4 pound Stilton Cheese, sliced 1/8" thick
2 cups Heavy Cream
2 tablespoons Thyme, fresh, leaves only
1/4 cup Butter, chilled, cut into pieces

SAUCE INGREDIENTS

Reserved Poaching Liquid
1 cup Heavy Cream
1 green Bartlett Pear, cored, peeled,
    sliced 1/8" thick
1/4 cup Thyme, fresh, leaves only

ACCOMPANIMENTS

6 Fresh Thyme Sprigs
Fanned Pear Slices, dipped in lemon juice to
    reduce discoloration
Sugar Cages, optional (recipe follows)

:: Chef's Note

To slice the Stilton cheese, use a knife with a
sharp, clean blade that has been warmed in
boiling water.

PROCEDURE

1. Preheat the oven to 350°F. Combine the sugar, water, cinnamon stick, and cloves in a medium saucepan to create the poaching liquid. Bring the contents just to a boil.

2. Immediately reduce the heat and add the 6 sliced pears. Cook until the pears are tender but not falling apart, approximately 7 minutes. Make sure to replace the water in the poaching liquid as it evaporates so that it does not get too thick at this point.

3. Remove the pears to dry and cool. Lay the slices flat, in a single layer, on top of waxed paper. Reserve the poaching liquid.

4. Fill the tart shell with layers of the candied pears alternated with the shavings of Stilton—pear, cheese, pear, cheese—in concentric circles until it's completely filled.

5. Drizzle 2 cups of cream around the surface of the tart, allowing it to drip down through the pears and cheese into the interior.

6. Sprinkle 2 tablespoons thyme leaves over the top.

7. Dot the surface of the tart with the small pieces of butter. This will give shine and richness.

8. Bake until the tart shell is golden brown and the cheese is melted, approximately 20 minutes. Remove the tart from the oven and allow it to sit where it can thicken and cool slightly.

9. Combine the reserved poaching liquid with the remaining cream, pear, and thyme. Reduce this mixture by half over medium-high heat.

10. Allow the mixture to cool slightly, then use a slotted metal spoon to remove and discard the cinnamon stick and cloves. (The mixture will burn your fingers.) Puree the sauce in a blender until smooth. Allow it to cool again slightly.

11. Transfer the sauce to a squeeze bottle and place in a warm-water bath.

12. Just before serving, squeeze the sauce onto the plate in a zigzag pattern, add a tart slice, and garnish with a fresh thyme sprig, a fanned pear slice, and the optional sugar cages (see following page).

STEP THREE: THE SUGAR CAGES (OPTIONAL)

Sugar cages are are fun to make. Although the sugar takes a while to come up to the proper temperature, the procedure itself is really simple. If you can drizzle syrup, you can make these cages. :: **CWM**

PROCEDURE

1. In a saucepan, combine the sugar and water and heat to 300°F.

2. While this is cooking, coat the backs of 15 soup spoons (30 if you have them) with nonstick spray. Lay them out, back-side up, on top of waxed paper laid on the countertop.

3. When the sugar reaches exactly 300°, swirl in the thyme. Remove the syrup from the heat before the temperature exceeds 320°.

4. Immediately dip a fork into the syrup and drizzle thin threads of melted sugar over the spoons to create a cage the same size and shape as the back of each spoon (see the illustration). As the sugar hardens, remove the individual cages and set them aside to free up the spoon to make a total of 30 sugar cages.

5. To garnish, arrange the cooled cages in a flower shape and lean them on the edge of the tart slice. Add a sprig of thyme, a fanned pear, and a zigzag of sauce to complete the plate.

SUGAR CAGE INGREDIENTS

24 ounces (3 cups) Sugar
7 1/2 ounces (1 cup – 1 tablespoon) Water
1/3 cup Thyme, fresh, leaves only

PROCEDURE FOR OTHER SUGAR PRODUCTS:

· Even though the pear tart recipe does not necessitate adherence to strict sugar melting procedures, it is important to know how to melt sugar without crystals forming in the pan. This is particularly important if you are making other sugar creations that require a very high level of luster in the resulting sugar product. In these cases, strict adherence to the rules of sugar melting must be practiced. If the sugar crystallizes, it will be impossible to manipulate the finished product into shapes with the sheen and translucency that make pulled sugar creations so beautiful.

WAYS TO AVOID THE CRYSTALLIZATION OF SUGAR DURING THE MELTING PROCESS:

1. Start with pure, clean granulated sugar. Make sure it contains no impurities or contamination from other products.

2. As the sugar is brought up to temperature on the stove, it must be given constant attention; to avoid splatters of sugar from bubbling up onto the sides of the pan and crystallizing on the edge. Even the tiniest amount of crystallization will affect the rest of the sugar in the pan. Using a spray bottle filled with water, you must occasionally spray down the tiny spots of sugar on the sides of the pan as well as on the sides of the candy thermometer. This does, however, increase the length of time to bring the sugar up to temperature, but it is necessary to do in order to ensure the integrity of the melted sugar.

3. Put a lid on the pan between the times you spray water onto the sides.

4. Add a couple of drops of pure tartaric acid mixed with equal parts water into the pan to reduce crystallization. Lemon juice may be used in place of the tartaric acid. Adding a monosaccharide also reduces crystallization.

5. Before the sugar reaches the boiling point, be certain to skim off the impurities that rise to the surface.

6. After the sugar begins to boil, stop any stirring or movement of the pan. If the contents are disturbed, crystals will begin to form. Also make sure the burner of the stove is on as high as possible, but does not reach around the edges of the pan or it will start to caramelize the edges by overheating that part of the pan.

7. Be sure to take the pan off the heat at exactly 320°F. If you don't, the sugar will begin to caramelize in the pan.

TO MAKE THE CAGES FOR THE PEAR TART

· Follow the directions in the Stilton Pear Tart recipe to create the simple syrup for the sugar cages.

· After the thyme has been incorporated into the poaching syrup, immediately dip a fork into the syrup and drizzle the fine streams of melted sugar over the backs of the prepared spoons.

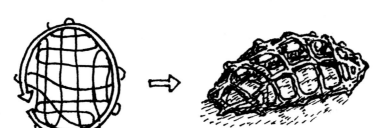

· The final drizzling motion surrounds the circumference of the spoon to finish off the cage pattern. Allow the cages to cool. The resulting cages form the structures that are used to garnish the plate.

TO PLATE THE DESSERT

· Begin by filling a squirt bottle with the creamy thyme pear puree. Draw a zigzag pattern of puree onto the plate. Then place a warm wedge of tart centered in the back ⅓ of the plate in the 12:00 position.

· Next place five sugar cages, arranged in a flower pattern, next to one corner of the tart in the 11:00 position. Take a thyme sprig and extend it outward from the flower to act as a leaf.

· Finally, fan three slices of pear and place them on the plate in the 4:00 position to balance the design.

THE CHEF AS TEACHER

A KINDER, GENTLER KITCHEN

Since Confectionery Showpieces falls near the end of the culinary school program, by the time students get to me they are generally exhausted from the grueling pace of the other classes. One beauty of creating showpieces is that our classroom does not have the same sense of urgency that you feel on the hot side of the kitchen. The focus behind our countertops is on mastering techniques, primarily with sugar, chocolate, and frosting, that require a great deal of time. Even though students are intensely engaged, the atmosphere is generally not frenzied.
It gives the students a chance to slow down, breathe, and experience a new way of producing in the kitchen. It gives a real opportunity for their creativity to flow and gives us the time to teach them very involved techniques.

I also try to give them a welcoming environment to work in. Students are generally very receptive to a nurturing workplace. I want them to see that as they go out to become chefs, they have options in their management styles. It's not just about ranting and raving. If you combine appreciation for people with a professional no-nonsense attitude about the food and rules of the kitchen, you end up with a level of respect that's deserved, not just demanded.

THE INTEGRITY OF FORTHRIGHTNESS

Chefs who hold back ingredients or techniques should be banned from the kitchen. The point is to share knowledge so that food and people evolve into something even better.

STAY OPEN TO EVEN THE MOST UNLIKELY INSPIRATIONS

I am constantly in awe of the number of ways a problem can be approached in the kitchen. Watching the inventiveness of my students gives me a chance to see the task from an entirely new perspective. One day we had a student who worked on pacemakers bring his tool kit to class—sterilized, of course—to work on the fondant cakes we make. These cakes require very intricate techniques to finish the detail work. He used his pacemaker tools to weave ribbon through the icing and carve

extremely delicate and beautiful patterns. It was probably the most precise work I had ever seen on that assignment.

KEEPING THE FAITH

Nothing is more heartbreaking than watching someone spend hours making a fragile sugar structure and then see it shatter in front of our eyes as the project is moved. I work to help my students understand certain principles that will allow their centerpieces to survive on top of a crowded buffet table. But it is trial and error that makes the lessons sink in—and it can be very painful to watch. Just like cooking on the savory side of the kitchen, it's the basics of technique that really mark the success of a project. In the end, if a product fails, it may feel traumatic, but remember, it's just sugar.

ADDITIONAL RECIPES

CHILLED CRANBERRY, GINGER, AND PEAR SALAD

From Chef Skip O'Neill

(SERVES FOUR)

Another way to use pears is in this simple salad recipe. The refreshing flavors make your mouth come alive. For this reason, it works well as an intermezzo between courses, served in a tiny, stemmed glass. Or serve on square black salad plates to accompany an Asian entrée. It even works with a traditional Thanksgiving dinner. :: CWM

INGREDIENTS

2 cups Sugar
¼ cup Balsamic Vinegar
1, 1" piece Ginger, fresh, peeled
1 stick Cinnamon
½ cup Orange Juice, freshly squeezed
2, 12-ounce bags Cranberries, fresh
2 firm Anjou Pears, peeled, cored,
    medium diced

:: Chef's Note
There are more than 5,000 different varieties of pears. The Anjou is a member of the Beurre variety. Its characteristic juiciness is enhanced by its soft, nongritty texture. It has yellowish green skin and is typically lopsided.

PROCEDURE

1. In a 4-quart saucepan, combine the sugar, vinegar, ginger, cinnamon stick, and orange juice.

2. Heat the mixture over medium high heat until it just reaches a boil, then immediately reduce the heat to medium.

3. Mix in the cranberries and pears and simmer for 15 minutes, or until the berries pop, the sauce thickens slightly, and the pears become al dente.

4. Discard the ginger and cinnamon stick and pour the contents of the salad into a serving bowl.

5. Chill for a minimum of 4 hours to allow the flavors to mingle. Serve chilled.

advanced cuisine

INSTRUCTOR: CHEF PHILIP SAYRE

I REALLY DON'T REMEMBER SLEEPING MUCH DURING CULINARY SCHOOL—THERE WAS SO MUCH TO DO.

Instead, I was able to think deeply, risk bravely, care profoundly, compare carefully, fail miserably, and succeed beyond my wildest dreams. In our last class, Advanced Cuisine, we worked in every location in the school's own restaurant—from the front to the back of the house, from prep cook to sous chef to executive chef—pulling together all of the lessons we'd learned. During this time, we looked to Chef Sayer for final wisdom. He looked outdoors for his inspiration. There he conceptualized new flavors, gaining inspiration from natural forces and revisiting his own philosophies of cooking and teaching. He taught us discipline and an appreciation for hard work, honesty, and commitment. Without a dedication to these principles, kitchens become chaotic and restaurants go under. As I drew upon his lessons in Advanced Cuisine, I cooked in every station in the kitchen with the drive necessary to succeed as a chef. Chef Sayer's lessons on working from my core will always be with me. As my final days in culinary school approached, I realized how much I would miss my fellow students. When you cook every day together, you learn the true nature of teamwork. You see each other's best and worst sides, and you grow to love all of it. I will also miss the instructor-chefs who filled my cooking with joy. I reminded myself to continue to seek out and connect my experiences in the world with the kitchen, where my thoughts on food and life converge. :: **CWM**

REFLECTIONS OF A CHEF

A MUSE EARLY IN LIFE

I don't know what it was about Julia Child that made me, at 12 years old, want to watch cooking shows instead of being outside playing football. The day she made estouffat was the day I got on my bike, rode to where my mom worked, and asked her for money to buy the ingredients. I stopped at the grocery store on my ride home, bought all the food, and pedaled frantically back to our house to make estouffat. It didn't turn out like Julia's. I burned it.

I wasn't discouraged, though; Julia was still my muse. From there I made pizzas, chicken Parmesan; anything I'd see her make, I'd want to try. I loved the creativity and freedom that cooking allowed you. I loved the joy it brought other people. I still love those things about cooking.

My food memories from those days are surrounded by images of family. Shucking oysters with my grandfather, savoring every moment with him as he taught me to exchange the art of oyster slurping for a more appreciative method of oyster chewing that allows the essential oils to release into your mouth. Or sitting down on fold-up chairs around long tables to accommodate the 40-some relatives who routinely gathered in my home for great food and quality time together. Food was meant to bring us all together.

THE MILIEU OF THE KITCHEN

The energy of the kitchen alone inspires me to create. The noises, the sounds, the rush, the smells, the intensity of the line, the person next to me, all inspire me to work harder. There's nothing better than walking into the kitchen in the middle of service and smelling all those deep, rich smells, and if you have a good nose they are smells that are individually distinguishable. I notice the pungency of cumin hanging in the air just below my nostrils or the meandering aromas of onions as they begin to caramelize, their smells swirling over the pan and drifting past my head.

If I could just bottle the energy that happens on a night that really rocks in a restaurant kitchen and sell it to chefs, I would be able to retire early. As the bottle is cracked open, the excitement would immediately escape and fill the room with an orchestration of movement. You'd feel the energy of the chef expediting on one side of the line, the sous-chef choreographing movements on the other, and the line cooks in the middle pumping out food at an incredible pace, but with fluidity and purpose behind every movement. You would be able to watch the flow that takes over as the cooks' conscious minds shut off and their subconscious minds take over. You would be overcome by the synchronicity of your surroundings, and reminded of music, dance, poetry in motion.

THE QUEST FOR GOOD EATS

I am interested in the flavors of real food. I love finding places with old crusty waitresses who have worked in the same restaurant for the past 20 years. What a treasure to find great truck stops with all-you-can-eat breakfasts or wonderful mom-and-pop take-out joints with the best lo mein noodles you've ever tasted. People who cherish cuisine know that real food is worth the search. Epicurean gems are scattered everywhere, not all gathered together in a few fine-dining restaurants.

An elderly woman who was a chef in a restaurant in Mississippi, where I went on a catfish tour, made every dish out of catfish. Each plate that came out of her kitchen was done perfectly. They were not fancy; it was straight 10 o'clock, 2 o'clock, 6 o'clock presentation, with every item gently poised around those positions on the plate. But it was cooked to perfection. She began her career selling smoked catfish at a flea market. She went from there to owning her own restaurant and eventually writing her own cookbook. This amazing old woman with perfect simple food: She was an inspiration.

PHILIP SAYRE

BENEFITS OF BEING A COOK

Working in the food industry can take you anywhere you want to go: You can choose from any focus of cooking, you can be your own boss. I can literally take a map, close my eyes, stick out my finger, and say, "This is where I want to find a job."

THE HAUNTED KITCHEN

Undoubtedly my favorite position when I was working in restaurants was cooking at an old lodge at the Grand Canyon. It was completely historic and undeniably beautiful, but absolutely unforgettable. In the early-morning hours I would go in to open the restaurant for breakfast. I was all alone in the kitchen. The walls were lined with pots and pans hanging from rows of pegs. At 4 A.M. those pans would rattle on the wall, without any apparent disturbance causing it to happen. Although I was the only one in the kitchen, there were sounds of chopping on the other end of the counter as if parsley were being chopped with a French knife. At first when it happened, I felt my hair standing on end as I said, "Who is that? Cut that out." After a while I just got used to the presence in the kitchen.

DON'T APOLOGIZE FOR AMBITION

When I begin in a position that allows the opportunity to advance, I look around the room at the other members of the staff. Then I say to myself, "In three months I'm going to have your job." I'm not ruthless; I just have ambition. I can't sit idly by waiting for good things to happen, I have to be a catalyst. My feeling is if other people want a position as much as I do, they also have to prove their determination. Otherwise that job is for the taking, because I know I would do the job well.

BECOMING IRREPLACEABLE

You must temper your ambition with humility or you will become far too impressed with your own abilities. I made that mistake once in my career and I'll never let myself forget it. I got cocky and said things to my chef that I shouldn't have. I quickly learned the repercussions for such an act of insubordination: I was demoted to the cafeteria. It was completely humiliating, and I never forgot the necessity for respect again.

You also have to be aware that there are situations in which you can do your job too well. At the point you become indispensable to your boss, you will lose the opportunity to advance to higher positions. Your boss will not want to retrain someone to do the job as well as you do. Therefore, it's a good idea to make your ambitions subtly apparent, to let people know your desire to achieve as well as your desire to do well in your current position.

THE EMOTION OF INTERNATIONAL CUISINE

I find that when I'm angry I eat more aggressively. I want a big steak, potatoes, and just some vegetables—food I can eat in big bites. When my emotions are on the other end of the extreme, I love pasta. It's more delicate, and I linger over it instead of just gulping it down.

Chinese food to me is very fiery, emotional cuisine, particularly with the Szechuan ingredients, the intensely hot fire, and the food that flies around in the pan. French food is more romantic with its beurre blancs, beurre rouges, and hollandaise that are all smooth and velvety. The sauces elicit trancelike responses as you hit the explosion of flavor and hear yourself unconsciously uttering "wow" beneath your breath. Italian food is both fun and formal. Indian food carries all the complexity of India itself with all its variations tied together into one entity. But regardless of the emphasis, it's all about family and friends enjoying the kind of camaraderie that's the key to great living.

I think every American should read about and experience Spanish food. The Spanish tradition of tapas is the social equivalent to our time around the water cooler at work, except the Spaniards know how to relax and do it in style. Tapas invite conversation after the workday, as people nibble on bites of lovely combinations of food and mingle with their co-workers and friends. The flat shapes of the original tapas were intended as coverings for the tops of their wineglasses, but now feature a beautiful tapestry of colors, textures, and flavors that work to sustain appetites as well as friendships as people digest the happenings of the day.

COOKING SECRETS

One product you see nearly universally around the world is eggs. There are great chefs in the world who initially form their opinion of your cooking based on your ability to cook a great egg. The secret to flipping eggs in a sauté pan is to start with plenty of butter added to a preheated pan. Use very fresh eggs so that there is more structure in the egg white. Swirl the eggs as they cook in the butter. Get the yolk to turn around so that when you flip it over, the whites flip first and all the yolks have to do is to fold over in the pan. It's an applied science, so practice is the only way to master the technique. Get a flat of eggs and flip them. You will fail many times, but then you'll find some success and soon it will start to feel natural. Cooking and life are successions of failure and accomplishment. What counts is learning to face challenges squarely in the eye, or in this case squarely in the yolk.

THE CHEF'S LESSON

INSALATA RUSSA (SHRIMP AND ROASTED BABY BEET SALAD)

(SERVES SIX)

I love beet salad as part of a warm-weather menu. This salad works perfectly for summer gatherings since baby beets are most widely available throughout the summer season and into fall. :: **CWM**

INGREDIENTS

Olive Oil Nonstick Spray
1½ cups Baby Beets, blanched, peeled,
    small diced
½ cup Butter
1½ pounds Shrimp, size 26/30, peeled,
    deveined, shells reserved
1 cup Green Beans, blanched, stemmed,
    small diced
2 large Red Potatoes, fork-tender, peeled,
    small diced
2 Carrots, cooked al dente, peeled, small diced
1½ cups Frozen Peas
2 tablespoons Capers, rinsed, drained
¼ cup Cornichons, roughly chopped
2 tablespoons White Wine Vinegar
¾ cup Mayonnaise
1 tablespoon Sugar
Kosher Salt and freshly ground Black Pepper

:: Chef's Note

Beets come in a variety of colors, from bright red and gold to white. They even come in a striped variety. Blanch them with their skins on to make the peeling process easier. When preparing the blanching water for beets, add 1 tablespoon vinegar per 2 quarts of water. The acid reacts with the red pigments, or anthocyanins, in the beets and causes them to turn a brighter red.

PROCEDURE

1. Preheat the oven to 450°F.

2. Preheat a baking sheet in the oven. When hot, remove it from the oven and coat with nonstick spray.

3. Spread the diced beets on the baking sheet in a single layer. Return it to the oven for 3–4 more minutes, stirring occasionally with a spatula, until the beets are crisp on all surfaces. Remove the pan from the oven, transfer the beets to a rack, and set them aside to cool.

4. Heat a saucepan and add the butter. When the butter is melted, add the shrimp shells and sauté until they turn pink. Reserve the butter in the pan but discard the shells.

5. Add the peeled shrimp to the shrimp butter in the hot sauté pan. Sauté until the shrimp curl and begin to look opaque. Do not overcook: The shrimp should still look plump and juicy.

6. Refrigerate the shrimp until they are cool enough to handle. Remove a third of them from the pan and cut into small dice. Reserve the remaining whole shrimp in the refrigerator. Put the diced shrimp in a large bowl and add the beans, potatoes, carrots, peas, capers, and cornichons. Mix well.

7. Mix the vinegar, mayonnaise, and sugar together in a separate bowl. Mix well; season to taste with salt and pepper, then add it to the bowl with the shrimp and vegetables. Finally, add the beets and stir gently to incorporate them evenly throughout the salad. Taste and season again if necessary.

8. Pack the shrimp salad into the bottom of a medium-sized, clean bowl, or mold, and chill for 1–2 hours.

9. At the time of service, invert the bowl onto a serving platter. Shake gently to carefully dislodge the salad. Leave it on the serving platter in the shape of the container. Arrange the remaining whole, cooked shrimp at the base of the salad. Or, for individual servings, place on a ½-cup serving of mesclun greens and garnish with toast points, capers, and fanned shrimp.

NEW MEXICAN CHILE CARNITAS WITH RICH TEQUILA SAUCE

(SERVES SIX)

Not many people think about the flavor profile of the beer they are drinking with their food. They just ice down their favorite standby. I am a fan of porter when it comes to beer, but I've learned that with really spicy foods, lighter beers work better. With this recipe a nice match would be a Corona, from south of the border. The flavor tempers rather than competes with the spices, and the connection of the regional food with beer from the same part of the world always makes sense. :: **CWM**

PROCEDURE

1. Season the pork with salt and pepper.

2. Heat a Dutch oven or large saucepot and pour in the oil or lard; make sure the pot's sides are high enough to contain the splatters. Heat the fat on high until the pan sizzles when the pork is placed inside. Brown the pork on all sides.

3. Reduce the heat to low and add the onion, garlic, chiles, and peppers. Cover and sweat with the pork for 4-5 minutes.

4. Deglaze the pot by pouring the tequila down the sides of the pan, then scraping the bottom to loosen and incorporate the brown, flavorful bits into the cooking liquid.

5. Add the stock and cumin. Simmer for 1½-2 hours or until the pork is fork-tender. Remove the pork from the pot and set aside to cool.

6. Using the same pot, reduce the cooking liquid by half. Then pour the contents into the blender and puree until smooth. Strain. Adjust the seasoning with salt and pepper and set aside.

7. The next step is what defines the carnitas: It turns them into "little browned pieces of meat." Deep-fry the pork in a pan of oil heated to 350°F, until the meat's surface is a medium brown color. This takes approximately 2-3 minutes.

8. To serve, place a portion of the pork on each plate and pour the sauce over it. Serve with warm flour or corn tortillas and cold beer.

INGREDIENTS

4 pounds Pork Butt, diced in 1" cubes
Kosher Salt and freshly ground Black Pepper
2 tablespoons Vegetable Oil or Lard
1 Onion, large diced
1½ teaspoons Garlic, freshly chopped
3 Dry New Mexican Chiles, reconstituted, seeded
2 Jalapeño Peppers, seeded, small diced
2 Anaheim Peppers, roasted, seeded, small diced
1 Poblano Pepper, roasted, seeded, small diced
½ cup Tequila
12 cups Pork or Chicken Stock
1 tablespoon Cumin, ground
Blended Oil, or Lard
12 Flour or Corn Tortillas

:: Chef's Note

The term *fork-tender* means that the meat falls away from the pork butt when it is lightly pulled back with a fork. It refers to a very tender stage of the food, generally produced in meat after very slow, prolonged cooking.

INSALATA RUSSA

· Although this salad has an Italian name, it is a Russian salad, typically characterized by cooked vegetables, a large amount of mayonnaise, and occasionally gelatin.

CLASSIC KNIFE CUTS:

BRUNOISE
(1/8" x 1/8" x 1/8")

SMALL DICE
(1/4" x 1/4" x 1/4")

MEDIUM DICE
(1/2" x 1/2" x 1/2")

LARGE DICE
(3/4" x 3/4" x 3/4")

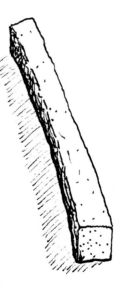

JULIENNE
(1/8" x 1/8" x 2–2½")

BATONNET
(1/4" x 1/4" x 2–2½")

MEDIUM DICE
(1/3" to 1/2" x 3")

HOT CHILES

JALAPEÑO:

· hot to very hot

· Named after Jalapa, Mexico, capital of Veracruz.

DRIED NEW MEXICAN CHILE:

· mild to hot

· Yellow, orange, red, and brown varieties with deeply wrinkled skin.
· The red variety is particularly wonderful for sauces.

·ANAHEIM:

· mild to hot

· Commonly found, this pepper is long, light green, and skinny.

POBLANO:

· almost mild

· This large chile is dark green with a bulky triangular shape.

· The temperature of a chile can vary depending on several factors. The seeds, veins, and flesh can all vary in temperature. The size of the pepper itself affects the heat-generally, the smaller the chile, the hotter it is. Even chiles from the same plant can vary from mild to hot. Taking out the seeds and veins is the only way to reduce a chile's intensity.

remove stem   ribs   seeds   flesh of the pepper

THE CHEF AS TEACHER

RUNNING A TIGHT SHIP

I believe in holding people accountable for their actions. But I'm strict for a reason. It's not intended to make someone's day miserable. It's to get people to respect the chef's jackets we both wear, to let them know the importance of taking our responsibilities seriously.

I look for truth and heart in young cooks. I look to see if they really want what they say they want. I watch to see if they are strong and committed enough to lay everything on the line. Someone with a little piss and vinegar, backbone and drive, who's not wishy-washy: That's who'll get my attention. I lay it on the line the first day: "If I am wrong, prove me wrong. Be willing to stand up for what you believe in." I don't give A's very often. But when I do, it's because they've been earned through sweat, dedication, respect, and a true understanding of what it takes to work from your core.

Besides the need to learn personal responsibility, my adherence to policy has to do with the need for consistency. Unless the conduct in your kitchen is superior, the results of your efforts will be inconsistent. When someone takes a bite of food in your dining room, that bite has your name on it. That's why professional chefs know it has to be perfect every time.

TRUSTING YOUR TONGUE

To know that a plate is ready, chefs need to learn how to trust their tongue. The idea is to strike a balance among the flavor sensations in your mouth: salty, sour, sweet, bitter, and a sort of savory response called umami. You have to understand the science behind the food. There's a reason why certain foods taste good together. It may be because the acids and alkalines in the food are in a particular balance. It may be the actual reactions of the food to the salt and pepper. You have to know how to taste properly so that you can identify the nuances that suggest a little more or a little less. You also need to know when a dish is in its greatest form. As a cook you need to be both artist and chemist in order to use all of your tools and knowledge to bring out the best in your creations.

NO ROOM FOR EXCUSES

When you're in school, you are intentionally faced with pressure. Working on the line in the field is as high-pressure as it gets, so you'd better learn to get used to it while you're in school. We specifically build in situations to heighten the sense of urgency. Your comfort level with competing demands is crucial, because regardless of how busy you are or how many covers you do a night, each plate out of your kitchen has to be your best. You never know when the diners who ordered your entrée are celebrating a once-in-a-lifetime event. You have to get it right or their evening is ruined, that moment is lost forever. It's your responsibility to make their lives' most memorable moments events they'll always cherish. There are no excuses.

ADDITIONAL RECIPES

MANGO CHORIZO STUFFED CHICKEN

From Chef Bob Peterik

(SERVES FOUR)

Here's another recipe with flavors from south of the border. The acids in the marinade really tenderize the chicken, causing the meat to almost slide off the bone. The chorizo adds the spice, but the mangoes help keep the entrée fresh. :: **CWM**

CHICKEN INGREDIENTS

3 large Mangoes, peeled, pureed
1 teaspoon Sugar
1 teaspoon White Wine Vinegar
1, 3–4-pound Chicken, washed, patted dry

STUFFING INGREDIENTS

1 Mango, peeled, pureed
½ teaspoon Sugar
½ teaspoon White Wine Vinegar
½ cup Basmati Rice, cooked
¼ pound Pork Chorizo Sausage, bulk
1 tablespoon Vegetable Oil
1 small Yellow Onion, chopped
2 Pickled Jalapeños, drained, stem and seeds removed, chopped
Kosher Salt and freshly ground Black Pepper
½ cup Butter, melted

:: Chef's Note

Sausages come in every imaginable variety: patties, links, bulk wrapped, with casings and without. The longer the sausage is dried, the firmer it is. The chorizo used for this dish is sold both in bulk and in casings. The type with casings can be used for this recipe if you pierce the casing and pull it off the sausage.

PROCEDURE

1. Combine the 3 mangoes, and 1 teaspoon each of sugar and vinegar in a bowl.

2. Place the washed chicken in a gallon-sized zipper-locking bag, pour in the mango marinade, and rub it all over the top and interior of the chicken. Place the bag in the refrigerator overnight, rotating every few hours.

3. Before you begin the roasting process, make the stuffing. The first step is to puree the mango and add it to a small bowl with the sugar and vinegar. Set aside.

4. Precook the rice and set it aside. Preheat the oven to 350°F.

5. Cook the chorizo in a sauté pan on medium-low heat until it is brown and crumbly. Pour it into a colander and drip out the excess fat. Using a paper towel, wipe out and discard the browned bits of chorizo in the bottom of the pan.

6. Reheat the same sauté pan. Add the oil and allow it to get hot.

7. Add the chopped onion and jalapeño and sauté until the onion just begins to turn translucent. Remove from the heat and cool slightly.

8. Combine the onion and jalapeño in a mixing bowl with the reserved mango mixture. Add the cooked rice and drained chorizo. Mix well. Season lightly with salt and pepper.

9. Remove the marinated chicken from the refrigerator, take it out of the bag, and place it in a roasting pan. Discard the excess marinade.

10. Stuff the chicken with the mango/chorizo mixture until it is as full as possible. Roast for about 1¼ hours, basting the top every half hour with a little melted butter.

11. When the chicken reaches an internal temperature of 165°, place it on the counter and allow it to rest for at least 5–10 minutes. Carve and serve with a portion of the stuffing.

advanced cuisine

BRAISED BEEF CALDILLO IN WARM FLOUR TORTILLAS

From Chef Michael Dudley

(SERVES EIGHT)

This Mexican stew is a great dish to make for an informal gathering of friends. Somehow when food is served with warm tortillas, it invites people to relax, use their hands, remove all pretenses, and just enjoy being together. :: CWM

PROCEDURE

1. Heat a large sauté pan and add the vegetable oil.

2. While your pan is heating up, toss the beef cubes in a pan of flour seasoned with salt and pepper.

3. Add the beef and diced onions to the hot sauté pan. Brown the beef on all sides.

4. When the beef is browned, add the beer and simmer for 3–4 minutes.

5. Add all of the remaining ingredients except the potatoes and tortillas. Simmer on low for approximately 2½ hours, or until the stew meat is tender.

6. Add the potatoes and simmer for 30 minutes more, or until the potatoes are tender and the stew is thickened.

7. Adjust the seasonings with salt and pepper and serve with warm flour tortillas.

INGREDIENTS

¼ cup Vegetable Oil
4½ pounds Beef Stew Meat, cut into 1" cubes
All-Purpose Flour
Kosher Salt and freshly ground Black Pepper
3 Red Onions, medium diced
2 cans Lager Beer
3, 8-ounce cans Diced Green Chiles, drained
¼ cup Cumin, ground
3 tablespoons Garlic, fresh, minced
10 cups Chicken Stock
1 tablespoon Oregano, dried
6 cups Beef or Veal Stock
4 Yukon Gold Potatoes, peeled, large diced

ACCOMPANIMENT

Flour Tortillas

ADVICE FROM A CHEF

LIFE LESSONS FROM THE KITCHEN

Being a chef is a state of mind. It is a consciousness that is characterized by constant mental mise-en-place. You have to be completely prepared before you walk into the kitchen every day: physically, mentally, and emotionally. You have to be willing to stay in your professional role despite anything that may arise in your kitchen. That level of commitment demands a full-time desire, not a part-time attitude. People respect what you do, not just the title that you have. Your staff depend on your ability to operate from a consistent level of integrity.

You have to be open to learning lessons from all stages of your life. My lessons on integrity came from taking care of livestock as a kid. The well-being of our animals depended on our commitment to their care. We couldn't just roll over in bed on early mornings just because our blankets were warm and there was snow on the ground outside. We got up, shoved our feet in our boots, and took care of them, without exception.

It's the same thing in the kitchen: Your commitment is the foundation upon which all other success of the business depends. To succeed in the food industry, the most important skills for you to learn have nothing to do with cooking: Dependability, reliability, accountability, respectfulness for people and products, honesty, cleanliness, and effective communication skills are the qualities that allow people to achieve. I know from my own experience as well as watching other chefs, real success is not measured solely by how well you cook, but by how well you live and live with others.

Everyone finds their own path as they go out to conquer the world of cuisine. But a few tenets are good to live by to make that journey richer. The following list is a collection of guidelines that other chefs and I have found helpful to our own career paths as well as those of many others:

- **Travel as much as you can.** Taste everything along the way. It's the only authentic way to build your repertoire of flavor.
- **Remind yourself why you love to cook.** Keep a picture in your mind of what people look like when they eat your food; imagine the joy that spreads across their faces and realize that you are directly responsible for that joy.
- **Stay focused.** No matter how busy you are, every plate you send out has to be your best work.
- **Push yourself.** Don't just question everything; learn from the answers.
- **Risk failure.** You have to fail in order to learn. You can't live your life walking on eggshells.
- **Risk success.** When an opportunity presents itself, go after it, don't be afraid to succeed.
- **Be consistent.** Your reputation follows you. If you say one thing and do another, your reputation will reflect that. Don't lose the ability to compromise, but stand tall in the process.
- **Be generous.** Work as a team player and pass on what you know to others. It's not only a good social choice, but also helps you delegate in the kitchen.

- **Maintain your ideals.** Even though you may work for people with lower standards, keep your own level of excellence high. Make them rise up to meet you.
- **Stay connected.** Keep in touch with chefs, co-workers, and fellow students. You never know when you may need a contact, a question answered, a referral, or a friend.
- **Be open to opportunity.** If you don't get the job you want, there is something out there that was meant for you to do. There's a reason things happen; be aware enough to know that gifts sometimes come in disguise.
- **Be whole.** No matter how much you love food, get out and experience other things. Live life in balance.

Above all, learn to appreciate the simple things in life. Be amazed at that roast chicken, exquisitely cooked, coming out of the oven, just the steam coming off it. Marvel at perfectly cooked asparagus, blanched and shocked, vibrant green, or at grill marks on a steak. Shrimp that is cooked to perfection is just beautiful. There can be grace in an ice cream cone, it's just how you are looking at it. It's not only cooking; there's beauty that is inherent in the ethereal art that we work with—taking all those raw beautiful foods and turning them into beautiful cooked products.

Just as it is with a great emulsion, you have to know how to combine life lessons in the proper proportions in order to have a balance that holds it all together.

:: CHEF GLENN HUMPHREY

CULINARY RESOURCES

CULINARY SCHOLARSHIPS

The following is only a partial listing of available resources.

American Culinary Federation
10 San Bartola Drive
St. Augustine, Florida 32086
(904) 824-4468 or (800) 624-9458
www.acffchefs.org

American Dietetic Association Foundation
120 South Riverside Plaza Suite 2000
Chicago, Illinois 60606
(800) 877-1600
www.eatright.org

American Institute of Wine and Food
304 West Liberty Street, Suite 201
Louisville, Kentucky 40202
(800) 274-2493
www.aiwf.org

Careers through Culinary Arts Program, Inc.
250 West 57th Street, Suite 2015
New York, New York 10107
(212) 974-7111
email: infor@ccapinc.org
www.ccapinc.org

Charlie Trotter's Culinary Education Foundation
816 W. Armitage Avenue
Chicago, Illinois 60614
(773) 248-6228
www.charlietrotters.com

Confrerie de la Chaine des Rotisseurs
444 Park Avenue South, Suite 301
New York, New York 10016
www.chaineus.org

FastWEB (Financial Aid Search Thrrough the Web)
www.fastweb.org

International Association of Culinary Professionals Foundation
304 West Liberty Street, Suite 201
Louisville, Kentucky 40202
(502) 581-9786 extension 264
email: tgribbins@htqtrs.com
www.iacpfoundation.org

International Foodservice Editorial Council
P.O. Box 491
Hyde Park, New York 12538-0491
(845) 229-6973
email: ifec@aol.com
www.ifec-is-us.com

International Food Service Executives Association
836 San Bruno Avenue
Henderson, Nevada 89015
(702) 564-0997
www.ifsea.com

Les Dames d'Escoffier
(each of the 20 local Les Dames d'Escoffier chapters of the IACP, International Association of Culinary Professionals, offers scholarships at various levels)
email: gjewell@aecmanagement.com
www.ldei.org

National Restaurant Association
175 West Jackson Boulevard, Suite 1500
Chicago, Illinois 60604
(312) 715-1010
www.nraef.org

Women Chefs and Restaurateurs
304 West Liberty Street, Suite 201
Louisville, Kentucky 40202-0300
(502) 581-0300
www.chefnet.com/wcr

A FEW OTHER IMPORTANT CULINARY RESOURCES

Peterson's Guide to Culinary Schools,
Thompson Peterson, Publisher
and
The Guide to Cooking Schools,
ShawGuides
Guides to domestic and international
culinary schools. Updated annually.

Slow Food Association
International Office
Via della Mendicita Istruita 8
12042 Bra (Cuneo), Italy
39 (0) 172 419 611
or (877)-SLOW-FOOD
www.slowfood.com
info@slowfood.it

Slow Food USA Office
434 Broadway, Sixth Floor
New York, New York 10013
(212) 965-5640
www.slowfoodusa.org
Supports sustainable agriculture, small
food artisans, and savoring our
moments at the table.

Mothers and Others for a Livable Planet
40 West 20th Street
New York, New York 10011
(888) ECO-INFO
www.mothers.org/mothers
Supports environmental health and
sutainable agriculture for families
and women.

Seed of Change
P.O. Box 15700
Santa Fe, New Mexico 87506
www.seedsofchange.com
Source for organic heirloom seeds and
organic food products.

Chez Panisse Foundation
1517 Shattuck Avenue
Berkeley, California 94709
(510) 843-3811
www.chezpanisse.com
Supports community and youth projects
in celebrating and respecting the land, the
self, the sense of community, as well as
the cooking, growing, and sharing of food.

Chef's Collaborative
282 Moody Street, Suite 21
Waltham, Massachusetts 02453
www.chefscollaborative.org
An organization of chefs that
encourages the use of local, artisanal,
and sustainable foods.

Sea Web
1731 Connecticut Avenue N.W.,
Fourth Floor
Washington, D.C. 20009
(202) 483-9570
www.seaweb.org
A source of information on diminishing
stocks of seafoods.

Oldways Preservation & Exchange Trust
266 Beacon Street
Boston, Massachusetts 02116
(617) 421-5500
www.oldwayspt.org
Preserves traditional methods of food
preparation and encourages healthy,
sustainable food choices.

The Farm at South Mountain
6106 South 32nd Street
Phoenix, Arizona 85042
(602) 276-6360

Garden Territory
(602) 268-1962

Quiessence Culinary Center
(602) 243-9081
www.thefarmatsouthmountain.com
Offers information as well as cooking
and gardening classes dealing with
organic produce. Also offers a restaurant
highlighting organic produce and hosts
seasonal farmers' markets.

PERIODICALS

American Brewer

American Gardener

Appellation

Art Culinaire

Art of Eating

Better Homes and Gardens

Beverage Digest

Bon Appétit

Caterer and Hotelkeeper

Chef

Chili Pepper

Chocolate News

Chocolatier

Cooking for Profit

Cooking Light

Cook's Illustrated

Country Living

Culinary Trends

Decanter

Delicious Living

Fine Cooking

Food Arts

Food for Thought

Food Management

Food Product Design Magazine

Foodservice Director

Food Technology

Food & Service

Food & Wine

Gastronomica

Gourmet

Herb Companion

Home Cooking

Hometown Cooking

Horticulture

Hospitality

Hospitality Design

Hotel and Motel Management

IACP Food Forum

Kashrus

La Cucina Italiana

Martha Stewart's Living

Meat and Poultry

Modern Baking

Nation's Restaurant News

New Living

Pizza Today

Prepared Foods

Restaurant Business

Restaurant Hospitality

Ristorante

Saveur

Slow

Spain Gourmet Tour

Veggie Life

Wine and Spirits

Wine and Vines

Wine Spectator

INGREDIENT CONVERSIONS

INGREDIENT	VOLUME	WEIGHT
Baking Soda	1 tablespoon	0.33 ounce
Butter	1 cup	8 ounces
Chocolate	1 cup	4 ounces
Cocoa	1 cup	4 ounces
Cornstarch	1 tablespoon	0.33 ounce
Cream, Heavy	1 cup	8 ounces
Eggs, yolk & white	1 large	1.75 ounces
Egg, whites only	1 large	1 ounce
Egg, yolk only	1 large	0.75 ounce
Flour, all-purpose, unsifted	1 cup	5 ounces
Flour, bread, unsifted	1 cup	4.75 ounces
Flour, cake, unsifted	1 cup	4.5 ounces
Milk	1 cup	8.5 ounces
Sugar, granulated	1 cup	7 ounces
Sugar, brown	1 cup	8 ounces
Sugar, powdered, unsifted	1 cup	4.5 ounces
Water	1 cup	8 ounces

CULINARY CLASSES

Although courses and course content vary tremendously from school to school, the following is a brief, general description of sample topics covered in a typical culinary program. It should not be read as definitive or all-inclusive of the course offerings; its purpose is simply to provide a basic idea of the material covered. This is by no means all that is taught in the course of a culinary school curriculum.

CULINARY BASICS

The information in these courses is the key to all other production in the kitchen. It generally focuses on the mastering of the basic principles of food and cooking. It includes such things as palate development, kitchen safety, operation of kitchen equipment, classic knife cuts, and proper cooking techniques. These courses also focus on the processes of selection, storage, fabrication, and cookery of vegetables, meats, fish, poultry, starches, stocks, sauces, soups, salads, and dressings.

MEAT FABRICATION

This course often covers both butchery and charcuterie. Butchery focuses on the identification, classification, and fabrication of meat, poultry, and fish. Charcuterie generally teaches about the production of pâtés, terrines, sausages, and forcemeats as well as the techniques of brining, curing, smoking, and aging.

SAUCIER

A saucier course covers the production of all types of stocks, soups, and sauces. It also emphasizes proficiency in sautéing techniques.

CATERING/GARDE MANGER

Catering teaches about the catering aspect of the food industry. It highlights areas such as buffet presentation, recipes, procedures and techniques, timing, planning and organization, themes, menus, and types of service as well as the business aspects of running a catering concern. A sampling of Garde Manger topics includes garnishes, hors d'oeuvres, canapés, aspics, chaud-froid, and ice carving.

NUTRITION

Both the science of nutrition and its implications within the food industry are generally covered in nutrition class. Dietary analysis, recommendations, lifestyle adjustments, and aspects of nutrition-related diseases as well as the application of the principles of nutrition to menu and diet planning are just some of the topics that might be covered.

BASIC BAKING

This course begins to answer the "whys" of baking as it addresses such topics as baking formulas, measurements, baking processes, gluten development, ingredient analysis, and mastering the basic techniques of baking. Here the basic procedures of breads, roll-ins, desserts, custards, and meringues are often introduced and practiced.

ADVANCED BAKING

The baking processes become more advanced as the more intricate processes of the production of cakes, desserts, pastries, decor, and plate presentation are introduced and practiced.

MANAGEMENT

Management class offers an opportunity to delve into the business and supervisory side of cooking. Typical topics include restaurant management and supervision, recruiting, hiring and firing, training, communication skills, diversity training, and delegating as well as other business aspects of the food industry.

RESTAURANT OPERATIONS

This course focuses on the front-of-the-house facets of a restaurant, such as the intricacies of proper service, menu development, and product analysis.

INTERNATIONAL CUISINE

Explores the dominant ingredients, techniques, customs, culture, and demographics of cuisine around the world.

CONFECTIONERY SHOWPIECES

This artistic course highlights such topics as advanced sugar techniques, tempered chocolate work, fondant cakes, wedding cakes, and advanced decorating techniques to create imaginative culinary showpieces.

WINES AND SPIRITS

An introduction to identifying, analyzing, producing, classifying, and using wines and spirits as both beverages and cooking ingredients.

ADVANCED CUISINE

Focuses on proficiency in all primary stations within the kitchen.

GLOSSARY

Al Dente Meaning "to the tooth" in Italian, this term refers to food cooked only until it maintains a slight resistance in the center.

All-Purpose Flour A blended flour that varies in the proportions of hard and soft wheat flours added to the mixture. For this reason, baking results are unpredictable, so it is generally used for kitchen purposes other than baking.

Arborio Rice A white, mild-flavored, short-grained rice with a hard core, used for making risotto.

Au Sec Cooked until almost dry.

Blanch To quickly submerge food in a boiling liquid or hot fat in order to very briefly and partially cook it.

Bouquet Garni A group of herbs and vegetables tied together and placed in a stock, sauce, or soup for flavoring. The bouquet—often parsley, thyme, celery, leeks, and carrots—are bound together so that they may be easily removed at some point during the cooking process.

Braising A method of cooking in which the foods are browned in hot fat, covered, and then cooked slowly over low heat in a small amount of liquid.

Bread Flour A strong flour with a high protein content, used for products requiring a high amount of gluten, such as bread or rolls.

Brining A method of preserving, curing, and/or flavoring food by submerging it into a salt-and-water solution.

Brunoise To cut food into cubes that are $1/8$" x $1/8$" x $1/8$".

Butterfly To split a food (such as lamb or shrimp) in half lengthwise but without cutting entirely through. The food is hinged in the middle and can be spread open, doubling its original width.

Clarified Butter Also known as drawn butter. Butter that has been melted, the milk solids skimmed off the top, and drained of excess water to result in pure butter fat.

Cake Flour A finely textured, low-gluten flour, used for products requiring a soft, tender texture, such as cakes or other delicate baked goods.

Caramelizing Heating foods containing sugars to temperatures of 310–365°F, causing the sugars to brown and intensify in flavor.

Carnaroli Rice A round, large, short-grained rice that has a high starch content, making it excellent for creamy risotto: The liquid absorbs evenly, but the kernels stay firm and separate.

Carry-over Cooking Cooking that takes place after a food is removed from the heat, caused by the residual heat left in the food.

Chaud-Froid A French term meaning "hot-cold," and referring to a technique of applying a thick sauce to a hot food, then chilling it and serving it cold.

Chiffonade To cut food into very fine shreds or slices.

China Cap A metal cone-shaped strainer with small perforations, used to strain liquids or, when used with a pestle, to puree foods.

Chinois	A metal cone-shaped strainer with a very fine mesh, used to strain liquids.
Cold-Smoke	A method of preserving, curing, and/or flavoring food by exposing it to smoke for a period of time at temperatures of 50–85°F. This method generally requires cooking after the smoking process is completed.
Corn Flour	Finely ground cornmeal.
Coulis	A hot or cold sauce made from pureed fruit or vegetables.
Crème Fraîche	A cultured cream that has a rich, tangy flavor with a slightly nutty essence. It can range in body from very thick to slightly thinner than sour cream.
Croquettes	Small shapes of pureed or finely chopped food such as potatoes or salmon that are held together with a sauce and deep-fried.
Deep-fry	A method of cooking in which foods are cooked by submersion in fat.
Deglaze	To pour liquids into a hot pan in order to dissolve the bits of cooked food on the bottom.
Denature	To alter a protein from its original state by means of a chemical or physical treatment using acids, heat, or a whisking process.
Dredge	To lightly coat a food with crumbs or flour.
Dutch Oven	A large kettle with a tightly fitting lid, often made of cast iron.
Emulsify	To mix generally unmixable liquids in a manner that keeps the ingredients uniformly distributed in a stable solution.
Enrich	Adding butter, cream, and/or egg yolks to enhance a sauce just prior to serving.
Flambé	To flame food briefly by igniting warmed alcohol that is in or on the food.
Flavoring	A product added to food in order to change and/or enhance the taste.
Flute	To carve decorative markings into a vegetable or fruit.
Foie Gras	The enlarged liver of a goose or duck.
Fold	To gently lift the bottom ingredients of a mixture up over the top ingredients using a slow circular motion.
Food Mill	A device that consists of a hopper, a hand crank, and a curved blade that forces food through a perforated disc. Used for straining and pureeing foods.
Fork-Tender	A degree of doneness that allows a fork to slide easily in and out of a piece of cooked food.
Ganache	Equal parts of chocolate and hot heavy cream mixed together until the chocolate melts. Used as a rich chocolate coating or filling.
Garde-Manger	The station in the kitchen where cold foods such as salads, cold appetizers, and garnishes are prepared. Also, the term used for the person responsible for the station and the food itself.

Gelatin Sheets	Also known as leaf gelatin, these thin sheets of unflavored gelatin look like translucent lasagne noodles.
Granité	Also known as granita in Italian. A frozen mixture made with sugar, water, and a flavoring ingredient that is stirred during the freezing process.
Haché	French term meaning "minced."
Intermezzo	A small course offered in between other courses of a meal to cleanse and refresh the palate.
Julienne	To cut food into planks that are 1/8" x 1/8" x 2" long.
Large Dice	To cut food into cubes that are 3/4" x 3/4" x 3/4".
Liaison	A mixture used to thicken and/or enrich a sauce, often but not always made with a combination of heavy cream and egg yolks.
Mandoline Slicer	A narrow, rectangular slicer containing a blade positioned at a 45-degree angle. It is operated manually to obtain very thin slices, waffle cuts, or matchstick shapes.
Marinade	A liquid that generally contains an acid, oil, and herbs and/or spices and is used to soak, flavor, and/or tenderize an ingredient before cooking.
Masa Harina	Dough flour made from dried corn that has been soaked and cooked in lime water.
Medium Dice	To cut food into cubes that are 1/2" x 1/2" x 1/2".
Mince	To very finely chop.
Mirepoix	A mixture of diced vegetables, generally carrot, celery, and onion, used in the preparation of stocks and sauces.
Mise-en-Place	The French term for putting everything in its place. It is the thorough preparation for cooking that involves the gathering of ingredients and utensils as well as the forethought necessary to carry out an organized cooking process.
Nappe	The consistency of a sauce or liquid that is just thick enough to lightly coat the back of a spoon.
Pan-Fry	A method of cooking on the stovetop that uses a hot pan and a moderate amount of fat.
Panna Cotta	Translated from Italian to mean "cooked cream." A simple molded custard made with gelatin.
Pastry Flour	A weak flour whose gluten content is lower than bread flour but higher than cake flour. It is used for products requiring a tender, crumbly texture such as pie doughs.
Pan Juices	Also known as pan drippings. The drippings are the juices and melted fat released when meat is roasted.
Pilaf	A method of cooking grains in which the kernels are first sautéed in hot fat, then cooked with a hot liquid (generally stock) until the liquid is completely absorbed.
Pin Bones	The tiny bones in a fish located just under the surface of the flesh.

Piping Bag	Also known as a pastry bag. A cone-shaped bag that can be fitted with tips of varying sizes and is used to apply icings, dough, whipped cream, etc., in decorative patterns.
Ramekin	A small ceramic soufflé dish that comes in varying sizes.
Remouillage	A weak stock made by rewetting the used bones from another stock.
Render	To cook meats or poultry until the fat is melted.
Roasting	A dry-heat method of cooking that surrounds the food with hot, dry air.
Rock Salt	Also known as ice cream salt or bay salt. A very coarse salt not generally used for consumption.
Rondeau	A wide, shallow pot with straight sides and loop handles. Also known as a brazier.
Roulade	A slice of fish, meat, or poultry that has been rolled around a stuffing.
Roux	Equal parts by weight of flour and butter, cooked together until it reaches a desired stage: white, blond, or brown.
Sauté	A method of cooking on the stovetop that uses a hot pan and a small amount of hot fat to quickly cook food over high heat.
Sear	To quickly brown a food over high heat.
Seasoning	A product added to food to enhance the natural flavor.
Self-Rising Flour	An all-purpose flour to which salt and baking powder have been added.
Shock	Also known as refresh. A method used to halt further cooking by submerging the food in ice water.
Slurry	A mixture of starch and cold liquid that is used to bind and thicken food.
Small Dice	To cut food into cubes that are $1/4$" x $1/4$" x $1/4$".
Stock	The foundation of French cuisine. A clear, unseasoned, unthickened liquid derived from the cooking of bones, bouquet garni, mirepoix, and occasionally other vegetables.
Sweat	To cook a food, covered, over low heat, with a small amount of fat until the food softens and becomes moist but does not brown.
Tatsoi Greens	Also known as rosette bok choy. A dark-colored green with round leaves and a rich mustardlike flavor.
Temper	A process of slowly mixing hot liquids into eggs in order to incorporate them without curdling the eggs.
Toast Points	Small, generally triangular pieces of toast with the crusts removed.
Water Bath	A container of water in a pan, used to surround the bottom and sides of other containers of food in order to allow them to cook or heat gently.

ACKNOWLEDGMENTS

First of all, to Alex, Anna, and Erin, who are the reasons this book began and whose unwavering love and support allowed it to come to fruition. A sincere thank-you to Nancy and Sean, for your amazing love and support throughout this project.

This book would not be in your hands were it not for Glenn Humphrey, Eileen Bailey, Erik Tieze, and Katy Tartakoff. Glenn lives, not only professes, what it means to be an extraordinary teacher, mentor, and friend. When it comes to his students, he hears every dream, he launches every ambition, he ignites every soul. It is because of his brilliance in the classroom that this book was created. There are not enough words to thank him for what he brings to us all. You would undoubtedly not be reading this book if it were not for my dear friend and mentor Eileen Bailey. From the moment I put pen to paper, she has been my absolute guiding light. She selflessly led me through the nuances of the publishing world and helped me to see that anything is possible. Her guidance and friendship will never be forgotten. Erik Tieze's gifts to the world are irreplaceable; his talent is limitless. I am endlessly grateful for his generosity in the creation of the gorgeous illustrations for this book, and for the joy that he brings to everyone's life. Katy Tartakoff's love and patience in teaching me how to see behind the lens of the camera opened up an entirely new world. Without her vision and generosity of mind and spirit, my best pictures would still be in my head and not transformed into beauty on film. Her belief in my work and my view of the world will be in my heart forever.

My heartfelt thanks go out to all of the chefs who participated in this project. Their generosity in sharing their lives, their food, and their passions resulted in the education of a lifetime and spawned a lifetime of new friendships. I'm eternally grateful to you all. Very special thanks to Darren Leite and Robert Wilson who are the co-founders of the Arizona Culinary Institute, along with Fife Symington. Their unwavering support allowed wisdom, staffing, and space to be offered for every stage of this project. Their commitment to this book is profoundly appreciated. At the Scottsdale Culinary Institute, a special thank-you to Jon Alberts and Creighton Schroeder, who supported my vision, who thought outside the box, and who ultimately helped make this project possible and my diploma a reality. Major thank-yous to Will Getchell for his constant encouragement and support, and to Allison and Martin Schroeder, who saved my computer more times than I care to count—and loved my children in the process. To Tracy and Ivan Flowers, who inspired and nourished me along the way with food and friendship that brought me to tears. To my classmates, whom I love, for your teachings of all kinds. Special thanks to Matt, Kristen, Joe, Maureen, Brian, Nate, Darin, Justin, Eric, Haley, Michael, Aaron, Theresa, B.B., Forrest, Mike, Craig, Efrain, Andy, Charlie, Reese, Corey, Jane, Jen, Jenny, Devon, Jon, Katie, and Dave, as well as to the members of the Dead Chefs Society for keeping me passionate about everything meaningful.

To Julia Child and Alice Waters, whom I thank for their contributions to the world of cuisine, and whose ideals inspire me as a woman and a chef. Sincere thanks to Robert McGrath, Eddie Matney, Jim Ranaldo, Kay Handal, Sylvia Long, Rachel Mersey, Cathy Johnston, and Fritz Pasquet for their special support and willingness to be involved as this book progressed. Deep gratitude is extended to John Zimmerman, who greatly influenced Glenn in his career, as well as to Elizabeth S. Leite, who founded the Scottsdale Culinary Institute and was instrumental to the success of many culinary careers. Dear thanks to my photographic family at Peter Fradin's 5 Star Image, to Photo Concepts in Phoenix, as well as to the amazing staff at The New Lab in Denver. Special thanks to LeRoy Ullman and Robert Humanski: Their gifts in the darkroom completely astound me. To Tom Algire for his photographic advice. To Susan Stockton and Georgia Downard at the Food Network for their time and generosity. Special thanks to Joan Houlton for her early guidance, and to Rosalee O'Donoghue, who inspired me from the beginning. To Bob Craig for his generosity. To Dick Kraft, who taught me what good teaching truly is, and to Cliff Hinderman and Glenn Humphrey, who showed me what that means. To Brooke Nixon and Deb Burney for their wonderful copyediting, and to all of my friends who listened ad nauseam to every detail about this book. To Becky, Lauren, Susan, Danielle, and Kaia for their loving assistance. To my dear friends who celebrated every morsel I lovingly created for them in the kitchen—and special thanks to my old friends who ate my food before I seriously got into cooking. To Irmgard, who is always supportive and my dependable source of a good read, and to Beth, Carole, and Karin, who helped inspire the artist within me. To my brother and sisters, Rita, Lynn, Peg, Jane, and Jerry, with whom I developed a true love of being in the kitchen, my dad for his flair for design, Uncle Tom for his cooking, and my mother, from whom I learned all things good.

Most importantly, my deepest thanks go out to my own family, whose constant patience with my pursuit of a dream is something I will eternally cherish. To Alex, whose journeys with me have clarified my visions, enhanced my photography, improved my palate, and nourished my soul.

Finally, a sincere thank-you to our editor, Ann Treistman, who immediately recognized the heart behind this book, to LeAnna Weller Smith whose gorgeous designs brought it to life, to Kevin Lynch and Chris Mongillo in The Lyons Press's superb production department who made a difference, and to Alan Kaufman whose guidance and generosity helped bring this book to you as well.

INDEX

:: :: ::